FOREIGN
DIRECT INVESTMENT
IN
CHINA

FOREIGN
DIRECT INVESTMENT
IN
CHINA

Phillip Donald Grub
AND
Jian Hai Lin

Q

QUORUM BOOKS
NEW YORK • WESTPORT, CONNECTICUT • LONDON

Library of Congress Cataloging-in-Publication Data

Grub, Phillip Donald.
    Foreign direct investment in China / Phillip Donald Grub and Jian
Hai Lin.
        p.   cm.
    Includes index.
    ISBN 0–89930–576–8 (alk. paper)
    1. Investments, Foreign—China.   2. Free ports and zones—China.
I. Lin, Jian Hai.   II. Title.
HG5782.G78   1991
332.6'73'0951—dc20   91–19

British Library Cataloguing in Publication Data is available.

Library of Congress Catalog Card Number: 91–19
ISBN: 0–89930–576–8'

First published in 1991

Quorum Books, One Madison Avenue, New York, NY 10010
An imprint of Greenwood Publishing Group, Inc.

Printed in the United States of America

The paper used in this book complies with the
Permanent Paper Standard issued by the National
Information Standards Organization (Z39.48–1984).

10 9 8 7 6 5 4 3 2 1

Contents

Figures and Tables

FIGURES

TABLES

Preface

The sleeping dragon that awakened in 1979, when China opened its doors for Western trade and investment, has moved forward at a cautious pace, sometimes backstepping and sometimes sidestepping, in its path toward achieving modernization of its economy. Inflows of capital, technology, and management through foreign direct investment by joint ventures and wholly foreign-owned enterprises have contributed significantly to China's development in the past eleven years. In spite of many obstacles, managers of these enterprises have been successful in transferring skills and technologies that have enhanced the pace of modernization. In so doing, production quality has been upgraded, new markets opened, and foreign exchange earned. However, progress has not been as rapid, nor has the outcome been as successful, as either the foreign investors or Chinese officials had hoped.

The future success or failure of China's modernization efforts rests with the present leadership. Decisions as to whether China moves forward with the open-door policy and accompanying reforms, or whether it reverts back to a highly planned system that ignores the role of market forces, will be crucial to China's overall development in the 1990s and beyond. In short, these decisions will determine whether or not China will be competitive in the world economy by the year 2000 or will have regressed to the roll of a bystander as other nations advance.

What China needs are informed and forward-looking leaders who will put personal gains and politics aside and chart a course of action that will streamline the economy and inspire the support of the nation. As the Chinese philosopher Lao-Tse, in 565 B.C., wrote:

> A leader is best when people barely know he exists.
> Not so good when people obey and acclaim him;

Worse yet when they despise him.
But a good leader, who talks little when his work is done;
His aim fulfilled,
They will say "We did it ourselves."

In doing research for *Foreign Direct Investment in China*, the authors interviewed countless Chinese and foreign joint venture and wholly foreign-owned enterprise managers in China, foreign corporate headquarters executives, and Chinese government officials at the state, provincial, and city levels. Few are named in this book; however, we are indebted to all persons for being willing and open to share their experience, ideas, and insights; without their cooperation, this book could not have been written.

In particular, we would like to thank senior personnel in the Ministry of Foreign Economic Relations and Trade, Ministry of Finance, Shanghai Municipal Government, Guangdong Province, and the Shenzhen special economic zone. It should be noted, however, that all views expressed in this book are those of the authors and do not necessarily reflect the views of the organizations with which we are associated.

Our enduring gratitude is extended to Catherina Z. Tonson, who undertook the task of processing numerous revisions and deciphering our writing, yet completing this project with a cheerful smile. Our thanks also go to Damaris W. King and Valerie Lee V. Buss, Aryamehr research assistants, who helped polish the final manuscript. Their many hours of extra effort on our behalf will always be remembered.

FOREIGN
DIRECT INVESTMENT
IN
CHINA

1

Introduction and Background

The changes that have taken place in the People's Republic of China since it opened its doors to the West have been dramatic, exceeding the expectations of the most optimistic China watchers. During the first ten years of the open-door policy, China's foreign trade rose by an impressive 300 percent, an unparalleled increase for any centrally planned economy and for most emerging economies of the world. During the same period, foreign investment reached about US $20 billion, increasing at an average annual rate of about 30 percent. Although expectations were shattered by the June events in Tiananmen Square, both trade and investment continued to grow rapidly in 1989 and 1990, with investment committed reaching about US $6 billion in each year.

From Kentucky Fried Chicken in Beijing to Lockheed Aircraft in Shanghai, along with other investments including automobile plants, consumer goods industries, hotels, and resource extraction in various parts of the country, technology has been transferred and capital invested by foreign firms at an amazing pace. Each time a new venture is inaugurated, it has been accompanied by numerous banquets, toasts, and fireworks to celebrate the occasion.

Structural changes have also been undertaken within the Chinese economy itself. Significant occurrences since 1979 include the following:

- Development of special economic zones and opened cities;
- Decentralization of decision making at the province and city levels;
- Privatization, including the breakup of communes and the return of private homes to their owners;
- Authorization of private ownership of property, along with transfer rights;

- Development of a flourishing private small business sector;
- Strong improvement in foreign investment laws;
- Implementation of bankruptcy laws;
- Passage of improved, but still inadequate, laws concerning intellectual property rights protection;
- Enhanced role for managers in state-owned enterprises, with greater authority for decision making and bottom-line profitability;
- Improved labor laws, especially for foreign-owned enterprises;
- Initial development of a stock and bond market; and
- Greater emphasis on infrastructure enhancement to meet modernization goals.

In the final phase of its seventh five-year plan (from 1986 to 1990), China attempted to modernize its massive economy through an infusion of technology transfers, management skills, and foreign capital despite the events that took place in June 1989. In most ministries and banks, younger and more technically trained leaders, many of whom received their education abroad, are replacing an older generation of leaders, whose accession to leadership positions was based heavily upon seniority and upon party loyalty. In industry, a transition has also taken place, with Chinese managers being held more responsible for bottom-line profitability, management innovations, quality control, and, in some firms, foreign exchange earnings.

In moving from the "common rice bowl" of the Cultural Revolution, China has become a land of contrasts. In some cases, individualism and entrepreneurship have produced a significant number of millionaires, while other segments of the economy have lagged behind and are as bureaucratic and dogmatic as ever. While per capita income has almost doubled in the last ten years, for every millionaire that has been produced, there are still many who go to bed at night hungry.

China is plagued by continuing inflationary pressures, a shortage of foreign currency earnings, massive hidden unemployment, overpopulation, and an industrial base that, for the most part, remains antiquated. Exacerbating these problems are massive infrastructure needs, inadequate communication facilities, and segments of the bureaucracy resistent to change. However, leaders who resist change are finding it more and more difficult to maintain their positions, since the majority of citizens are pushing China to become a newly industrialized economy by the year 2000, or shortly thereafter, with the opportunity to increase the welfare of the masses.

THE FOUR MODERNIZATIONS

At the onset of the seventh five-year plan, Chinese leaders singled out four areas for modernization: agriculture, industry, defense, and science and technology. A fifth area, educational reform, was added shortly thereafter. In all of these areas, China lags significantly behind most of its Asian neighbors, especially Japan and the newly industrialized economies of Korea, Taiwan, Hong Kong, and Singapore. Not only is China still noncompetitive in many of its exports of manufactured items, it often has to rely on scarce foreign exchange reserves to import food to feed its massive population.

To overcome some of China's problems in agriculture, communes were dissolved and the land distributed to the commune members. While the state is still the biggest buyer of all basic commodities, farmers are given the opportunity to sell on the free market. The results of this effort have indeed been positive; production increased and a significant number of farmers became rich in Chinese terms. Fresh fruits and vegetables, once luxury items in Beijing and the northern cities during the winter months, are now commonplace throughout the year. With more modern means of farming, refrigerated transport, and greater financial incentives, farmers have improved the quality as well as the quantity of products produced.

Mechanization has been introduced slowly, particularly in the production of wheat, rice, other grain crops, and cotton. Farmers are handicapped, however, by a lack of available local capital for loans and for the foreign exchange reserves necessary to import modern agricultural equipment and fertilizers, both of which are in short supply.

The modernization of industry is a major challenge for the further progress of China's economic reforms. Still strapped by massive bureaucracy in some state enterprises, managers have also been hampered by an inability to dismiss unneeded or unproductive workers as they attempt to reform their enterprises into more profitable operations. It has been estimated that at least a quarter of the work force employed in state-owned factories is not needed at either the worker or staff levels. Retraining and relocation programs are either nonexistent or minimal at best. Accustomed to the cradle-to-grave security, many workers simply refuse to transfer even though incentives may be offered.

With the labor reforms of 1987 and 1988, managers supposedly have the right to hire and fire at will, and workers are also supposed to have the right to move from one company to another. In practice, however, it is not that clear-cut. If a worker chooses to leave a factory and take a position in another firm, the worker needs the permission of the present employer. In general, the better trained and more efficient workers are those who wish to make the change, and companies are reluctant to let them go. On the other hand, if a manager wishes to release an employee because of a lack of productivity or need, it is virtually impossible to do so. As a result, managers of state enterprises complain that the factories cannot become profitable and competitive under present policies.

The same situation occurs where differential pay rates have been implemented. A major aspect of the "common rice bowl" policy, which existed for decades, was that workers were paid the same wages regardless of productivity or responsibility. Major complaints arise as managers try to implement incentive programs to improve productivity and to maintain quality control by rewarding the most efficient workers. Western joint ventures and private Chinese enterprises find this to be a lesser problem because they have more flexibility; however, for the state-owned enterprises, it still remains a major constraint.

Where workers are given incentives to improve production and quality control, their pay is supplemented by performance bonuses. In some cases, salaries have almost doubled. Union groups, however, still have a major impact on management/labor decisions and dissuade allowing these discrepancies to occur.

The majority of workers still live in factory subsidized housing. Moreover, there is no nationwide social security system or pension plan. As a result, when a worker takes a position with another firm, retirement and other benefits do not transfer; these benefits must be absorbed by the new factory. Furthermore, the worker may have earned the right to a larger and more modern housing facility because of acquired seniority. Consequently, although incentive systems, labor mobility, and other labor reforms have been made possible by legislation to improve both the efficiency of operations and labor productivity, the goals that were envisioned by the Chinese leadership have not been realized.

A major advantage of the decentralization process is the factory manager's ability to set prices and to retain profits. For example, prices can be adjusted up or down based on production efficiencies and market competition. With retained earnings, factory managers are able to purchase the equipment necessary to upgrade production facilities and enhance the modernization of their plant or to financially reward personnel.

This situation is more prevalent in export-oriented industries because of their ability to obtain foreign exchange earnings. While the government still sets minimal profitability targets that are renegotiated with the enterprise, earnings beyond that amount can be used at the discretion of the factory manager. In turn, this has led factories to develop strategic marketing plans that target new markets that could be entered because of the increased quality of the goods their factories are producing. Factories that once exported to low income South Asian and Middle Eastern countries, or sold goods solely in the Chinese marketplace, are now targeting sales for Japan, the newly industrialized economies of Asia, and even the United States and Europe.

CHALLENGES OF CHANGE

Overall, China's financial picture has improved in the last few years. For example, foreign exchange reserves are now estimated at more than

US \$26 billion, up from the low levels of 1985–86. Gold reserves are estimated at US \$4.2 billion. China had a deficit in its trade account for 1989 and also suffered a major drop in foreign exchange earnings in the tourism sector. As of summer 1991 the once fully booked hotels, for the most part, languish at low occupancy rates, and businesses that depend on sales to the foreign travelers suffer badly.

In 1989, China's trade deficit stood at US \$5.6 billion. Since June 1990, however, the trade deficit narrowed due to the tightened credit policy and resulted in a surplus of almost US \$5 billion for the year. However, there has been an estimated loss of more than US \$2 billion a year in tourism inflows for both 1989 and 1990. Furthermore, China is already one of the largest importers of grain, and due to adverse weather conditions, China has often had to increase its purchases from abroad in order to feed its population, thereby further exacerbating its trade problems.

Textiles, light industrial goods, and crude petroleum currently dominate China's exports. China is seeking to expand its export base on a broader scale, however, as it moves into the 1990s. The textile industry is being transformed from producing low cost, mass consumption goods to high fashion, often on contract from foreign buyers. Instead of an export dependency on footwear, novelties, and handicrafts, China is making strides in the exportation of household goods such as refrigerators, freezers, and other kitchen equipment sold overseas under Chinese brand names. Other products, ranging from automobile parts to computers, furniture to military gear, and hardware items to surgical equipment, are also making inroads into the international marketplace. By the late 1990s, China hopes to be exporting automobiles, trucks, and agricultural equipment, as well as cutting heavily into the global market with a vast variety of products ranging from light aircraft to container ships.

IMPACT OF THE OPEN-DOOR POLICY

In its quest for development, China has a number of advantages. Compared to much of the developing world, China has a vast supply of natural resources to fuel its industrial needs. The average Chinese person is basically self-motivated, highly intelligent, and in favor of change that will improve standards of living and individual prosperity. During the past decade, China's gross national product has more than doubled as has its per capita income, far ahead of most of the developing world.

The initial reforms set forth by Deng Xiaoping in the open-door policy led to many of the changes that have taken place within China in the past fifteen years. By the thousands, Chinese have gone abroad to study, primarily in the United States, Japan, Canada, Western Europe, and Australia, bringing back the knowledge of economies that are indeed a contrast to their own. Furthermore, the Chinese leadership has demonstrated over the past decade its willingness to experiment by developing private enterprises that compete head on with state-owned enterprises. An expansion of the limited number of stock exchanges and the development of a national stock exchange as a means to raise new capital and absorb excess local capital and to put it to more productive use are still under debate. On the extreme side, there are even those who suggest the opening of China's capital markets to foreign investors.

The special economic zones (SEZs) and opened cities have benefited most from the open-door policy. With liberalized policies and special incentives that include tax holidays, improved infrastructure facilities, preferential foreign exchange treatment, long-term and favorable land lease privileges, and special labor policies, the investment environment has significantly improved and has proven attractive to foreign investors. Initial investors were primarily from Hong Kong and Macao. However, they were quickly joined by firms from Japan, the United States, and various countries of the European Economic Community. In the past three years, there have also been significant inflows from both South Korea and Taiwan.

Shenzhen, located only a short hydrofoil ride across the border from Hong Kong, has been a particularly attractive investment location. When combined with the nearby special economic zones of Zhuhai and Shantou, Shenzhen has now become a major industrial and export base along the Pearl River delta extending to Guangzhou. Port facilities continue to be upgraded, and increased emphasis is being placed on improved rail and highway transport, communications facilities, and energy sources. Consequently, the economic zones provide an example of policies that have worked.

Concurrent with the process of modernization, China began a process of decentralization of authority in the first half of the 1980s. By giving more autonomy to city and provincial officials, as well as the state-owned enterprises therein, they have garnered mixed results. Provinces ranging from Guangdong in the south to Tianjin in the north have seized the opportunity to attract foreign capital, increase infrastructure development, upgrade their technological base, enhance their workers' skills, and develop strong export industries. On the other hand, decentralization has led, in some cases, to open competition between provincial leaders as they vie to attract foreign investment and establish priorities that may be in contradiction to those of the central government.

As an example of misguided priorities, leadership of a major state-owned factory found that the best way to enhance its profitability was to export production rather than satisfy domestic needs. As a result, the bulk of production was sold abroad, sometimes at below-market prices, in order to obtain foreign exchange which, in turn, was not used for plant modernization. Instead, the foreign exchange was used to purchase a wide variety of products, including automobiles, refrigerators, VCRs and television sets, which were then resold on the Chinese market at a substantial profit. The profits were used to give major bonuses to both management and workers alike. On the other hand, the firms that needed the products that were exported for their operations were forced to turn to the foreign market, paying prices far in excess of those obtained by the factory for its exports. In some cases materials imported from foreign trading companies were of Chinese origin. Consequently, it is not difficult to see why, with action like this, prices have spiraled in the past several years. Although some of this activity has been curbed in the past two years, it still continues.

The location of industries in itself presents another problem for China. Some provinces have attempted to make themselves autonomous and have built factories that have excess production capability. While there may be a demand for their products within the Chinese domestic market, the lack of infrastructure development and transportation facilities has made some products less competitive in the local market than foreign goods that can arrive from abroad at a less expensive price. In fact, transportation costs are so exorbitant within China that it is sometimes cheaper to ship goods from overseas to Shanghai than from Beijing.

The process of decentralization, combined with the removal of restrictions on market pricing, also permitted unlimited development of private enterprises. On the positive side, this sector accounted for an estimate of more than 25 percent of total industrial output in 1988 due to the efficiency of operations and modern management techniques. Many of these firms became foreign currency earners as they developed quality products for export. Bank loans to the private enterprises increased at a rapid pace because they offered better credit records than many large state enterprises.

On the negative side, the economy became overheated, producing an inflation rate that, depending upon which source is contacted, is admitted to have been about 35 percent for 1988; however, in some areas inflation was nearer the 50 percent mark. Inflation grew at about 16 percent for 1989 and dropped to below 5 to 6 percent for 1990. At the end of the first quarter of 1991, inflation was again on the rise.

Rapid price inflation during 1987 and 1988 created a major problem as wages simply could not keep pace. This disparity has been felt most significantly in the urban areas where wages are fixed, in contrast with the farmers from the rural areas who can sell much of what they produce on the open market as well as the self-employed who, according to Chinese estimates, earn five times the annual salary of a government employee. For example, the average mid-level government worker's monthly salary in Beijing will buy the equivalent of five pounds of prime seafood, with only enough currency remaining to pay the meager monthly rent and nothing left for other necessary purchases. The situation is even more dramatic for a low-level clerk or secretary in a government office. For these individuals, many of whom have college degrees, making ends meet is virtually impossible unless the individual has a second job, even with subsidized housing, medical care, and basic staples.

PRIVATIZATION

No one really knows how many private sector enterprises there are, although estimates range from several thousands to several million. Private enterprises range in size from one individual working in his/her small apartment to organizations that are, in Western terms, major conglomerates. As mentioned earlier, China has acknowledged that more than a quarter of the gross national product is derived from these private sector enterprises. Many of these firms now have joint ventures with Western partners and rank among the most efficient and profitable enterprises within the country.

The curtailment of credits, along with the abrupt change of policy following the May-June 1989 demonstrations, has negated further growth in this sector for those firms that were not linked to foreign joint ventures. Many small-sized private enterprises either have gone bankrupt or have been forced to close down partially since then. While this figure is small in terms of the estimated number of private enterprises in China, it has added to the overall unemployment problems in the country.

COUNTRY PROFILE

China is one of the most diverse demographic, economic, ethnic, and cultural nations in the world. Situated on the eastern side of the Asian continent, with a landmass of more than 9.6 million square kilometers, its population approximates 1.2 billion, or almost one fifth of the total world population.

To the east, the Pacific coastline stretches more than 18,000 kilometers from the Soviet Union to Vietnam. It is blessed with many natural, deep harbor ports that are complimented by rivers that may be navigated well inland. Its topography is diverse, ranging from the fertile basins situated in the east and southeast sectors of the country, accounting for a fifth of the total landmass, to the mountainous regions that cover over a third of the country and include Mt. Everest, the world's highest peak, which towers over the Himalayas.

The climate is equally diverse. While China is dominated by monsoon winds, there are significant variations throughout the country due to its sheer size, topography, and geographic location. From October through March, the northern part of the country is influenced significantly by the Siberian winter winds that sweep down from the Soviet Union, creating long cold, dry winters. This contrasts with the coast, which is influenced by warm and humid air masses that bring high temperatures and heavy rainfall to much of the eastern and southeastern sectors. As a result of the wide range in temperatures and landmass, China is able to produce a wide variety of agricultural products and by-products for both domestic consumption and export.

Mandarin is the official language; however, there are several hundred dialects spoken throughout the country by its multi-ethnic population. The largest of the ethnic groups, the Han, accounts for more than 90 percent of the total population. Mongolian, Hui, Tibetan, Uygur, Zhuang, Miao, Manchu, Li, Bai, and Dai are other significant ethnic groups, which are located primarily in the northwest, southwest, and the border areas with other countries. Aside from Mandarin, the Cantonese, Fujianese, and Shanghai dialects are spoken by large masses of the population. This diversity sometimes makes it necessary to have an interpreter present at meetings between Chinese delegations.

IDEOLOGY AND THE MODERNIZATION

Since 1949, ideology has been a significant factor in China's development as an industrial nation. While it has been influenced by the military, in both positive and negative fashions, significant strides have been made in both industrial development and modernization in the past four decades. As a nation where the bulk of the populous was once at starvation levels, China has attained a level where its citizenry is fed, clothed, and educated, for the most part, far better than that in some of the other centrally-planned economies, and certainly than many other developing countries. On the other hand, ideological extremism contributed to China's severe economic crises during the Great Leap Forward (1958–62), the Cultural Revolution (1966–72), and the Tiananmen Square uprising (1989). In all these instances, the military played a key role in overruling those with more progressive and external-looking points of view. The events of Tiananmen Square and its aftermath are frequently referred to as the "Great Leap Backwards."

The fear of foreign domination is, and always has been, a major concern of China's leaders. Following the bitter civil war between the Communist and the Nationalist Parties (1946–49), the Communists came to power in China during a period of rampant inflation marked by both economic and political chaos. Their appeal was meshed in the policies and aspirations that touched the hearts of the people: freedom from foreign domination, overall economic development, more equitable distribution of wealth to create a better life for all concerned, and nationalism that would include rule by the masses. These philosophies had their roots in the peasantry that formed guerrilla groups to overthrow the Japanese. These groups

were then convinced to join in with the communists by promises of achieving the aforementioned goals. Furthermore, with no class distinctions and
with a close comradery that has complete dedication to the cause, this
ideology brought forth a unity that led to the overthrow of the Nationalists
and to the emergence of a new political form throughout the Chinese
mainland.

As time progressed, however, two differing opinion groups began to
materialize. There were the traditionalists who, then and now, still cling
to the older ideology of utilizing military force to preserve and maintain
the status quo, enabling their power and positions to be maintained and
passed on to future generations. On the other hand, there are those who
see the need for change in both political ideology and economic reform
in order to develop an economy capable of raising the standard of living
of a massive population while competing globally in the 1990s and beyond.

THE ECONOMIC AND MANAGERIAL SYSTEM

The leadership that came to power in 1949 quickly gained the confidence
and the loyalty of the Chinese population with its efforts to build a strong,
independent, modern China that would be powerful economically, politically, technologically, and militarily, thus ensuring its independence from
the rest of the world. To enforce the ideology of independence, focus was
placed on class struggle, equality, distribution of wealth, national controls
on the means of production, and party political solidarity, which was
reinforced by the party cadre throughout the nation. This ideology appeared to be compatible with the aspirations of the masses because of the
focus on equality, economic development, improving standards of education and living, as well as the deeply rooted nationalistic feelings toward
independence.

The Great Leap Forward in 1958 saw a move away from the unity of
the people toward a system of control by the party dominated by Mao
and his close associates. Consequently, a merger of politics and ideology
became the focus of economics, management, and all aspects of daily life.
Neither the Communist party nor the people realized that the leadership
that came to power through utilization of military tactics did not have the
skills to enhance agricultural output through agrarian reforms, run complex industrial and commercial enterprises, or manage the various facets
of the national economy.

There was a belief on the part of the leadership that self-sufficiency
could be obtained by producing everything necessary for national economic welfare through the use of sheer manpower and primitive agricultural and industrial equipment and methods. Furthermore, this was
attempted at a time when there were very few skilled engineers, technicians, economic planners, or commercial and production managers avail-

able to assist in commercial and industrial development. Experimentation was encouraged, and huge quantities of labor were utilized in place of machinery and newer technologies. Both criticism of others and self-criticism were encouraged to promote efficiencies, and "heroes" were rewarded by praise for their initiative, innovation, and accomplishments. Decision making became more and more highly centralized and any deviation from the party line was quickly suppressed.

A result of the Great Leap Forward program was the de-emphasis of monetary incentives, as well as the elimination of class distinctions through both ideological and political education campaigns, with slogans calling for harder work and greater sacrifice for the masses. Those who showed resistance met with an increased use of punishment and coercion, which became the means of controlling the population. Anti-intellectual campaigns subjected those experts and professionals who disagreed with party policies to public ridicule and expulsion from the Party. Furthermore, the masses began to recognize that there were no rewards, which in turn led to both frustration and demoralization that compounded the lack of efficiency in all aspects of the economy. The policies set forth by the leadership resulted in a strong separation between ideology and reality.

Throughout this period, however, the citizenry as a whole remained loyal to Mao. Party leadership placed much of the blame for failures on "enemies of the people" within the country, as well as on disasters resulting particularly from poor weather that, in turn, diminished agricultural output. Blame was also placed upon the Soviet Union, which became an enemy after its pullout from China in the early 1960s. In reality, among the chief reasons for the collapse (which also impacted on the Soviet withdrawal) was the failure by the Chinese leadership to recognize the need for both political and economic changes. Instead, the leadership relied on irrational policies, using slogans and coercion instead of reforming the economic system and developing sound management practices, business and commercial expertise, an innovative scientific community, and an open policy toward the outside world.

In the first half of the 1960s, however, impetus was placed on developing managerial effectiveness and industrial progress. Ideological extremism came to the fore with the beginning of the Cultural Revolution in mid–1966. This disastrous period in China's development virtually led to serious civil conflicts. The "enemies of the people" were expanded to include anyone who resisted any edict of the Party, which included a substantial majority of the population. Policies promulgated during the Cultural Revolution led to economic and social disaster, resulting in hardships and sacrifices that the masses were no longer able to tolerate. Intellectuals, who could have brought about the necessary reforms in a positive fashion, were banished to the countryside and remote areas of the country to work at hard labor and "cleanse themselves from their

bourgeoise tendencies.'' Unqualified party leaders were placed in charge
of industrial enterprises, banks, and agricultural communes. The educational systems were completely disrupted. Administrators and faculty
were replaced by members of the party cadre who focused solely on
political education and ideological indoctrination. The result was chaos
throughout the nation.

Following the Cultural Revolution, emphasis again was placed on modernization, with a major focus on the industrial sector. Stress was placed
on managerial effectiveness and innovations in operations that would
enhance productivity.

By 1968, China had begun to make use of trade fairs, primarily in
Eastern Europe, to promote its own industrial and consumer goods. This
presented an opportunity to obtain scarce foreign exchange, as well as to
observe the types of equipment being displayed at these fairs by European
and American companies. Not only did Chinese intelligence gathering
focus on industrial equipment, it also turned to management technology
as well. In 1968, at the Budapest trade fair, five management and technical
experts from the Chinese exhibit team sat in on the seminars given by a
U.S. business team that focused on managerial, production, and marketing
techniques, as well as technology transfers. A similar group participated
in the seminars given at the autumn fair in Bucharest, Romania, in 1970.

In the early 1970s, renewed emphasis was placed on management education and training in various sectors of the economy. In 1972, for example, the Beijing Institute of Foreign Trade, located on the outskirts of the
city, accepted its first class of students since the Cultural Revolution. Curricula were designed to provide export-import specialists for Chinese trade
organizations, banks (including the Bank of China and the People's Bank),
and governmental institutions, particularly the Ministry of Finance and the
Ministry of Foreign Economic Relations and Trade. In addition, a wide
range of foreign languages was offered and each degree candidate had to
be fluent in one or more languages. Institutes of Foreign Trade were also developed in Tianjin, Shanghai, and Guangzhou. In the early 1980s, the Beijing
Institute revised its undergraduate curriculum to correspond to that of the
AACSB (American Association of Collegiate Schools of Business) schools in
the United States, and by 1985 it had a well-developed MBA program. It
changed its name to the University of International Business and Economics
and has grown from an institution of approximately 200 degree candidates in
1972 to one of nearly 5,000. A doctoral program has been inaugurated in cooperation with two U.S. universities and one Canadian university.

MANAGEMENT CHANGES AND THE ROLE OF THE
COMMUNIST PARTY

During the 1949–57 period, a balance was drawn between the role of
the Communist party and of management in Chinese industry. The Com-

munist party was responsible for mobilizing, organizing, and motivating personnel, whereas management was responsible for meeting production quotas. During this period an industrial structure was developed, patterned after the Soviet system. This structure provided stability to both the industrial and economic systems of the country. However, intermediate positions in both industry and government were filled by individuals whose rise in the hierarchy was based on party loyalty and not necessarily on expertise. As a result, bureaucracies increased and there was resistance to change, a situation that still exists, to some degree, today.

From 1957 through 1966, in conjunction with the Great Leap Forward, the macromanagement bureaucracy was dismantled and power rested with the management of the enterprise. This was reversed during the Cultural Revolution, when party loyalty took precedence over managerial effectiveness. The irrational directives issued by party committees resulted in downturns in productivity (because of irrational changes induced by inadequately qualified personnel). To compensate for the masses of unemployed, factories were ordered to take on far more workers than was necessary for production efficiency. This was true in almost every business and governmental entity within China. These labor surpluses, combined with the realization that there were no rewards and the distaste for management by slogan, resulted in an overall economic downturn. The inability to make decisions at a local level further complicated this situation. Decision making had to be deferred through the party structure via a massive government bureaucracy. More often than not, multiple ministries would be involved in a single factory decision, a situation that in many instances still prevails in 1990, particularly where Western joint ventures are concerned.

Since 1970, however, China has looked to the West for innovations in management technologies. President Nixon's visit to China in 1972 created a flurry of interest in a massive market that had been opened to the world in terms of trade and investment. Entrepreneurs from around the globe began to seek a foothold in what they hoped would be the world's largest consumer and industrial market of over a billion people. However, the realities soon became evident. While the door had been opened, actual purchases from the West would be few in number due to a lack of foreign exchange hampered by an unwieldy bureaucracy. The Chinese view on foreign investment carried with it strong constraints. Examples included unrealistic demands for the transfer of modern technologies, training, infusion of foreign capital, and the requirement that a significant amount, if not all, of production be exported, except for selected import substitution products.

Early visitors to China soon learned that they had to go through a maze of bureaucracies regardless of the project and that negotiations, even for small deals, required months if not years of time and effort. China was handicapped by a lack of foreign exchange reserves and by laws, policies, and an infrastructure unable to accept a rapid inflow of foreign investment. Because of financial difficulties, the Chinese often insisted on making payment with Chinese goods or raw materials in lieu of hard foreign currency, a practice that still exists. Furthermore, sales made in Chinese currency could rarely be converted into hard currency. As world markets now illustrate, there is indeed a limit to the amount of Chinese handicrafts desired by Western buyers. Consumer products produced by emerging economies from Bangladesh to Brazil are competing effectively in world markets with Chinese low-technology, consumer-oriented exports.

Despite the difficulties presented by a country with erratic policies and a massive bureaucracy, trade and investment grew slowly in the early 1980s and then rapidly accelerated between 1984 and 1988. The 1979 law on joint ventures, combined with the implementing procedures promulgated in 1983, gave investors greater confidence in making investments on the mainland. Special economic zones and selected cities were opened to foreign investment with such special concessions as the duty-free import of machinery and equipment, lower taxes on profits that were extremely competitive with other Asian countries, favorable labor regulations, and, in some cases, Chinese government financing at low interest rates. Decentralization policies that placed decision-making authority with local governments and allowed selected foreign investments favorable access to raw materials, energy sources, and other materials essential for their operation facilitated the attraction of foreign investors.

The government emphasized investments for infrastructure development, including airport modernization to accommodate large commercial aircraft, expansion and upgrading of existing roads and highways, modernization of ports and construction of new port facilities, and enhancement of communication networks. Agricultural communes were dissolved and land distributed to the citizenry. Privatization was encouraged, and state industrial enterprises began to be managed more professionally, with factory managers being held accountable for bottom-line profitability. From Guangzhou to Tianjin along the China coastline, and inward to cities like Beijing and Wuhan, the country took on the image of a vast construction site. Hotels, office buildings, apartment houses, and shopping complexes sprung up in unprecedented numbers in every major city. Farmers who became rich in short periods of time by producing poultry and selling it at the open markets of large cities like Beijing and Shanghai made the headlines in local news media. Individuals who had had their bank accounts restored to them in Chinese currency quickly pooled their money and invested it in commercial projects, setting up private companies and engaging in foreign trade transactions as importers and exporters, using old linkages to the Western markets. In short, the 1984–88 period was one of uncontrolled expansion in both the public and private sectors.

It was during this period that inflation began to skyrocket. Prices rose more rapidly than wages, and shortages appeared everywhere. An active parallel market began to flourish in all major cities, not only for hard currency and luxury items, but also for needed raw materials and component parts. Factories soon learned that it was much easier and more profitable to export their products, obtain foreign exchange, and bring luxury goods back into the country where they would, in turn, sell them for hard currency or at greatly inflated prices for local currency. In some instances, factory output was sold to foreign buyers, who simply resold it to some other factory in another part of China that had a shortage of that material. Local financing bounded out of control and, although the government took steps to curb lending and thereby dampen inflationary growth, these attempts were not fully successful.

This instability, combined with rising political discontent, culminated in the infamous Tiananmen Square confrontation in June 1989. Following the military crackdown, the economy entered a slump from which it is slowly recovering in 1991. Bank lending was curtailed heavily, impacting both domestic and foreign joint venture companies alike. Since factories producing component parts could not get loans to purchase raw materials, they could not meet their production commitments. This inability to supply the necessary goods or component parts resulted in the end users' missing their deadlines as well. Consequently, foreign investment was decreased severely, and many local small-scale industries went bankrupt.

The following chapters are designed to provide a framework for the policy maker, practitioner, and researcher to gain insights into the policies and practices involved in foreign direct investment in China. As such, a practical guide to investing in China is provided, as well as insights into the evolving open-door policy, foreign investment motivations and incentives, organizations involved in foreign investment, and joint venture strategies.

2

The Open-door Policy, Special Economic Zones, and Opened Cities

The open-door policy has had a major impact on advancing technologies in the People's Republic of China; however, the policies for utilizing foreign capital have yielded mixed results. China's open-door policy, which has been pursued since 1979, consists of several major components. Efforts to attract foreign investment constitute one of the most important parts of this policy; other major elements include active involvement in international financial markets and the liberalization of China's foreign trading system. These policies have differed substantially from the pre-reform stage when external financing was limited, trade highly centralized, and foreign investment prohibited. Positive results include improving their management system as well as expanding production and export capacity for the country.

THE OPEN-DOOR POLICY

The deficiencies of China's centrally planned economic system prior to 1979 created the need for an open-door policy. The pre–1979 system was characterized by widespread market distortions, including irrational pricing policies and practices, large bureaucracies, an unmotivated labor force, and a noncompetitive and inefficient marketplace. In order to overcome these problems, various policy initiatives were adopted by the government aimed at reforming the economic systems in both agriculture and industry and opening the economy to the outside world. The major objective of the reforms was to make the economic system function more efficiently by relying more on market forces, while the purpose of the opening to the outside world was to acquire capital, technology, and other necessary production inputs to support the economic reform. The overall objective of these policy measures was to help achieve the goals of the modernization program started in the late 1970s.

The open-door policy started in the spring of 1979. In a broad sense, these efforts consisted of several major policy changes designed to broaden economic and financial contacts with the rest of the world. They included:

1. Reducing the trade controls that prevailed for about three decades between 1949 and 1979 and gradually abolishing state monopolies on foreign trade by permitting more active participation by the private sector in external economic activities;
2. Active interaction in international financial markets, utilizing foreign capital from various sources;
3. Encouraging foreign direct investment inflows, primarily through equity joint venture arrangements;
4. Adopting other trade practices, such as leasing, compensation trade, export processing, and assembling in order to rapidly expand external trade; and
5. Encouraging overseas equity investment by Chinese industrial companies and financial institutions in order to broaden the export base and marketing network for Chinese products.

In a more narrow sense, the open-door policy focused on two major areas: a more liberal policy toward external financing in order to mobilize foreign capital necessitated by the economic reforms to meet modernization goals and a firm commitment on the part of the government to develop measures that would encourage foreign investment inflows, thereby acquiring the essential capital, technology, and managerial expertise to increase domestic production capacity. To promote these foreign investment inflows, significant steps were taken by establishing four special economic zones and opening fourteen major coastal cities, as well as Hainan Island, to foreign investors.

EXTERNAL FINANCING POLICIES

External Financing Policies before 1979

China's presence in international financial markets prior to 1979 was minimal because, in large part, it was predominantly a cash trader. External credits were rarely used and, if any, were mostly provided by foreign governments. This conservative borrowing policy and practice in the past reflected largely the strict political and economic philosophy of self-reliance under which the use of external funds to finance imports could only be justified as a temporary step on the road to economic independence. The use of foreign capital for other purposes was considered to be ideologically unacceptable; therefore the use of foreign private credits was virtually impossible.

From the early 1950s through 1971, China paid for virtually all of its foreign purchases in cash. Business transactions with foreign firms were mainly paid for using letters of credit. Countertrade was used only (in the 1970s) for some large equipment transfers from Eastern European countries. Toward the late 1970s, deferred payment mechanisms were adopted for large turn-key projects. These arrangements typically called for a down payment of a certain percentage of the contract amount (normally 20 to 30 percent), with the remaining balance (70 to 80 percent) being paid upon the completion of shipment. The establishment of mutual deposit accounts in the 1970s, between the Bank of China (BOC) and its counterparts in foreign countries, came closest to direct external borrowing of any measures undertaken. This approach allowed the BOC to accept deposits from foreign banks to finance imports.

External Financing Policies after 1979

After the government began efforts in 1979 to accelerate modernization, it realized that a closed-door policy would make it impossible for the country to attain its ambitious development goals that had been established without using external financing. The funds demanded by the modernization programs exceeded those available internally by a large margin. Therefore, obtaining external financing would be critical as a means of supplementing the domestic savings, and, therefore, supporting the modernization efforts.

In order to accomplish this goal, it became clear that China would have to adjust its traditional, negative attitude toward foreign investment and adopt new policies to attract external financing. Based on these considerations, several measures were taken:

1. Opening all possible financing channels (bilateral credits, loans from international financial institutions, private commercial borrowing, and financing through international bond issues);
2. Seeking the most favorable financing terms (interest rates, maturities, amounts available, etc.) from among these financing sources;
3. Matching foreign borrowing with domestic funds available, thereby avoiding possible shortfalls in total financing; and
4. Ensuring the ability to service the external debt repayment.

Most importantly, foreign borrowing was encouraged for those projects either with export potential or with the capacity to produce goods that could serve as import substitutes. Strict rules applied to foreign borrowing

Table 2.1
External Borrowing, 1979–89

Sources	1979-82	1983	1984	1985	1986	1987	1988	1979-88
	(In Millions of U.S. Dollars)							
Foreign Governments	5233	716	723	486	841	798	1179	9977
International Organizations	1791	73	183	604	1342	715	1123	5832
Buyer's Credit	501	106	133	127	178	473	888	2405
Commercial Borrowing	7560	0	122	527	1495	2580	2435	14718
Other[1]	505	170	125	762	1159	1239	862	4822
Total	15590	1065	1286	2506	5015	5805	6487	37754
	(In Percent of Total)							
Foreign Governments	33.6	67.3	56.2	19.4	16.8	13.7	18.2	26.4
International Organizations	11.5	6.9	14.2	24.1	26.8	12.3	17.3	15.4
Buyer's Credit	3.2	9.9	10.4	5.0	3.5	8.1	13.7	6.4
Commercial Borrowing	48.5	0.0	9.5	21.0	29.8	44.4	37.5	39.0
Other[2]	3.2	15.9	9.7	30.4	23.1	21.4	13.3	12.8
Total	100.0	100.0	100.0	100.0	100.0	100.0	100.0	100.0

Source: Almanac of China's Foreign Economic Relations and Trade, various issues.

[1]While total borrowing for 1989 was US $6,286 million, disaggregated data are not available.
[2]Borrowing from issues of international bonds.

that would be used to finance the central or local government budget deficits or be used for consumption purposes. These policies paved the way for rapid development in external financing activities.

As Table 2.1 indicates, between 1979 and 1989 China's total external borrowing amounted to about US $44 billion. Altogether, official credits from foreign governments and international financial organizations accounted for more than two fifths of total borrowing. Official loans of this type, while prominent in early years, declined noticeably as a percentage of total borrowing in the latter period. Instead, borrowing from private foreign commercial banks increased substantially, accounting for about two fifths of the total by 1989. External private borrowing normally took two forms: international syndicated loans arranged through the BOC, the China International Trust and Investment Corporation (CITIC), and local financial institutions in the Eurocredit market; and project financing through banks in Hong Kong, which aimed at providing financing for specific large industrial and infrastructural projects. During this period, financing through foreign and Eurobond issues also rose substantially due to the increased need for funds domestically and the active participation of domestic financial institutions in international financial markets.

Loans from Foreign Governments

Official loans from foreign governments were, in fact, not new to China. In the 1950s, China borrowed a significant amount of money from the Soviet Union; and in the 1970s, it used trade credits from industrial countries to finance high-volume imports. However, it was not until the late 1970s and early 1980s that China began to substantially tap these official sources of financing.

For the Chinese government, the use of official loans had several advantages:

1. They were generally available in large amounts, allowing the government to undertake massive infrastructure projects that could not be financed through commercial borrowing;
2. The interest rates charged on these loans were usually fixed and low, thereby enabling the government to reduce the interest risk that it would otherwise face and to lower the overall financing cost;
3. The loans usually had long maturities, thereby permitting China to service its interest payments and have the principal amortized over an extended period;
4. Technically, these borrowings were easy to monitor and manage as they were based on official agreements; and,
5. In many cases, loan agreements were tied to commodity purchases from creditor countries, which could help China save foreign exchange that would otherwise be necessary to finance these purchases.

Loans from International Financial Institutions

China began to utilize financing from international organizations in the late 1970s. The United Nations Development Program became one of the first such groups to earmark funds for the country. Later, other agencies such as the Population Activities Office and the Disaster Relief Office of the United Nations started providing grants and assistance. In 1980, China joined the International Monetary Fund (IMF) and the World Bank. This permitted it to have access not only to short-term balance-of-payments financing if needed, but also to long-term financing for development programs and projects.

China first obtained the IMF credit in 1981 and later in 1986, primarily because of the balance-of-payments difficulties it experienced in these years. However, it has not actively used IMF resources since then for two principal reasons. First, it has not experienced any serious short-term balance-of-payments problems. Second, there has been no need to request longer-term structural program loans from the IMF because most funding needed for economic reform efforts during this period has been satisfied from other sources, both official and private, without much difficulty, and given the large quota China has held in the IMF, sizeable borrowing from the IMF could easily deplete the institution's financial resources, which would otherwise be made available to other smaller member countries. China has, however, benefited from the IMF membership in a number of other ways, including economic advising on policies and reforms, technical assistance to improve data bases and management, and seminars and training programs for Chinese officials.

Since it joined the World Bank, China has actively utilized the financial resources available at the bank. The membership in the World Bank has also qualified it to be a major borrower of long-term and low or zero interest rate financing from the International Development Association, which is a part of the World Bank Group. Prior to June 1989, China was one of the largest borrowers from the World Bank, with annual borrowing amounting to about US $1 billion on average. The World Bank's financing covered a wide range of projects from industry, agriculture, and infrastructure projects to social development, including education. In addition, the bank has provided valuable technical assistance and training programs to update the managerial expertise of the Chinese staff working on these projects. Loans from the World Bank are customarily large in amount and long in maturity, with interest rates lower than those charged in the international financial markets. While loan disbursements to China were suspended in June 1989, resumption began on a selective basis in late 1990; hence the World Bank will likely remain one of the principal sources of external financing for China in the 1990s.

China has also obtained help from the International Finance Corporation (IFC), another sister organization of the World Bank. The IFC specializes in investing in private sector projects and providing technical assistance to develop domestic financial markets. While detailed information is not available, there are indications that the IFC was quite active in investments in joint ventures in China prior to June 1989. Assistance has also been provided to develop Chinese securities markets, particularly the stock market.

Foreign Commercial Borrowing

In 1979, China began borrowing massively, making more extensive use of commercial loans from Eurocredit markets and other private sources. These loans were used primarily to pay for imports of machinery and equipment, as well as for turn-key projects. By using these forms of commercial borrowing, China has been able to finance major projects through international syndication in a single package since individual financial institutions are unable to handle these transactions by themselves and, more importantly, the funds may be used freely at the borrower's discretion.

Financing through Foreign and Eurobond Issues

Foreign bonds (bonds are denominated in the currency of the country/ market in which they are floated) were first issued by the CITIC in the Tokyo capital market in 1982. However, it was not until November 1984 that the BOC, China's main foreign exchange bank, began issuing public bonds in Japan. Since then, the use of bonds to raise financing has become quite extensive. In October 1985, the BOC floated a Eurobond issue in the Tokyo market (bonds were denominated in U.S. dollars). This was considered a quite important move since only highly qualified financial institutions could issue Eurobonds in the international financial markets.

Financial institutions in large cities, including Shanghai, Tianjin, and Guangzhou, as well as Fujian Province, also have floated bonds in various foreign financial markets. Between 1982 and 1988, thirty-nine bond issues were arranged, of which fourteen were in the form of Eurobonds and twenty-five in the form of foreign bonds. Tokyo has been the most important market for floating foreign bonds—a total of twenty-one issues were floated in this market during the past ten years. Other Asian markets include Singapore (five issues) and Hong Kong (four issues). European markets include Frankfurt, Luxembourg, and London (four, three, and two issues, respectively, as shown in Table 2.2).

Financing from bond issues has enabled China to enjoy several advantages: bonds usually carry medium- and long-term maturities, permitting the country to diversify the maturity profile of its external borrowing; bonds have been denominated in dual currencies, therefore helping to reduce the exchange rate risk; and some bond issues were made with fixed interest rates, which have proven to be more advantageous than the floating rates charged on commercial bank financing.

Prior to June 1989, bonds floated by the Chinese financial institutions were extremely highly rated. The BOC bonds were assigned "AAA," the highest rating given by the Japan Public and Corporate Bond Institute, a prime Japanese rating agency. CITIC's bonds were rated "AA," while bonds issued by other financial institutions were all rated "A or above," still a very trustworthy credit rating for a financial institution to receive. The assignment of these credit ratings was based on two principal factors: China's political environment and economic development, and the issuer's financial history, current financial position, and future repayment ability. Given the relative political stability and the ongoing economic reforms during the first part of the 1980s, together with the monopolistic position of these financial institutions, the high ratings that the Chinese financial institutions had received prior to June 1989 were not unexpected. These

Table 2.2
Issuance of Foreign and Eurobonds, 1982–88

Date of Issue	Issuer	Amount	Term (years)	Interest (%)	Market
Jan. 1982	CITIC	Yen 10 billion	12	8.7	Tokyo
Aug. 1983	FIEC	Yen 5 billion	10	8.5	Tokyo
Nov. 1984	BOC	Yen 20 billion	10	7.0	Tokyo
Jan. 1985	CITIC	Yen 30 billion	10	6.6	Tokyo
Apr.	BOC	Yen 20 billion	10	7.1	Tokyo
June	BOC	DM 150 million	7	7.0	Frankfurt
July	CITIC	HK$ 300 million	5	9.375	Hong Kong
Sept.	CITIC	DM 150 million	6.6	6.25	Frankfurt
Oct.	BOC	US$ 150 million	10	10.0	Tokyo
Oct.	BOC	Yen 30 billion	10	6.1	Tokyo
Dec.	FIEC	Yen 10 billion	10	7.10	Tokyo
Dec.	CITIC	US$ 100 million	10	9.625	Tokyo
Feb. 1986	SITC	Yen 25 billion	10	6.6	Tokyo
Feb.	CITIC	Yen 40 billion	10	6.3	Tokyo
Apr.	BOC	Yen 20 billion	10	7.2	Tokyo
Apr.	BOC	Yen 50 billion	12	5.3	Tokyo
July	BOC	US$ 200 million	10	L+1/16	Frankfurt
Sept.	CITIC	HK$ 400 million	7	7.875	Hong Kong
Sept.	CITIC	Yen 20 billion	10	6.1	Tokyo
Nov.	FIEC	US$ 50 million	10	8.0	Singapore
Dec.	TITC	Yen 10 billion	10	6.0	Tokyo
Jan. 1987	CITIC	Yen 20 billion	5	7.875	Tokyo
Mar.	CITIC	Yen 10 billion	5	1.0	Singapore
Apr.	CITIC	Yen 30 billion	10	4.9	Tokyo
May	BOC	US$ 200 million	10	L+1/16	Singapore
July	FIEC	Yen 10 billion	10	4.8	Tokyo
Aug.	BOC	Yen 15 billion	5	5.2	Tokyo
Aug.	CITIC	US$ 50 million	5	8.5	Hong Kong
Sept.	BOC	US$ 200 million	5	L+1/16	London
Oct.	MOF	M 300 million	5	6.0	Frankfurt
Jan. 1988	CITIC	Yen 15 billion	5	5.625	Luxembourg
Mar.	BOC	Yen 15 billion	5.25	5.0	Luxembourg
May	CITIC	Yen 20 billion	5	5.125	London
June	SITC	Yen 15 billion	7.25	5.25	Luxembourg
July	Bank of Communications	HK$ 200 million	5	5.30	Hong Kong
July	CITIC	Yen 15 billion	5.25	5.25	Singapore
Aug.	Bank of Communications	US$ 100 million	5	9.375	Singapore
Sept.	FIEC	Yen 15 billion	10	5.9	Tokyo
Dec.	TITC	Yen 10 billion	10	5.1	Tokyo

Source: Vetro China Newsletter, no. 82, 1989, p. 10.

BOC: Bank of China
CITIC: China International Trust & Investment Corporation
FIEC: Fujian Investment Enterprise Corporation
MOF: Ministry of Finance
SITC: Shanghai Investment & Trust Corporation
TITC: Tianjin Investment & Trust Corporation

high credit ratings paved the way for quite impressive borrowings in the later years.

Since June 1989, the credit ratings for bond issues have been lowered, and all bond issues placed in the Tokyo capital market have been put under "credit watch." This change has undoubtedly placed Chinese financial institutions in a difficult position to raise new long-term financing through bond issues on the Tokyo market. It also indicates the concern of the international financial community about the current political and economic environment in China, which has not given evidence of the stability required by analysts and investors alike.

External Financing Policy Assessment

Although China has substantially increased external borrowing since 1979, its overall policy has, by and large, been cautious, and the total borrowing and debt services have so far remained at prudent levels. Total debt outstanding in terms of GNP, for example, accounted for only about 10 percent during the mid–1980s and increased slightly to about 13 percent in 1989. Measured by export earnings, debt service ratio has also been about 10 percent, far below the 20 percent prudent level. Looking ahead, even with projections that external debt were to accumulate further, debt service ratio in the immediate future would still be within the 15 percent limit.

Several factors may have contributed to the relatively conservative management of external borrowing. First, the painful experience of repaying the Soviet debt in the late 1950s and early 1960s provided a strong lesson about the problems associated with foreign indebtedness. Second, the ideological effect of the Cultural Revolution may still influence the use of foreign capital. Third, the debt problems experienced by Latin American countries in general, and by several Eastern European countries, particularly in the early 1980s, provided another caution to the Chinese authorities that excessive borrowing could be dangerous. Finally, unlike in many other countries, the Chinese realized the importance of a balanced use of debt and equity financing. In fact, the authorities believed (and still believe) that foreign direct investment financing could be more advantageous to economic development through the infusion of not only capital, but technology, management, and an expansion of their external market.

Since the late 1970s, much emphasis has been placed on the improvement of the investment environment to attract equity investment inflows, and foreign borrowing has been minimized to the extent possible. While it is expected that foreign equity inflows could not entirely replace the importance of foreign debt financing, it is likely that foreign direct investment will continue to increase at a rapid rate while foreign commercial borrowing will remain relative limited, even though China may not experience much difficulty in raising debt financing in the international financial markets.

SPECIAL ECONOMIC ZONES

The establishment of four special economic zones (SEZs) has been one of the most widely publicized aspects of China's open-door policy. The first zones were established in 1979 in the two coastal provinces of Guangdong and Fujian, adjacent to Hong Kong, Macao, and the South China Sea. Of the four zones, three are located in Guangdong Province and one is located in Fujian Province. The short-term objective of establishing the zones was to promote inflows of foreign investment, technology, and management know-how. Their long-term objectives, were, however, more ambitious—to act as laboratories for China's economic reforms. It was hoped that the more market-oriented approach to business operations would be tried in these zones first, with successful experiences later being passed on to the rest of the country. Since their establishment, significant progress has been made in this direction.

Motivation for Establishing SEZs

"Special economic zone" is a term that describes designated legal and geographic areas in which commercial activities, including manufacturing, exporting, processing, banking, and assembly, take place between the local and foreign companies under special conditions that provide a variety of incentives that are not available in other parts of the country. More importantly, an investment environment had to be developed that was considerably more liberal than elsewhere in China, which would allow foreign investors to take either a minority position in an investment project or own up to 100 percent subject to the approval of the local government. Additionally, foreign firms would be given high levels of autonomy in managing operations, face minimal controls in both capital and goods movements, and be allowed to export and import freely when needed.

Two policy considerations motivated the Chinese government's decision to establish the SEZs. First, the opening of these SEZs was understood to be the first step in China's overall open-door policy and practices. Until it opened to the outside world in 1979, China had been a closed economy, both politically and economically, for about thirty years. To avoid unnecessary mistakes and drawbacks, the government decided to establish these special zones to serve as centers for observation and experimentation. Isolated geographically, the zones were viewed as incubators of economic reform, permitting the country to learn how to deal with market economies in a controlled environment. The purpose was to provide a testing ground for integrated economic development that would include infrastructure, regulation and law, industrial projects, construction, tourism, and foreign investment. If the SEZs became successful, such experiments would be adopted in other parts of the country. If the SEZs failed, the problems could be identified and avoided elsewhere.

Second, these zones were designed to benefit economically the overall Chinese economy. The zones were viewed as a window through which to introduce foreign technology, capital, and managerial techniques, as well as Western production, marketing, and information systems. The government hoped that these zones would provide better investment incentives and the more liberal environment necessary to attract foreign investment more quickly than would be possible in other less accessible areas of the country.

The SEZs were set up, not only to encourage export processing and assembly businesses, but more importantly to encourage foreign investment in major projects, which include those in the manufacturing, construction, and service sectors. In the process, the government hoped that these zones would become major industrial and export bases for the country.

The location of zones was also of great significance in the overall decision of their establishment. The selection of Guangdong and Fujian provinces as sites for the initial SEZs was made for several reasons:

1. These coastal zones could potentially facilitate the importation of raw materials and finished products necessary for export processing and assembly operations;

2. Guangdong Province is the home of many overseas Chinese who reside in Hong Kong, Macao, and Southeast Asian countries. For these overseas Chinese, the opportunity to assist in the economic development of their hometown and, at the same time, make a profit on their investment would have both sentimental and practical appeal;

3. The proximity of the zones in Guangdong Province to Hong Kong would provide investors with easy access to the zones and would permit the SEZs to tap the infrastructural resources of Hong Kong, particularly as a transit port;

4. China's choice of Guangdong Province as the location for three of the four SEZs was also politically motivated. Since Hong Kong shares the border with the Shenzhen SEZ (the largest of the four), promoting economic integration between Hong Kong and the southern parts of China would ultimately benefit China's move to unify Hong Kong after 1997 by accelerating the pace of economic development on the Chinese side; and

5. The rationale to designate Xiamen as a SEZ, one of the four zones in Fujian Province, was both political and economic. Politically, the Chinese government hoped to attract Taiwanese investment since many Taiwan residents had emigrated from Fujian Province and still had close family ties there. The expansion of this process ultimately could unite the two parts of China. Because Fujian Province is well connected with Chinese living in other parts of the world

Table 2.3
Economic and Investment Indicators in SEZs, 1989 (In Millions of U.S. Dollars)

Indicators	Shenzhen	Zhuhai	Shantou	Xiamen	Total
Industrial output	2478	621	1391	1160	5650
Exports	2174	365	747	648	3933
Foreign exchange earnings	830	100	374	140	1444
Number of FDI contracts	647	225	285	225	1382
FDI committed	489	242	256	835	1822
Actual FDI inflows	458	169	157	238	1023

Source: China Economic News, April 30, 1990.

(particularly in the United States), the zone would be attractive to them as a place to develop their investment and trade linkages.

Investment Policies and Measures

To encourage foreign investment inflows to the SEZs, the Chinese government has undertaken numerous measures since 1979. These measures are designed to either remove regulatory restraints on foreign investment or provide attractive incentives to foreign investors. On the regulatory side, the aim has been to reduce government intervention and to create an environment in which foreign investors could operate in a more Western market-oriented approach. Toward this end, various regulations and rules were enacted which stipulate that foreign investors in the SEZs have considerable freedom in the production, financing, and marketing activities of their companies. Incentive programs, which are discussed in detail in chapter 3, were focused on tax concessions, tax holidays, and exemptions from import and export duties. These incentives were designed to help foreign investors reduce their operating and tax cost, thus making their operations more profitable.

Economic and Investment Indicators

Since their establishment, the SEZs have made remarkable achievements in terms of overall economic development, utilization of foreign capital and technology, and the growth of both exports and imports. In fact, before these areas were designated as the SEZs, three of the four (except the Xiamen SEZ) were small fishing villages with no infrastructure and no industrial facilities, and they had very small populations. Today these zones have become modern cities, comparable to those in the newly industrialized countries. For instance, economic indicators for 1989 (Table 2.3) indicated that total industrial output for the four SEZs reached US $5.7 billion. In terms of the utilization of foreign investment, a total of 1,382 contracts were signed and the amount of new investment pledged amounted to over US $1.8 billion.

The Shenzhen SEZ has outpaced all other zones in terms of development, accounting for almost 50 percent of economic growth among the other SEZs. In 1989, for example, the Shenzhen SEZ's total industrial output was about half of the total industrial output of all the zones combined. In terms of foreign investment committed in the same year, the Shenzhen SEZ accounted for over one quarter of the total while it also accounted for over 55 percent of total exports for all zones.

OPENED CITIES

Based on the successful experience and remarkable performance of the SEZs, in 1984 the Chinese government took a further step in its open-door policy and liberalized fourteen coastal cities for foreign investment. Following a similar approach as in the SEZs, the opened cities were allowed to prepare their own investment regulations and incentive programs and to operate more flexibly. Most importantly, the central government's control was relaxed and the autonomy granted to local governments substantially increased. Reflected in investment regulations, local (municipal) governments were permitted to approve all foreign investment projects within certain upper limits.

Characteristics

At the time of their designation, these opened cities differed considerably from the SEZs in a number of ways:

1. They were far larger than the zones in terms of population, geographic size, industrial output, and other economic indicators;
2. They were also located in coastal areas of China but where there were already relatively well-developed industrial infrastructures as well as a fairly good, diversified industrial and trade base;
3. They possessed far more convenient and modern transportation facilities and communication systems;
4. They were equipped with relatively well-educated technicians and labor; and
5. They had a long tradition of being engaged in international trade and investment.

Therefore, the opening of these cities to foreign investment reflected, to a large extent, China's determination to pursue an open-door policy with a long term perspective. Another difference between the opened cities and SEZs is that within each opened city there is a separate area that is designated as an economic and technical development zone (ETDZ). More generous incentives (than other parts of the opened city) are usually made available within the ETDZ designed to attract technology-oriented foreign ventures.

Motivation for Designating Opened Cities

Although the reasons for designating opened cities for foreign investment were similar to those for establishing the SEZs, the Chinese government's expectations and emphasis between the opened cities and SEZs were somewhat different. As discussed earlier, the most important policy consideration for creating the SEZs was to use them as a testing or experimenting place for the open-door policy, whereas the primary motivation for designating opened cities was to attract foreign capital, technology, and management so as to improve the overall economic development in these coastal cities where present plants and equipment were either outmoded or obsolete. Another important motivation was to utilize foreign investment to develop an export base to penetrate the external markets and thereby generate foreign currency earnings for development purposes. Furthermore, foreign investment inflows could help resolve the unemployment problems that each opened city has encountered in recent years. Therefore, if the establishment of the SEZs was motivated by both political and economic considerations, the designation of the opened cities was mainly the result of economic considerations.

Investment Policies and Measures

In addition to the preferential treatment opened cities can provide to foreign investors (discussed in chapter 3), municipal governments were given greater autonomy in managing foreign investment policies. For example, local authorities were given the right to approve most foreign investment projects (within certain limits) without having to obtain approvals from the central government. Large opened cities such as Shanghai and Tianjin have the authority to approve foreign investment projects up to US $30 million, while smaller cities can also approve investment up to US $10 million, in contrast to a lower limit, usually US $3 million for unopened city provinces. This autonomy has greatly simplified the approval procedures for foreign investors. In addition, opened cities are in a better position to provide other services, such as financing and marketing assistance, to facilitate foreign investors in their perspective regions.

Economic and Investment Performance

Compared with the SEZs, the opened cities are much larger in terms of overall economic activity. In 1989, for example, the combined industrial output of the fourteen opened cities was ten times greater than that of the four SEZs, whereas the industrial output of Shanghai alone was more than four times greater than that of all the SEZs combined. Although Shanghai has been the largest open city in terms of the industrial output, smaller cities, such as Zhengjiang, Ningbo, and Huizhou, have experienced more rapid growth in the past few years. Total foreign investment inflows to the opened cities were about three times greater than those of the SEZs during the same years, with Shanghai, once again, outnumbering its counterparts.

HAINAN ISLAND

Hainan Island, formerly a county in Guangdong Province, was declared an independent province in 1988. The decision to elevate the status of Hainan Island was ambitious; the central government wanted to create a zone that would provide an even better investment environment and more incentives than were available in the SEZs to enhance development on this undeveloped island. In the same year, the central government and the Hainan provincial authorities passed two pieces of legislation that outlined the basic incentive programs the island would provide to foreign investors. Like those available in the SEZs and opened cities, investment incentives on Hainan Island have focused on tax concessions for foreign investment as noted in chapter 3.

A COMPARISON OF THE SEZs IN CHINA AND OTHER COUNTRIES

While the concept of SEZs is relatively new in China, foreign trade zones, economic activity zones, or free zones in other countries have existed for quite some time. A typical foreign trade zone is established by a host country to promote export and import business through low or nonexistent import and export duties (Table 2.4). To the same extent, these zones are established as a part of major efforts to develop an export manufacturing base or a worldwide distribution center for the host country, as well as a means to employ local labor and to benefit from the transfer of technology.

Foreign trade zones in the United States, for example, offer tax deferral mechanisms for goods consumed in the domestic market and duty-free status for imported components that are traded within the trade zone and re-exported. But the trade zones are still subject to U.S. foreign trade regulations, such as export controls. As such, U.S. foreign trade zones play even a lesser role in the U.S. economy.

Economic activity zones, on the other hand, provide more economic and investment incentives and more business opportunities for foreign

Table 2.4
A General Taxonomy of Economic Zones

Type of Zone (Z)	Usual Features	Applied to	Examples of
Free Banking/ Insurance Zones	Freed from most/ all regulations	Services for foreign/ domestic markets	Eurodollar market and the Asian dollar market
Export Process- ing Free Trade, and Foreign Trade Zones	No tariffs, tax exemptions, less red tape	Mainly manufacturing activities for export	Shannon (Ireland) Bataan (Philippines) Kaohshiung (Taiwan)
Free Port	No tariffs, no taxes, less red tape	Basically storage and transhipping facilities	Hamburg (Germany) Penang (Malaysia)
Bonded Warehouse	No tariffs, no taxes, less red tape	Storage of goods	USA, Malaysia, Indonesia
Duty Free Shops	No tariffs, no taxes, less red tape	Sale of goods to be exported or consumed by foreigners/ travelers	Airport, boats, planes, special stores
Enterprise Zone	Reduced taxes and less red tape	Most types of economic activities	Great Britain
Industrial Estate Industrial Park	No specific	Most types of economic activities	Great Britain, USA, Taiwan, Malaysia
Science Park	No specific, often near universities	High technology industries, research facilities	USA, Singapore, Taiwan
Special Economic Zones	Reduced income tax, tax holidays, free of imports & export duties. Simpli- fied procedures and regulations. All economic activities encouraged. No restrictions on domestic sales vs. export.	All types of economic activities, investment, manufacturing, service industries, etc.	Shenzhen, Xiamen, Shantou, Zhuhai (China)

companies. Particularly popular throughout Asia, these zones are established for the purpose of generating foreign exchange earnings, renumer-
ating factors of production, and supplying intermediate/nonconventional
inputs, as well as capitalizing economies of scale for the host country. In
Ireland, investment in their export zones is a major factor in the total
GNP; the same holds true for the maquilladora region of Mexico. Therefore, these zones provide important impulses for the industrialization
process and ensure a more efficient allocation of resources in the host
country than otherwise may be attained. Although China's SEZs share
some similarities with the foreign trade and economic activity zones else-

where in the world, striking differences also exist in the way that they are developed, located, and function.

Rationale for Establishment

The first difference between the SEZs in China and those in other countries is the rationale on the part of government for which they were established. As analyzed earlier, the major policy consideration for initiating SEZs in China was their use as testing centers for China's open-door policy. Economic considerations, such as building the infrastructure and industrial facilities and enhancing foreign exchange earnings capability in the long run, were secondary. Also, the rationale for establishing the Chinese SEZs was influenced by a variety of other factors, including political and ideological reasons unique to China. In other countries, however, economic motivation has usually dominated all other policy considerations of their host governments.

Geographical Scope

China's SEZs are much larger in geographical size than their counterparts in other countries. In fact, China's Shenzhen SEZ is the largest zone in the world. Table 2.5 shows that even the smallest SEZ in China (the Zhuhai SEZ) may be several times larger than many of those in other Asian countries.

Business Activities

Business activities differ greatly between the Chinese SEZs and those in other parts of the world. In the Chinese SEZs, foreign companies are encouraged not only to engage in the exporting and importing business, but also in manufacturing, banking, insurance, real estate, and other business operations. In fact, most of the foreign business firms located in the Chinese zones were to take advantage of low labor costs available locally and were to produce goods for the Chinese domestic market. In other countries, however, foreign companies are only permitted to engage in foreign trade-related activities within the zone. Even in the economic activity zones in most Asian countries, foreign companies are more restricted than are those situated in the Chinese SEZs. For example, in most economic activity zones, foreign companies are required to export a certain percentage of their products or face heavy duties when goods are imported into the host country. In many countries, foreign business is simply not permitted to market any of their products in the local market, whereas in China decisions are made on a case by case basis.

Table 2.5
Basic Data on Economic and Trade Zones in Selected Countries

Name/Country	Date Established	Area/Acres
China		
Shenzhen	1980	81,875
Xiamen	1980	32,750
Shantou	1980	15,625
Zhuhai	1980	3,790
Indonesia		
Batam Island	1978	9,143
Jakarta/Tanjung Priok	1978	82
Malaysia		
Senai	1977	100
Melaka/Batu Berendam	1973	52
Tanjong Kling	1973	170
Penang/Bayan Lepas	1971	304
Prai	1972	416
Prai Wharf	1972	42
Pulau Jerajak	1972	406
Selangor/Ampang Ulu Klang	1973	50
Sungei Way - Subang	1972	141
Telok Panglima Garang	1974	49
Philippines		
Central Luzon/Bataan	1972	853
Central Visayas/Mactan	1979	294
Northern Luzon/Baguio	1979	156
Singapore		
All industrial areas	1960	21,994
Taiwan		
Kaohsiung/Kaohsiung	1966	168
Nantze	1970	222
Taichung	1971	57
Thailand		
Lard Krabang	1980	69

Sources: The China Investment Guide, Longman Publishing Company, 1986, pp. 65–77, and Dean Spinanger, "Economic Activity Zones—Objectives and Impact—Some Evidence from Asia," *Working Paper*. Kiel Institute of World Economics, November 1983, p. 13.

Incentives

Compared with the economic activity zones in other Asian countries, the Chinese SEZs provide far more comprehensive incentive programs in terms of tax concessions and tax holidays. China also provides cheaper labor and lower land-use fees for foreign investors. Most importantly, it does not impose any special requirements or restrictions on foreign companies' ability to export from the zone to other parts of the world.

SUMMARY

China's new external financial policies and strategies, as well as its establishment of special economic zones, opened cities, and Hainan Island as windows for investment, are an important part of the open-door policy. When the SEZs were first established, many in and outside of China wondered why the Chinese should take such a step—unprecedent in a nonmarket economy and far ahead of the Soviet Union and other Communist countries.

The modern methods of mass production and the formation of international markets have led to production and consumption on a world scale. To offset the weaknesses of each nation, extensive economic cooperation and technical changes must occur between developed and developing countries. The Chinese understand this very well. While relying mainly on its own forces to bring about modernization, China, as a developing country, has to win foreign assistance, actively develop economic cooperation, and reasonably use and absorb foreign technology useful to its overall economic development. For these reasons, China forged ahead with its decisive policy to set up SEZs and designated fourteen opened cities to attract world resources.

It is obvious that the SEZs and opened cities have performed the functions set out for them to the extent possible at this stage of their development. Foreign capital, technology, and equipment have been introduced, competition has been promoted, and the training of personnel has occurred. Indeed, the SEZs and opened cities represent the focus of a substantial share of all foreign investment flows to China, and significant economic development has been achieved. More important than their enormous vitality in absorbing and utilizing foreign capital and importing advanced technology, the SEZs and opened cities represent a significant pioneering undertaking by China in carrying out the policy of opening the country to the outside world and in serving as experimental centers in economic structural reform to create a completely new set of conditions for economic development. As such, a new avenue has been opened, creating opportunities for foreign investors wishing to become involved in a rapidly expanding Chinese marketplace.

3

Investment Policies and Incentives

Factors affecting an investment environment are numerous. First and foremost, a stable political situation, a stable social order, and consistent policies to attract foreign capital are essential. There should also be good profit-making opportunities—a prime concern of foreign investors—the legitimate rights and interests of foreign entrepreneurs should be protected, and incentives should be offered.

The investment policies and incentives provided by the Chinese government are generally positive and flexible depending on the particular investment and where it is placed. Covering a wide range of areas, they include:

1. variances in the degree of foreign ownership
2. flexible project duration
3. free choice of investment sectors
4. flexible size of investment project
5. free choice of investment location
6. lower corporate tax rates
7. flexible policies on land use
8. relatively flexible management, employment, and wage systems
9. flexible policies on product pricing structures
10. variable terms for financing and remittance of profits

INVESTMENT POLICIES

Flexible Foreign Ownership

In contrast to foreign investment in some developing countries, the claim that unilateral direct foreign investment is discouraged and that some sort of local participation in investments is mandated does not hold true for China. A unique characteristic of the investment policy in China is an acceptance of equity investments up to and including 100 percent ownership by foreign investors. This is significant because foreign investors in would-be joint ventures often face difficulties in selecting or even discovering experienced or appropriate Chinese joint venture partners. Depending on the type of venture, flexible ownership permits foreign investors to choose between a joint venture with a local Chinese partner and a wholly owned subsidiary. The foreign investor's ability to have majority ownership and management control of the venture, as desired, ensures adequate flexibility in production, management, financing, marketing, and other important operational decisions of the venture.

Flexible Project Duration

The Chinese legislation does not impose any formal limit on the duration of the investment project, allowing investors to plan their investment on either a short-term or a long-term basis. This is important for certain large-scale manufacturing and raw material development projects that require a substantial outlay in the initial investment stage and have a relatively long payback period. The primary objective of many investors is to maintain a presence in the Chinese market over a long period. Flexible durations allow them to achieve this strategic objective.

Choice of Investment Sectors

The Chinese government encourages foreign investment in all industrial sectors. With diversified foreign investment, a more balanced distribution in different industries may be attained. Hence, a variety of investments are encouraged, and all industrial sectors may benefit. Due to minimal restrictions on the choice of investment, joint ventures have been established in various sectors, ranging from high-technology-oriented industries to raw material exploration and extraction, as well as in hotels, consumer goods, construction, and other service-oriented operations.

Flexible Size of Investment Project

Legally speaking, there is no restriction on the size of a foreign investment project in China. This policy not only encourages large multinational companies to locate their resources in China, but it enables medium- and even small-sized companies to tap the Chinese market through the form of joint ventures. In fact, most of the joint ventures already established are small operations with initial equity investments of less than US $1 million. Some are even as small as US $100,000 in size, yet others are as large as several hundred million U.S. dollars.

Choice of Investment Locations

Another unique characteristic of China's foreign investment policy is the freedom of choice given to foreign investors to invest wherever they want and in any locations they consider best. Foreign investment has been particularly encouraged in the coastal areas where investment opportunities, as well as the business and social climates, are generally better than those of the inner part of the country. This policy is in sharp contrast to the foreign investment policies of many developing countries whose intention is to stimulate economic growth in lesser-developed remote areas rather than in the well-developed metropolitan areas. The objective of the Chinese investment policies, however, is to provide the most attractive part of the country to foreign investors in the initial stage, and when these areas are developed, it is believed that investment flows to the lesser-developed areas will follow.

Relatively Flexible Management Systems

Management systems for foreign joint ventures differ vastly from those of domestic Chinese enterprises. In most domestic enterprises, there is a lack of independent rights and adequate autonomy. The management system in a joint venture, however, is much more Western oriented because joint ventures have the right to manage themselves, provided that they observe the investment laws and related regulations, and joint ventures are managed by their own boards of directors. In general, the government does not interfere in the administration of these ventures. Wholly owned ventures, of course, have complete autonomy for internal operations.

The board of directors is typically the highest decision-making body in a joint venture. Under its supervision, the general manager is responsible for carrying out the day-to-day business activities. A representative administrative structure for a joint venture is shown in Figure 3.1. Foreign investors should recognize, however, that in the Chinese environment, many management decisions of an investment project still have to be made in conjunction with either the local or central government, or both. For example, a joint venture may not be free to determine prices for its products that are considered important to the Chinese economy and sold

Figure 3.1
Organizational Structure of a Joint Venture

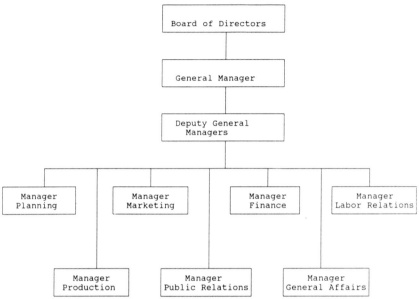

in the local market. Likewise, it may be difficult for the venture to market its products freely in the Chinese domestic market due to government-imposed restrictions set forth in the agreement under which the venture was approved.

Employment and Wage Policies

Legally speaking, joint ventures are free to employ any required personnel. According to the investment laws and regulations, all hiring is contractual and employees are subject to warnings, demerits, wage cuts, or dismissals. Wage systems can be based on an hourly, daily, monthly, or annual basis. Normally, the total wage consists of basic wages, which are similar wages earned by workers all over China and support the basic needs of workers and their families, and wages appropriate to jobs and specific posts that reflect the amount of labor and quality of work and are determined by the worker's labor intensity and the technical level of working conditions. The administrators' salaries are determined by the importance of their posts and the degree of difficulty in their work. Additional considerations include education, housing, medical insurance, retirement, labor welfare, service fees, and general welfare. Subsidies are provided to workers to help them cope with the rising housing, living, and other costs. Floating wages, generally in the form of bonuses, are determined by the workers' contribution to the performance of the joint venture. No formal ceiling is imposed on such bonuses.

The average proportion of these four types of wages is as follows: basic wages account for 40 percent of the total wage, specific wages 30 percent, subsidies 10 percent, and floating wages 20 percent. Since only basic wages and subsidies are fixed, 50 percent of the total wage workers and staff receive remains flexible.

In 1989, the average monthly wage of a worker in a foreign joint venture located in a non-SEZ was about 400 to 500 RMB, or approximately US $85 to 100. Among the total wage, the basic wage was equal to US $40, the bonus equal to US $10 to 15, the supplements for education US $1, housing US $10, retirement insurance US $7, labor welfare US $7, medical insurance US $5, service fees US $5, and other welfare US $5. In the SEZs, however, the unit labor cost is about US $250 to 300 per month, much higher than in other parts of the country.

Pricing Policies

The product pricing of joint ventures is basically determined by the market forces and is set by the factory management. Except for a few product categories, in which the prices are determined by the state, prices are allowed to fluctuate according to the local market supply and demand conditions. State-determined prices are subdivided into fixed prices and floating prices. Fixed prices are determined by the central government and cannot be changed by individual joint ventures. Floating prices are set by the central government but are allowed to fluctuate within preset margins, which are determined by the central government and cannot be changed by a joint venture. Market prices include negotiated prices and free prices. The former is decided through consultations between the local governments and joint ventures, while the latter is determined by the joint ventures themselves.

A few important commodities (such as grain, oil, fuel, and medicine) and certain service charges (such as rent, electricity, tuition, and mass transit) have their prices fixed by either the central government or the local government. The prices for steel, cement, timber, coal, and other major capital goods are priced on a floating basis. The floating margin is usually between 10 and 30 percent. Aside from these products, the joint ventures can either freely determine prices for their products sold domestically or in foreign markets.

GENERAL INVESTMENT INCENTIVES[1]

Almost all Asian countries offer a complex set of direct and indirect incentives to attract foreign investment. Before discussing the specific investment incentives offered to foreign investors in China, it will be helpful to review the role of these various measures as a means to attract foreign investment.

Direct incentives can be described as offering either commodity or factor protection to foreign investors. Commodity protection, which aims to alter the prices of goods and services bought or sold by a foreign firm, usually takes the form of reductions in or exemptions from both import and export duties. Factor protection, which attempts to reduce overall operating costs, consists of a broader range of measures that typically include tax holidays, investment allowances, and sometimes even subsidies for training local labor. Indirect incentives, which can take many forms, include the following:

1. simplified investment application and approval requirements and procedures
2. guarantees of capital flows and profits remittances
3. legal protection of industrial rights, such as patents and copyrights
4. political and commercial risk insurance schemes

In essence, direct incentives are aimed at helping foreign firms reduce their operating costs in host countries and therefore at enhancing the profitability of such operations. Indirect incentives are directed at lowering the overall risks of the investment environment by reducing the regulatory requirements and by minimizing policy changes and government intervention.

The type and size of incentives offered by a country depend on the market orientation of the investment it wishes to attract and on the degree of competition it faces from other countries in the region in attracting such investment. For instance, direct investment can be oriented toward production for worldwide export or for the domestic market of the host country. Naturally, competition to attract foreign investment tends to be more intense in countries competing for worldwide export markets. Incentives involving factor protection are more important and often used among competitors concerned with attracting export-oriented investments, while commodity protection incentives (particularly protection from competing imports) are more important for countries primarily concerned with attracting investment to serve the domestic market.

The variety and complexity of incentives make it difficult to evaluate their effectiveness. Incentives are, perhaps, important in two areas: a country might stand to lose new investment were it to abolish all of its incentives unilaterally, and a country might stand to gain investment were it to increase incentives unilaterally. Although numerous studies have been conducted on the role of investment incentives, no firm conclusions have been reached. Researchers undertaking a detailed investigation of new investment locations in a cross section of developed and developing countries concluded that in two-thirds of the cases analyzed the choice of investment location was influenced by the incentives provided, in the sense that the investment would have been located elsewhere without the incentives.[2]

Other researchers, however, have concluded that incentives have had only a limited, if any, role in attracting investment. A study conducted by the Organization of Economic Cooperation and Development (OECD) supports this view by observing that economic factors in the host country, such as the size of the market, economic growth, and price stability, were by far the most important determinants of productive foreign investment, and that even if incentives had a direct impact on investment, it would be quite limited in comparison with the impact of the previously mentioned factors. In particular, due to the temporary nature of most investment incentives, these factors might only affect the timing of an investment, without having a lasting significant effect on the level of total capital stock.[3] In a survey of the foreign direct investment decisions of major multinational companies conducted by the Group of Thirty, only 13 percent of the respondents ranked host-country incentives among the top three factors affecting direct investment in developing countries.[4] Individual research has also supported the view that at the initial stage of foreign investment decisions, incentives offered by host countries were considered important by investing firms.[5]

Whether a country can attract significantly more direct investment by making small increases in its existing incentives is even less clear, especially if such increases are matched by other countries competing for the same investment. Moreover, there are indications that incentives become less effective as their complexity and revisions increase since such factors serve to exacerbate the uncertainty facing potential investors. Indeed, a study on foreign direct investment in China indicated that frequent policy changes in the early 1980s served as disincentives to foreign investors, even though many of these changes were aimed at improving the investment climate.[6] Moreover, incentives can be costly, and increases in these incentives imply a potential loss in fiscal revenues and, to some extent, increased protection provided to foreign firms.[7]

Incentives, Disincentives, and Policy Implications

Since the role played by investment incentives is not clearly known while the costs (foregone fiscal revenue and protectionism) are quite obvious, the issue of the appropriate level of investment incentives should be considered. If one assumes that incentives play no role in attracting new investment, the introduction of new incentives would not be logical. It would also be true that existing incentives could be abolished if they were not considered important by foreign investors. Indeed, a recent Malaysian survey indicates that the relatively low labor costs, combined with a sophisticated labor force, are the most significant considerations of foreign firms when investing in Malaysia, followed by the country's well-developed infrastructure. Incentives are cited only as a minimal factor.[8]

On the other hand, if incentives are believed to be important, at least in the sense that they could be used to offset any major move by competitor host countries, the answer would be equally clear: maintain or even strengthen the incentive measures whenever necessary. A simple regression test indicates that incentives *do* have influence, in the case of Singapore, on investment decisions by foreign firms. The empirical results reveal that foreign investment inflows are inversely related to increases in relative unit labor costs and inflation rates while positively correlated to investment incentives.[9]

However, the view opposing the maintenance of incentives is also well founded. According to this view, a country's ability to compete for foreign investment should not only be assessed on the type of incentives it provides but on the type of disincentives (or restrictions) it may have. To the extent that incentives promote foreign investment by lowering a firm's operating costs, hence improving profitability, disincentives discourage and limit investment activities by imposing more uncertainties, therefore higher risks, which firms must face. Major disincentives to foreign investment include ownership requirements, restrictions on capital flows and profit repatriation, restrictions on the access of foreign firms to local capital markets, and specific performance requirements for foreign firms.

When determining the adequacy of incentives, it is important to understand how foreign investors make investment decisions. The decision on a foreign investment is principally determined by two factors: potential profitability and risk. Investment incentives would likely enhance the expected profitability of foreign investment while disincentives could add to the risk of the same investment. Assuming that conditions in competitor countries remain unchanged, that is, there is no change in the structure of their incentives and/or disincentives, a reduction in incentives in a country would be unlikely to seriously affect the expected profitability of investment operations since it would be unlikely to significantly alter the mix of profit versus risk in the investment decision. In this context, new incentives may be effective only in a very limited way in promoting new investments. However, if conditions in other countries change, that is, either they provide a better incentive package or further liberalize their investment environments, the determination of the appropriate level of incentives would become more difficult for the same country. In this case, maintaining its competitiveness through more generous incentive measures to match its competitors' moves would appear to be logical.

Any decision regarding whether the existing incentives are sufficiently adequate to retain a country's competitive position for foreign investment should be based on consideration of the following factors: the competition with other countries vying for the same investment, the orientation of its economic and industrial policies, and in a larger context, its overall economic and investment climate for foreign investment. Factors that call for further strengthening of the investment incentives may include rising competition with other economies in the region, declining competitiveness due to rising labor costs, and the strategy for directing the economy into high-technology and high value-added industries. On the other hand, the costs associated with such incentives and their ambiguous role argue that there is no need to further expand the existing program. Moreover, the disadvantages stemming from a less favorable incentive program, if any, could well be offset by the attractiveness of the free and conducive investment climate a country could offer. Although it appears difficult to assess the effectiveness of investment incentives and, therefore, the desirability of maintaining and/or expanding them, countries may mutually benefit from an agreement to limit competitiveness in granting incentives.

INVESTMENT INCENTIVES IN CHINA

China's incentives for foreign investment have focused on fiscal measures that are designed to reduce the tax burdens of foreign investors. These measures include tax holidays, concessionary rates, and exemptions from import and/or export duties. In addition to tax incentives, the SEZs, opened cities, and many provinces also offer preferential land-use fees to foreign investors.

Tax Incentives in SEZs

The corporate income tax is normally lower in the SEZs than in other parts of China, except for the opened cities and Hainan Island, which have almost equal preferential arrangements. The flat income tax rate is 15 percent for joint ventures and wholly foreign-owned companies. In most cases, foreign companies in the SEZs may also benefit from more advantageous tax holidays than those offered under the national tax legislation.

Depending on such factors as the amount of investment, nature of the technology, and duration of the project, tax holidays of up to five years are available. Generally, tax reductions or exemptions of 20 to 50 percent are alloted to those enterprises that have invested within two years after the promulgation of the Guangdong SEZ regulations (i.e., until August 26, 1985), invested more than US $5 million in a single project, and introduced advanced technologies that were not available locally.

Firms that reinvest their profits in the SEZs are exempted from income

Table 3.1
Tax Incentives in SEZs

	Special Economic Zones
	1. Income tax is 15% for manufacturers contracting for business periods of 10 years or more; fully exempt for two years after first making profits, and a 50% reduction for three years thereafter. 2. Services with foreign capital of US $5 million or more and contracting for business periods of 10 years or more; fully exempt for one year after first making profits, and a 50% reduction for two years thereafter.
Local Income Tax	Local governments decide on tax reduction measures in SEZs
Remittance Tax	Exempt
Income Tax on dividends, interest, leasing and loyalties (in cases where no office is maintained in China)	1. Exemption where provided for by existing laws. 2. 10% for income not falling within category 1 above. 3. Local governments can adopt further preferential tax reduction measures for firms supplying funds and facilities under preferential terms or transferring advanced technologies.
Industrial and Commercial Tax on Imports	1. Production facilities and raw materials are exempt. 2. Tax collected for means of transport and other durable consumer goods subject to import restrictions. 3. 50% reduction for mineral oils, tobacco, liquor, other daily necessities.
Industrial and Commercial Tax on Exports and Domestic Sales	Exempt (except on export restricted items) 1. Special Zones taxes for mineral oil, tobacco, liquor are reduced by 50%. Regular or reduced taxes are collected on products designated by local people's governments. Other products are exempted.
Transport Services	Reasonable quantities tax exempt.
Industrial and Commercial Tax on Business	1. Ordinary tax rates applied to earnings from commerce, communications and transport and services. 2. 3% for banks, insurance concerns. 3. Tax reduction measures can be adopted by local governments for firms such as those cited above in the early stage of their operation.

tax on the investment amount as well. For enterprises with over US $5 million of foreign investment, involving high-technology transfer, or that may have a slower return on investment, income tax may be exempted for up to five years. Enterprises operating in the tourist and service sectors are exempt from income tax for three years, and those in the transportation and communications fields are exempted for five years.

The tax on the income obtained from dividends, interest, rentals, royalties, and other sources in the SEZs by investors who do not have establishments in China is charged at a flat tax rate of 10 percent (Table 3.1). Other tax rates vary with the type of investment, resources used, and other factors determined by investment regulations.

The individual income tax in the SEZs is levied on the monthly income above RMB 800 (about US $150) at the progressive rates as tabulated in Table 3.2.

Table 3.2
Individual Income Tax Rates in the SEZs

(Monthly income, in Yuan)	Tax Rates
Below 800	Exempt
801 - 1500	3%
1501 - 3000	7%
3001 - 6000	15%
6001 - 9000	20%
9001 - 12000	25%
above 12000	30%

Individual income derived from remuneration for personal services, royalties, and property leasing is allowed an expense deduction of RMB 800 for incomes of less than RMB 4,000 and a deduction of 20 percent for expenses for incomes above RMB 4,000. After these deductions, the remainder is taxed at a rate of 15 percent. However, the following items may be exempt from individual income taxes: prizes and awards for scientific, technological, or cultural payments; insurance indemnities; retirement pay; tax-free income as stipulated in international conventions to which China is a party and in the agreements China has signed; and all incomes from Hong Kong, Macao, or foreign countries.

Tax Incentives in Opened Cities

Like those of the SEZs, foreign investors in the opened cities enjoy a variety of benefits. For enterprises involving foreign investment, the Chinese government offers not only preferential treatment in taxes, but it also provides a variety of conveniences to facilitate operations. For example, local governments can facilitate the acquisition of plant sites and expedite the building of the necessary infrastructure and the connecting of utility and communication lines to the plant site. Also, the negotiation time required for gaining approval from local and state authorities can be shortened significantly and sometimes eliminated.

As compared to unopened cities and areas in China, there are many tax and other concessions.

Income Tax. The income tax rate is set at 15 percent for technology and knowledge-intensive investment projects, as well as for large-scale projects whose total investment may exceed US $30 million (Table 3.3). According to China's tax law, a joint venture is exempt from income taxes during the first two years after it begins to earn a profit and pays only half the required taxes for the third through fifth year. If a joint venture

Table 3.3
Tax Incentives in Opened Cities

	Economic and Technical Development Zones	Opened Cities
Income Tax	Income tax for firms engaged in production is 15%. Firms contracting for 10 years or more are exempt from income tax for 2 years after first making profits, and from 50% of tax for 3 years thereafter.	1. Income tax is 15% for technology oriented, knowledge intensive projects of a projection nature with foreign capital of US $30 million or more and a long period of investment recovery, as well as for energy, transport and port construction projects. 2. Income tax is reduced by 20% for the following firms which do not fall in the category 1 above. (i)machinery, electronics industries (ii) metallurgical, chemical construction material industries (iii) light industry, spinning industry (iv) medical equipment, pharmaceutical industries (v) agriculture, forestry, livestock and breeding industries and associated processing industries (vi) construction industry Tax reduction measures for these industries are subject to the effective periods and limitations specified in the income tax law for joint ventures and foreign enterprises.
Local Income Tax	Municipal governments decide on tax reduction measures in development zones.	Municipal governments can adopt tax reduction measures.
Remittance Tax	Exempt	Exempt

is a high-technology enterprise, it is required to pay only half of its income taxes due during the sixth through eighth year.

Industrial and Commercial Tax and Export and Import Duties. Production facilities and equipment, parts and raw materials involved in the production of export goods, packaging materials, transportation-related equipment and office equipment, and daily necessities for foreign personnel are all exempt from industrial and commercial taxes. Exemptions of import and export duties are also available.

Preferential Treatment in Economic and Technical Development Zones (ETDZs). In addition to the basic preferential measures provided in the opened cities, the following two preferential treatment measures apply to foreign investment in the ETDZs of the opened cities: the income tax rate is set at a uniform 15 percent, and 10 percent of the profit remittance tax is exempt.

Table 3.3 (continued)

	Economic and Technical Development Zones	Opened Cities
Income Tax on dividends, interest, leasing and royalties (if no office is maintained in China).	1. Exemption where provided for by existing laws. 2. 10% for income not falling within category 1 above. 3. Municipal governments may adopt further preferential tax reduction measures as Economic and Technical Development Zones needed for firms which supply funds and equipment under preferential terms or transfer advanced technology.	1. Exemption where provided for by existing laws. 2. 10% for income not falling within category 1 above. 3. Municipal governments may adopt further preferential tax reduction measures as needed for firms which supply funds and terms or transfer advanced technologies. Open Cities
Industrial and Commercial Tax on imports, leasing and royalties (if no office is maintained in China)	1. Production facilities, raw materials exempted. 2. Tax-exempted raw materials used in manufacturing products for domestic sale are subject to the stipulated tax rates.	1. Equipment, raw materials means of transport exempt. 2. Tax-exempted raw materials used in manufacturing products for domestic sale are subjected to stipulated tax rates. Reasonable amounts of personal effects, means of transport of investors, tax exempt.
Industrial and Commercial Tax on Exports & Domestic Sales	Exempt (except on export restricted items) 1. Special Zones Taxes for mineral oil, tobacco, liquor are reduced by 50%. Regular or reduced taxes are collected on designated products by local governments. Other products are also exempt.	Same as column 1 Tax collected

Tax Incentives on Hainan Island

The corporate income tax rate on Hainan Island is also 15 percent, while the remittance tax of 10 percent is exempted for foreign enterprises. In addition, Hainan Island provides the following incentives for foreign investors:

1. *Exemption from local income tax.* In contrast to the SEZs, where the local governments still retain the discretion to impose a local income tax, all non-financial enterprises on Hainan Island are exempt from a local income tax.
2. *Extended tax holidays.* Tax holidays are extended to foreign enterprises investing in infrastructure projects and in minority areas. Enterprises that plan to invest for at least a fifteen-year period in development projects, including ports, airports, wharves, roads, power plants, water conservation projects,

Table 3.3 (continued)

	Economic and Technical Development Zones	Open Cities
	2. Unified industrial and commercial tax collected upon entry into China of cargoes transhipped from special zones and previously exempted, and on products carried in to China after being produced in special zones. Reasonable amounts of personal household effects carried into ordinary areas from special zones.	
Industrial and Commercial Tax on imported household goods, means of transport and daily necessities	1. Reasonable quantities tax exempt.	Same as column 1
	Economic and Technical Development Zones	Open Cities
Industrial and Commercial Tax on Business	1. Ordinary tax rates applied to earnings from commerce communications and transport, and services. 2. 3% for banks, insurance concerns. 3. Tax reduction measures can be adopted by local governments for firms such as those above in the early stage of their operations.	

coal mines, and agricultural projects are entitled to an income tax exemption of five years, beginning with the first profit-making year. They also enjoy a 50 percent reduction in income tax for the following five years.

Foreign enterprises that invest in specially designated remote minority areas for a minimum of ten years are to be granted a ten-year exemption from income tax following the first profit-making year and a 50 percent reduction in income tax for the succeeding ten years. The local governments of these remote areas are given automony to further lower tax charges for projects in tourism if they so desire.

3. *Tax refunds for reinvested profits.* Like those in both the SEZs and opened cities, foreign enterprises that plan to reinvest profits on Hainan Island are entitled to a 40 percent refund. Furthermore, those that reinvest profits in infrastructure and agricultural projects (as outlined above) will receive a 100 percent tax refund.

4. *Exemption from the withholding tax.* Enterprises earning dividends, interest, royalty fees, rentals, and other fee incomes, but without establishments on

Hainan Island, can apply for an exemption from the withholding tax, which is normally 10 percent elsewhere in the country.

5. *Sales tax.* The investment regulations of Hainan Island stipulate that foreign enterprises operating on the island are not subject to the industrial and commercial tax when they sell goods on the island. Instead, they pay the same taxes, such as the value-added, product, and business taxes, as their Chinese counterparts do. More importantly, with the exception of a few items (mineral oil, cigarettes, liquor, and sugar), the sale of all other goods on the island is exempt from taxes.

6. *Import and export duties.* Like the SEZs and opened cities, the Hainan Island government allows industrial machinery, equipment, raw materials, and spare parts, as well as communication and transportation equipment, to be imported duty free. Products that are imported for sale on the island enjoy a 50 percent reduction in customs duty. Export goods with a 20 percent or more local content are also entitled to an exemption from customs duty and tax. In addition, other provinces have provided various incentives for attracting foreign investment. Often, they adjust tax incentives in order to keep their competitiveness, not only within China but also with other zones in Thailand, Malaysia, and Indonesia. Foreign investors should, therefore, always check with a given province for the latest local guidelines regarding tax incentives. Depending on the type, size, and importance of the investment project to the local economy, most tax incentives can be negotiated between the foreign investor and local authorities.

Preferential Land-use Policies and Fees

A foreign investor who needs land for a potential investment project in China must first obtain the right to use it. Although foreign individuals and companies are officially prohibited from owning land, they must apply for and be granted fixed-term land-use rights by the Chinese government. If the proposed project is a joint venture between a foreign company and a Chinese partner, it is usually the Chinese partner that goes through the complicated and time-consuming process of applying for the land-use rights. However, if it is a wholly foreign-owned enterprise, this burden falls on the foreign investor.

As noted earlier, a good relationship with local authorities can be most effective in expediting this process. To acquire the use of land, the land-use rights must first be surrendered to the government by the current user and then reassigned to the venture either by the central or local government, depending on the nature and the scope of the project. If there are persons with homes or apartments on the land, they must be compensated and assisted in moving. Firms must often acquire living facilities for them or construct the new apartments where they are to be relocated. Again, this can be a difficult and time-consuming process.

Given the complexity of land acquisition, commonly the potential

Table 3.4
Land-use Fees in the Shenzhen SEZ

Purpose	Lease Period (years)	Annual Fee (in RMB)/ Square meter
Industry	30	10-30
Commerce	20	70-200
Housing	50	30-60
Tourism	30	60-100
Agriculture	20	Fixed Separately
Scientific, cultural and educational institutions	50	Fixed Separately (more preferential)

Source: Interim Provisions of the Shenzhen Special Economic Zone for Land Management, chapter 3, articles 16 and 17.

Chinese joint venture partner is already a landholder. Therefore, the Chinese partner may contribute land as part of the capital investment in the venture. In this case, the venture would not have a land-use problem and could avoid the land acquisition process; however, the foreign partner should be aware of some potential problems associated with this alternative. First, it may be difficult to make a fair assessment of the land value contributed by the Chinese partner as a capital investment. Second, even though the land is part of its initial investment, the joint venture may still have to pay a land-use fee after operations have begun because of China's complex regulations.

When a Chinese partner does not have the needed land for the joint venture, or if the joint venture prefers not to take the land from the Chinese partner as part of the capital contribution, the venture should apply for land-use rights from the local governmental land management department. This department will issue a contract that will be signed by the joint venture and the department. Normally, an official certificate is issued specifying the terms and conditions for land use by the venture.

The joint venture, of course, must pay for the right to use the land it acquires. The land-use fee differs according to the type of investment project, as well as the location. Joint ventures in the SEZs and ETDZs of the opened cities enjoy some of the land-use incentives and usually pay lower land-use fees compared to ventures in other parts of the country (Table 3.4). In addition, joint ventures relating to educational, cultural, scientific, technological, medical, health, and public welfare projects pay even lower land-use fees. Export-oriented and technologically advanced projects can also apply for better terms of land-use fees in various cities and provinces. Consequently, it is in the best interest of the venture to consider several alternative locations in order to secure the best terms for its project.

Although the incentives relating to land-use fees vary widely, most provinces offer exemptions from these fees during construction and start-up periods, and sometimes further reductions are possible for an extended time period for the venture. Investment projects located in downtown areas of major cities are not qualified for any of these incentives. Instead, the types of investments that can be located in urban areas are restricted, and they must pay high land-use fees. Many cities (e.g., Shanghai) discourage certain manufacturing enterprises within the central part of the city due to congestion and pollution.

Foreign enterprises on Hainan Island and in the Xiamen SEZ can lease land for up to seventy years, a longer period than those of other zones and opened cities. As practiced elsewhere, enterprises are allowed to sell and transfer the rights to land use and may use these rights as a mortgage for financing collateral.

In addition to the land-use fees, many cities charge other fees, including site development fees; connection fees for sewage disposal and treatment; public utilities fees for water, gas, and heating facilities constructed off the site; public utilities construction fees covering utility construction on the site; and charges for any additional public construction undertaken to meet the joint venture's requirements, including roads, bridges, and port facilities.

Potential joint ventures and wholly foreign-owned ventures should also be aware of a recent and significant land reform experiment. Beginning in late 1987, some major cities, including Shanghai, Shenzhen SEZ, and Tianjin (in 1989), started to lease land-use rights to foreign companies for commercial development. Basically, foreign companies may lease a piece of land on a fixed-term basis (normally fifty years, but it can be renewed) from a municipal government. During this period, the foreign company can construct industrial, commercial, and residential properties and sell, lease, or mortgage the buildings and land-use rights.

This practice, which was popular in Shanghai before 1949, allows foreign investors flexibility in utilizing the land for a variety of investment projects. In doing so, investors can lease the land needed at the beginning of a deal and, therefore, avoid some of the problems associated with the normal ways of acquiring land use. Wholly foreign-owned ventures are particularly pleased with this new policy since applying for land-use rights is problematic for them in most cases.

Land lease is still new in China. Many provinces and cities are following the example of Shanghai and the Shenzhen SEZ and are adopting similar policies in their own regions. Shanghai has even opened up a large area in the eastern side of the city (Pudong) for foreign investors. This is expected to substantially reduce the time and cost that joint ventures would otherwise need and, therefore, increase the attractiveness of the sites·to potential foreign investors.

NEW INCENTIVES AFTER 1986

Despite the increasingly liberalized investment policies and favorable incentives provided during the first part of the 1980s, foreign investors often complain about the Chinese investment environment. These complaints have focused mainly on the currency nonconvertibility problem (local currency earnings could not be freely converted into hard currencies), employment restrictions and the difficulty of dealing with local bureaucracies, as well as other operational problems. As a consequence, overall foreign investment declined sharply in 1986 due to foreign investors' dissatisfaction.

In order to renew the interest of foreign firms, and attract continuous foreign investment inflows, the State Council issued a set of new regulations in October 1986, later known as the "twenty-two regulations," designed to provide additional investment incentives to foreign investors. These incentives included further reductions in the income tax rate, easier access to the financial resources available domestically, increased access to the domestic labor market, and more autonomy and flexibility in hiring and firing, as well as other related decisions. Management was granted more autonomy in seeking raw materials from the domestic market and in making production, financing, and marketing decisions. Additionally, controls over the remittance of profits in foreign currencies abroad were reduced.

Principally, China had two purposes in issuing the "twenty-two regulations": to improve the overall investment environment and to provide special incentives for the investment projects it particularly wanted. These incentives, made available to all foreign investors, were directed toward specific ends, such as facilitating exports or giving joint ventures additional options for solving foreign exchange imbalance problems. But the real benefits, such as exemptions from certain payments and lower costs, were given only to those joint ventures that could fulfill one of China's two major goals for attracting foreign investment: to expand exports and to introduce advanced state-of-the-art technology.

Benefits for All Investment Projects

One of the major purposes of the new regulations was to help foreign joint ventures resolve their foreign exchange imbalance problems. Joint ventures are encouraged, for example, to use their Chinese currency earnings to purchase local products for export to other countries. In this way, joint ventures spend their Chinese currency earnings while earning the hard currencies they need. To do so, however, the joint venture must first obtain permission from the local government. Such permission is usually granted for a one-year period, and the value of local products purchased and exported cannot exceed the amount of foreign exchange required for the joint venture's production, operation, and profit remittance.

This policy certainly helps many joint ventures that have surpluses of

Chinese currency earnings. However, new problems also occur in practice. First, to find a suitable product with export potential is very difficult for several reasons:

1. Some major products such as rice, soybeans, cotton, tobacco, silk, tea, oil, and coal that have ready export markets are subject to central government control and therefore cannot be purchased and exported by foreign joint ventures;

2. Some less important products are subject to export licensing or quotas; therefore, if a joint venture plans to purchase this type of product, it must obtain prior approval from the central government;

3. The purchase of products, in general, is permitted only in the province where the venture is located. If the venture is interested in products that are available in other provinces, additional approval must be obtained from the specific provincial government, which is usually difficult, and

4. Those products that have export demand are either in short supply or already committed for sale by a state enterprise.

Second, the process of purchasing local products for export may prove to be expensive for a joint venture. Usually, the joint venture must organize a team whose special functions are to identify potential local products for export, negotiate with concerned local governments, obtain the necessary administrative permissions, and arrange necessary export details, including packaging and transport. All of these activities are in addition to finding foreign buyers. Normally, joint ventures are not designed to handle unfamiliar products and to sell them in world markets. An alternative is to sell them to an intermediary, but this reduces the profit potential.

Another way the new regulations alleviate the foreign exchange problem is to encourage the establishment of foreign exchange adjustment centers in major cities. These centers assist joint ventures with temporary foreign exchange balance difficulties by converting some of their Chinese currency earnings into hard currency. The centers also help ventures adjust their foreign exchange surpluses and deficiencies on a more regular basis as needed.

Like stock exchanges, foreign exchange centers are physical locations where sellers and buyers of foreign currencies meet and conduct transactions. Exchange rates, however, are determined by the centers and reflect market supply and demand conditions of the various currencies. Generally, the market rates tend to be about 20 percent higher than the official exchange rates quoted by the government. Currently, the official rate is RMB 5.30/US $ while the market rate is about RMB 6.00/US $.

The following example (Table 3.5) illustrates the legislation establishing a foreign exchange center.

Table 3.5

Interim Provisions of Shanghai Municipality Concerning the Business of Mutual Adjustment of Foreign Exchange among Enterprises with Foreign Investment[10]

Article 1: In order to encourage enterprises with foreign investment to actively export and generate foreign exchange and to promote the circulation of foreign currency funds among enterprises with foreign investment, the Shanghai Foreign Currency Adjustment Center for Enterprises with Foreign Investment was established under the supervision of the State Administration of Exchange Control in order to handle the business of mutual adjustment of foreign exchange (cash) among enterprises with foreign investment.

Article 2: All foreign exchange adjustments conducted in Shanghai by enterprises with foreign investment established within and outside of Shanghai must be carried out at the Shanghai Foreign Currency Adjustment Center for Enterprises with Foreign Investment (hereafter, the "Adjustment Center").

Article 3: Enterprises with foreign investment may apply to the Adjustment Center to register to sell any or all of their foreign currency revenue.

Article 4: Enterprises with foreign investment may apply to the Adjustment Center to register to buy any or all of the foreign exchange required within the scope of their business operations, as well as the funds for such items as the repayment of loan principal and interest and the remittance of profits.

Article 5: The prices for the adjustment of foreign exchange shall be freely negotiated by the buying and selling parties in question.

Article 6: After the conclusion of an adjustment transaction, the Adjustment Center shall collect from each of the buying and the selling parties a handling fee of 0.1 percent (of the total amount adjusted). The minimum handling fee shall be RMB 10, and the maximum shall be RMB 10,000.

Article 7: An enterprise with foreign investment may not buy or sell foreign exchange privately; nor may it use the foreign exchange obtained through adjustment transactions to engage in commercial foreign exchange resale activities outside the scope of its business. Violations will be handled in accordance with the Penal Provisions for Violation of Foreign Exchange Control Regulations and relevant stipulations.

Article 8: For the time being, the Adjustment Center shall be open for business for one day (every Thursday). Should the volume of business grow, business hours may be adjusted at a later date.

Article 9: The Adjustment Center is provisionally established at the main business hall of the Bank of China, Shanghai Branch, No.23 Zhong Shan Road. The Shanghai Bureau of the State Administration of Exchange Control shall be responsible for supervising foreign exchange adjustments.

Article 10: The power to interpret these Interim Provisions is vested in the Shanghai Bureau of the State Administration of Exchange Control.

Source: Provided by the Shanghai Municipal Government.

Incentives for Export-Oriented and Technologically Advanced Projects

According to the twenty-two regulations, joint ventures receive additional preferential treatment if they are categorized as either export-oriented or technologically advanced projects. To qualify as an export-oriented project, a joint venture must meet two primary requirements. First, it must export more than 50 percent of its annual production value, and second, it has to have either a balance or surplus in its foreign exchange receipts and expenditures. Foreign exchange surplus generated in the previous year may be carried over to the following year's computation of its foreign exchange balance. A technologically advanced project must meet the following conditions:

1. It must be in the sector that China has targeted for foreign investment;

2. It must process technology and have production processes and equipment that are advanced in nature;

3. Its technology must be new and in short supply in China; and

4. The venture must help China produce new products, upgrade domestic products, increase exports, or produce an import substitute.

Based on these definitions, an export-oriented venture is identified by a straightforward statistical measure of exports as a proportion of total output. Determining whether a venture is a technologically advanced project, however, tends to be very subjective. Usually, before the project becomes operational, the venture partners must apply for and obtain a special status for their project.

Once granted this status, both export-oriented and technologically advanced projects may enjoy several important incentives.

1. *Exemption from paying State subsidies.* As mentioned in earlier sections, foreign joint ventures usually have to pay subsidies to their employees to cover some of the benefits the Chinese workers receive from the Chinese government. Export-oriented and technologically advanced projects are two types of joint ventures that are exempt from all but the housing subsidies, thereby reducing the total operating cost of these ventures.

2. *Priority in receiving Bank of China loans.* These two types of ventures are also given priority for securing short-term loans from the Bank of China, which can be used either for working capital, or for other financing purposes essential to operations.

3. *Profits remitted abroad exempted from tax.* Normally, a 10 percent remittance tax is placed on any profit remitted abroad by the foreign partner of a joint venture. These two types of joint ventures, however, are exempted from this tax.

4. *Extended reduction period for income tax.* The new regulations grant a tax holiday in the first two profit-making years, followed by three years at a reduced rate of 50 percent of the original income tax. After these tax benefits are exhausted, an export-oriented venture exporting over 70 percent of its output in any one year will have its income tax cut by an additional 50 percent. Technologically advanced projects are granted an additional three years with a 50 percent reduction in income tax.

5. *Additional tax benefits for reinvested profits.* If the joint venture uses part of its profits to reinvest in an export-oriented and technologically advanced project, it can receive a full refund on the income tax paid on the reinvested funds in the previous years.

In addition to these benefits, joint ventures can enjoy further reduced land-use fees, as well as priority in obtaining utilities, transport, and communications facilities at local rates. All incentives are aimed at further reducing the cost of joint ventures and, therefore, encourage more export-oriented and technologically advanced projects to be established in China.

Import-Substitution Projects

Import-substitution projects are those ventures that produce products that China needs to import. The products produced by these joint ventures, therefore, can serve as import substitutes. In this manner, China actually saves the foreign exchange that would otherwise be spent on these imports. The regulations for this type of joint venture stipulate that if needed the Chinese government will be responsible for providing foreign exchange assistance in balancing a project's foreign exchange receipts and expenditures. Certain conditions, however, must be met if the joint venture wants to qualify for such benefits:

1. The joint venture's need for foreign exchange must be temporary in nature, occurring in the initial period of operations;
2. The joint venture's products must be made with most materials obtained inside China, that is, with Chinese inputs;
3. The joint venture's products must be regarded as products that would otherwise have to be imported;
4. The product specifications, performance, delivery time, technical service, and training must meet the requirements of the Chinese inspectors. A quality inspection and testing center in China must certify that the venture's product meets the same quality standards as the import product;
5. The price for these products cannot be higher than the prevailing price in international markets; and
6. Approval for such a venture may be required from the central government.

The regulations on import-substitution projects have paved the way for many foreign investors to form joint ventures in China and have been a major step in resolving the foreign exchange problems of foreign investors. Before making a firm investment commitment, however, foreign investors should first determine whether or not the potential project will receive import-substitution project status.

NOTES

1. Part of this discussion is based on International Monetary Fund [IMF], *Foreign Private Investment in Developing Countries*, Washington, D.C., 1985.
2. IMF, *Foreign Private Investment in Developing Countries*, occasional paper no. 33, Washington, D.C., January 1985.

3. Organization of Economic Cooperation and Development, *Investment Incentives and Disincentives and the International Investment Process*, 1983.

4. Group of Thirty, *Foreign Direct Investment*, 1973–83, New York, Group of Thirty, 1984.

5. See Yair Ahroni, *The Foreign Investment Process*, Boston: Harvard University Press, 1966.

6. A typical example is that a firm might choose to locate its investment in a special economic zone even though the infrastructure in the zone might be less developed than that of a major urban industrial area. Later, the foreign investors might realize that their initial choice of location was a mistake when similar incentives were offered in the urban areas. See Phillip D. Grub and Jian Hai Lin, "Foreign Investment in China: Myths and Realities," *Journal of Economic Development*, vol. 13 (December 1988); 17–40.

7. Incentives provided to foreign investors could create unfair competition for domestic firms and for those foreign firms that had undertaken investment prior to the new incentives. Therefore, additional investment, if any, generated by the new incentives would have to be balanced against the cost arising from the protection provided to these foreign investments.

8. Jian Hai Lin, unpublished working paper, 1990.

9. The model measures foreign investment flows into Singapore relative to those in selected countries, mainly Malaysia, Thailand, and Indonesia, against several key variables including the relative real GDP growth (RGDP), relative inflation rate (RCPI), and relative unit labor costs (RULC), as well as investment incentives (IC). A dummy variable for incentives (IC) is also used as it is believed that many incentives were introduced in 1986 in Singapore.

10. Issued by the Shanghai Foreign Currency Adjustment Center for Enterprises with Foreign Investment on November 5, 1988.

4

Motivations and Modes of Investment

Foreign investment involves a great variety of political, economic, commercial, and cultural complexities of host countries, in addition to the internal strengths, resources, and constraints of each individual investing firm. Entering into a foreign investment arrangement, such as a joint venture in a nonmarket economy like China, presents additional problems and uncertainties. These arise because the Chinese investing partner of a proposed joint venture is ultimately the State, whose motives and purposes in embarking upon the venture may differ vastly from those of a foreign investor. Also, the Chinese have had little historical experience in conducting collaborative projects with foreign firms. More importantly, under a centrally planned environment, rigid political and economic systems, together with different management practices, may pose potential difficulties for a "marriage" between a Western private market-oriented enterprise and a state-owned and operated organization.

Why have so many foreign firms invested in China, with still many planning to do so, despite the recent political and economic uncertainties caused by the events of June 1989? To understand this development, one must first consider the motivations of both the Chinese and foreign investors.

INVESTMENT MOTIVATIONS

Chinese Motivations

The promotion of foreign investment by the Chinese government is motivated by a variety of factors that include the following:

- Obtain foreign technology;
- Acquire foreign capital;
- Obtain foreign management expertise;
- Obtain foreign marketing experience and marketing networks;
- Increase foreign exchange generating capacity;
- Develop and promote joint research activities; and
- Raise the standard of living for local communities.

In the late 1970s it was clear to the Chinese government that much of their technology and industrial facilities were out of date, if not obsolete. Most technology and industrial equipment was imported in the 1950s from the Soviet Union, which was then China's major political and economic ally. As a result, the acquisition of technology, especially in the areas of electronics, computer hardware and software, production processes, energy development, telecommunications and transportation equipment, was given high priority in the national economic development policy programs. This was especially evident in the sixth and seventh five-year plans.

While China could develop some of these technologies independently, it would not only be time-consuming but extremely costly in terms of research and development. Additionally, China has faced, and continues to face, another key problem—a lack of foreign exchange—which has prevented it from importing the needed technology and equipment at will. Therefore, foreign investment, joint ventures in particular, is considered a logical alternative to either the purchase of foreign technology or the development needed to upgrade and modernize its own technological base.

As discussed earlier, from the 1950s through the 1970s, China obtained much of its foreign capital through credits from foreign governments. The Chinese government saw foreign investment as an ideal source of external funding that would attract the desired technology and other production inputs, including management expertise. The government sought to diversify its sources of borrowing and obtain a desirable balance between debt and equity financing. This led to a heavy emphasis on technology transfer through joint venture arrangements. These arrangements would not only facilitate technology transfers and increase production capacities, they would also attract appropriate transfers, thereby raising the quality of products being produced. It would also make the ventures more competitive in both domestic and foreign markets. Through their contact with foreign partners, Chinese companies would be able to accrue the following benefits:

- Obtain firsthand exposure to modern management practices and production processes;

- Gain insight into techniques for quality control and product design;
- Better understand international marketing and promotion techniques for market penetration;
- Gain access to established marketing networks of foreign partners; and
- Develop collaboration with their joint venture partners in third markets.

As a result, many of the goods and services developed by joint ventures can be sold more effectively in international markets, thereby increasing China's foreign exchange earning capacity and improving its trade balance through import substitution and export diversification. In keeping with these motivations, foreign investment projects in China have been focused on one or more of the following:

1. Technologically advanced projects that are engaged in developing new products and upgrading and/or replacing present machinery and equipment;
2. Export-oriented projects that can potentially export a large portion of their products to third markets so as to generate foreign exchange surpluses after deducting foreign exchange expenditures incurred in their operations;
3. Import substitution projects, which produce goods and services China currently imports, thereby reducing foreign exchange spending;
4. Other projects that may require substantial fixed capital investment, particularly in the manufacturing sector, where most of current Chinese technology lags well behind that of industrial countries;
5. Raw material exploration projects that would locate and develop production facilities for oil, gas, coal, and other raw materials; and
6. Service-oriented projects catering to foreign tourists and business executives, as well as office facilities and housing for executives and their families stationed in the country.

Foreign Investors' Motivations

Foreign investors' motivations for investing in China may vary, but they certainly include one or more of the following:

1. Receive assurance of a share of China's potential market and the rapid growth of its economy;
2. Reduce production, labor, and other costs, including benefits from China's investment programs;
3. Obtain raw materials available in the Chinese market that can be either used to meet production needs or be sold in third markets;
4. Meet their competitors' move to China and/or forestall or reduce competition from other firms' earning markets in the same geographical area;

5. Test the Chinese market as a potential for large scale investments at a later stage; and

6. Fulfill sentimental and other reasons, such as returning to their homeland.

It is not surprising that China's market potential is considered a prime factor by foreign investors. With a population of over one billion people and a relatively rapid rate of economic growth during the past ten years, the potential for future market growth appears attractive. Furthermore, with incomes rising and increased discretionary income, the demand for consumer goods has grown rapidly in recent years, and the prospects for future growth remain excellent. Because of China's import substitution policy, there has been an equally strong market for industrial goods and infrastructural development.

In order to attract foreign investment projects that would assist China in reaching its planned goals, the Chinese government guaranteed selected joint ventures the opportunity to sell a certain percentage of their products domestically. In many cases, this guaranteed sales allowance would provide sufficient domestic funds for local joint venture needs, such as the purchase of raw materials and production inputs as well as for wages and salary expenses. In some cases, companies are allowed to sell in the domestic market and be paid in hard currency thus enabling foreign joint venture partners to make profit remittances in convertible currencies.

Since China lacks sufficient foreign exchange reserves to import everything it needs, foreign investment is considered by many investors as the only possible way to penetrate the Chinese market. Many firms also hope that by gaining a foothold in this market they will be able to build an operational base for competitive sales to other countries because of the production efficiency they obtain.

The relatively low operating costs (labor, raw materials, and other production inputs) have attracted investors not only from industrial countries, but also from Hong Kong and other nearby economies, including South Korea and Taiwan, whose labor cost is much higher than that of China. Although the actual labor cost in China appears to be much higher than many had originally expected, it remains, nonetheless, well below that of the major industrial countries and most neighbor Asian countries. The availability of local factory facilities and a trainable, stable labor force have provided an additional incentive for relatively labor-intensive operations.

China's rich deposits of oil, gas, coal, and other raw materials are another attraction to foreign investors. Many multinational firms from major industrial countries have been actively involved in oil exploration in the South China Sea and gas and coal mining in the central part of the country.

In order to promote foreign investment, the Chinese government has

Table 4.1

A Comparison of Tax Rates in China and Selected Countries

Country	Income Taxation
China	Corporate income tax: 15% in SEZs and opened cities and 10% withholding tax on remitted dividends; in other areas, corporate income tax is 30%
Hong Kong	Corporate income tax: 18.5% Other entities: 17% Taxes are levied on profits and interest arising in or derived from Hong Kong
Malaysia	Corporate income tax: 35% Development tax: 5% Excess profits tax: 3%
Singapore	Corporate income tax: 31% Withholding tax: 33% on dividends earned in Singapore
South Korea	Corporate income tax: 0-30%
Thailand	Corporate income tax: 35% Business tax: 1.5-40% Remittance tax: 20%

made a considerable effort to provide various investment incentives. Relatively low tax rates are a good example. China's current corporate tax rate for joint ventures is 15 percent in most areas, compared with an average tax rate of 30 percent or more in most neighboring developing countries (Table 4.1).

Some firms, however, have invested in China without a specific reason or objective. Their investment may have been motivated by a similar move by their competitors or by a desire to initiate an investment project in China on a trial basis—if the first project operates successfully, they may either expand their existing operations or commit to new investments. For this reason, a majority of joint ventures to date have been quite small in scale. Indicators show that most joint ventures are less than US $1 million in size. Only a handful of them have an investment exceeding US $10 million.

MODES OF FOREIGN INVESTMENT

Foreign investment is more broadly defined in China than in the Western world. Under the Chinese definition, foreign investment includes not only

equity investment (both wholly foreign-owned and joint venture investment) but also contractual investment (contractual joint ventures and oil
exploration ventures), and other forms of activities, such as compensation
trade, processing and assembling arrangements, and international leasing.
Aside from equity and contractual investment, the other forms of investment are largely recognized outside China as different forms of trade.
Compensation trade, for example, has been widely used in the Eastern
European countries to prevent spending scarce foreign exchange when
trading with the West. In recent years, it has also been used in many
developing countries as a means of saving foreign exchange or as a means
of developing export industries. At the same time, compensation trade
helps to acquaint local industry with new foreign markets and gain inter-
actional marketing expertise.

Although this book focuses primarily on foreign equity and contractual
investment, it is essential to discuss other forms of investment activities
in order to present a complete picture of the foreign capital inflows to
China in recent years.

Equity Joint Ventures

Equity joint ventures, often understood as equity investment, are the
most important form of foreign investment in China. In general, equity
joint ventures refer to those projects established between foreign companies and/or individuals and the Chinese companies according to the
Law on Joint Ventures Using Chinese and Foreign Investment promulgated in 1979. Under this law, an equity joint venture is a limited liability
company with a board of directors composed of individuals selected by
both the Chinese and foreign joint venture partners to manage operations.
The number of directors representing each partner is determined by its
share of capital contributed. In earlier years (1979–87), the chairman of
the board was, in most cases, Chinese, while the vice-chairman and general manager were from the foreign partner. After 1988, however, the
new regulations have allowed joint ventures to be chaired by the foreign
partner.

A foreign partner's capital contribution to a joint venture usually takes
the form of machinery and equipment, technology, cash (in convertible
currencies), industrial property rights, and managerial experience. The
Chinese partner usually contributes land, factory buildings and facilities,
raw materials, and cash in local currency as its share of the capital.
According to Chinese investment law, the foreign partner's contribution
must not be less than 25 percent of the total equity investment, but it has
no upper share limit. In other words, the foreign partner may contribute
more than 50 percent of the total capital required, depending on the negotiations and agreement between the two parties. In fact, foreigners can

contribute up to 100 percent of the capital to a project, in which case the venture becomes a wholly foreign-owned enterprise. Buyout provisions are also permitted, if agreed to and approved in advance.

An equity joint venture has two basic characteristics: the Chinese and foreign partners manage the project jointly on a daily basis, and both partners are responsible for the risks involved as well as the profits or losses of the enterprise. For example, let "A" be the Chinese partner and "B" be the foreign partner. If both A and B agree that each will contribute 50 percent of the capital needed to form an equity joint venture, then each partner would assume 50 percent of the risk in operating the venture. In other words, if losses occur, both A and B would have to share the losses proportionally according to the share of the capital they each contribute (in this case 50 percent each). Profits are also shared and distributed in the same fashion.

Existing Chinese laws and regulations protect equity joint ventures above all other forms of investment. In most cases, equity joint ventures also enjoy the most attractive investment incentives provided by the government (see chapter 5).

Contractual Joint Ventures

Contractual joint ventures, also known as cooperative joint ventures, refer to an arrangement whereby the Chinese and foreign partners cooperate in joint projects and activities according to the terms and conditions stipulated in a venture agreement. These terms and conditions spell out the liabilities, rights, and obligations of each partner. The key difference between an equity joint venture and a contractual joint venture is that investment partners in the latter form of joint venture do not assume the risk or share profits according to their respective capital contributions. Rather, risks and profits are predetermined by the terms and conditions laid down in the venture agreement.

Using the same example, assume that A and B agree they will form a contractual joint venture, stipulating that A will contribute 60 percent of the required capital while B will contribute the remaining 40 percent. However, both agree in their joint venture contract that A and B will share potential profits or losses equally despite the different amounts of capital contribution. In this case, profits will be distributed according to the stipulation of the agreement rather than in proportion to the shares of the paid-in capital.

In late 1988, the Chinese government promulgated a set of laws governing contractual joint ventures. It is interesting to note that, in most cases, this type of joint venture does not necessarily involve the creation of a new legal entity. It can take any form agreeable to both partners. It is possible that the two partners may appoint a third party to manage the venture (often the case in the hotel industry) or that the foreign partner may entrust the Chinese side with the management of the project and be involved in the day-to-day operations.

The major advantage of this type of joint venture is the flexibility of both partners to form a joint venture based on their common interests and needs. A contractual joint venture, however, is not as well protected by Chinese laws and regulations as is the equity joint venture. Therefore, if disputes arise, solutions may depend only on consultation and negotiation between the two partners, rather than on legal procedures and court settlement. The lack of an adequate legal framework may result in foreign investors' becoming confused about their obligations, benefits, and other rights in this type of joint venture.

Joint Venture Structure

A typical joint venture, whether equity or contractual, usually involves only two parties, a foreign partner and a Chinese partner. However, a joint venture may also be multi-party, in which there is more than one foreign company with only one Chinese partner, or one foreign partner with several Chinese companies, depending on the nature, scope, and needs of the joint venture. There can be as many foreign and Chinese partners as the venture needs and the participating companies agree upon. In general, the larger manufacturing joint ventures tend to have more partners than smaller ones or than less sophisticated projects. Obviously, partner cooperation is easier under the two-party structure than under a multi-party structure. A two-party joint venture, therefore, has a greater chance of being successful than does a multi-party joint venture in most instances, depending on the partners' relative strengths and abilities (as well as the degree of cooperation achieved between themselves).

In a two-party equity joint venture, the foreign partner must contribute at least 25 percent of the total equity capital of the proposed joint venture. For a multi-party joint venture, however, there is no fixed ownership level for each partner so long as the total foreign ownership exceeds 25 percent of the required total equity capital. This practice differs from those in many other developing economies where foreign ownership often cannot exceed 49 percent.

The most common type of equity joint venture is organized as shown in Figure 4.1. As mentioned earlier, the foreign partner generally provides the technology, management expertise, and capital as its equity share of the venture, while the Chinese partner provides the factory site, existing industrial equipment, and other facilities. The joint venture is usually designed to market its products or services in both the Chinese and foreign markets, including the foreign partner's home country. The foreign partner is usually responsible for selling products in foreign markets as it usually

Figure 4.1
Two-Party JV with Cash Compensation

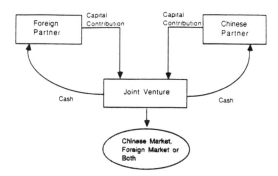

has already developed marketing channels and networks in its home country and abroad. Hence, the foreign partner does not have to create a new market for the joint venture's products. On the other hand, the Chinese partner is responsible for marketing goods in the Chinese domestic market through its own channels. Both partners, therefore, utilize their specific advantages, experience, and pre-established networks in marketing the goods produced by the joint venture.

Under this agreement, the foreign currency earnings generated through foreign sales can be used to purchase raw materials and production components or equipment from abroad that the joint venture needs in its production process. Hard currency earnings may also be used to pay the salaries and wages of foreign managers and workers. The remaining foreign currency income may then be distributed to the foreign partner as dividends from the venture or held in reserve for future needs. If a joint venture generates more than adequate foreign currency earnings, it may distribute earnings in both Chinese and foreign currencies to the partners. Hence, decisions on distributing profits are also flexible as to their use as well as to the currencies involved.

Income derived from sales by the Chinese partner in the local market can be used effectively by the joint venture. First, local employees can be paid salaries and wages from the local currency account, and needed supplies may be purchased on the local market. Most foreign employees also receive part of their salary in local currency, which can be used for local expenses, housing, and entertainment. Finally, these local currency earnings may be used to pay for utilities, raw materials, and components purchased from Chinese sources as well as for the dividends paid to the local partner.

Sometimes a joint venture is organized simply to take advantage of the relatively low costs of labor and raw materials in China (Figure 4.2). In this case, the joint venture may aim at marketing all of its products abroad,

Figure 4.2
Multi-Party Joint Venture

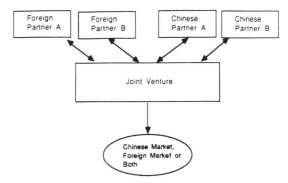

with both the Chinese and foreign partners receiving foreign currency earnings as dividends from the venture. So far, this type of joint venture is most welcome in China and enjoys the most comprehensive set of investment incentives available. Not only is the foreign partner guaranteed to receive its return on the investment paid in hard currency, but the local partner is also assured of hard currency reserves for meeting its needs.

Another type of joint venture can be designed to produce and market all of its products inside the Chinese market (Figure 4.2). Under this structure, special arrangements must be set forth in the initial agreement concerning the earnings of the foreign partner. There are four possible ways in which the foreign partner may be compensated:

1. Receive Chinese currency earnings and reinvest them in the same joint venture or other projects;
2. Receive Chinese currency earnings, buy Chinese products and sell them elsewhere;
3. Receive Chinese currency earnings and swap them into a foreign currency through one of the foreign exchange adjustment centers; or
4. Receive foreign currency earnings provided by the Chinese authorities as stipulated in the joint venture agreement.

In order to qualify for the last option, a joint venture must be regarded as either a technologically advanced or an import-substitution project. It must also obtain a certificate of guarantee from the concerned authorities prior to commencing operations (see chapter 6).

When a joint venture is engaged in the exploration and development of raw materials, the foreign partner may simply take the product (in this case raw materials) as profits (Figure 4.3). This occurs often in the coal, gas, and oil industries. It is also possible for the foreign partner to buy

Figure 4.3
JV Partners with Noncash Compensation

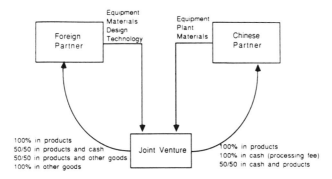

Figure 4.4
Joint Venture with a Specialized Trading Company

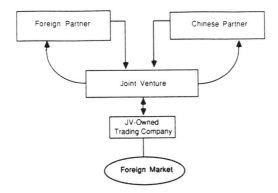

the product at a predetermined price from the joint venture. In this manner, the foreign partner is assured of a continuous supply of this particular product at a fixed price for a guaranteed period of time. Foreign currency earnings obtained in this manner are often shared with the Chinese partner.

Finally, a joint venture may establish a specialized trading company to be responsible for marketing its products overseas. Foreign currency earnings generated through this trading company would be shared by the Chinese and foreign partners (Figure 4.4).

Wholly Foreign-Owned Enterprises

A wholly foreign-owned enterprise (WFOE) may be established by a foreign company using entirely its own capital, technology, and management. The enterprise is responsible for all risks, gains, and losses. The

Figure 4.5
Wholly Foreign-Owned Venture

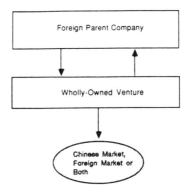

advantage of this type of enterprise is its flexibility and the ability of the foreign owner to manage and operate the enterprise as desired. Currently, priority is given to technologically advanced or knowledge-intensive projects. Certain labor intensive industries, where all production is exported, also quality for priority benefits.

A WFOE can take one of several forms as shown in Figure 4.5. Most often, the enterprise is organized inside China and markets all its goods and services in the Chinese domestic market. For this type of enterprise, the goal is to establish a presence in the Chinese market and expand its market share, rather than to generate profits in a foreign currency in the short run. However, an enterprise can also be established to sell products both domestically and overseas. This may enable the enterprise to generate some of the foreign currency earnings needed to cover expenditures in that currency. Still, an enterprise can produce in China while marketing all of its products overseas. Although it is rare, a WFOE may be organized simply to take advantage of lower production costs available locally. In this case, the company must sell 100 percent of its products in foreign markets. Several such ventures have been established for this purpose in Guangdong Province, primarily by Hong Kong, U.S., and Japanese firms.

The basic law governing WFOEs was adopted in 1986, but detailed regulations are still being drafted and revised by Chinese authorities. Compared with joint ventures, WFOEs have enjoyed less favorable investment incentives, often having to pay higher income taxes and face more stringent requirements on balancing foreign exchange earnings and expenditures. Furthermore, funding usually has to be sourced outside of China. Nevertheless, WFOEs may be more advantageous than joint ventures to foreign investors, in at least two aspects: flexibility and independence in managing production, financing, and marketing decisions; and more adequate protection of technology and trade secrets. Firms tend to establish WFOEs in those industries in which they have dominant positions internationally and, therefore, have been reluctant to share their technology with Chinese counterparts through joint ventures.

In exceptional cases, a joint venture investment may be classified as 100 percent foreign owned even though it has a Chinese partner. This situation occurs when a foreign investor takes a 75 percent or more equity ownership but includes a Chinese joint venture partner that is headquartered outside China. In most cases, this occurs with a mainland Chinese enterprise that has a Hong Kong company in which it is a full or majority owner. The view of the Chinese government is that this company is indeed a foreign company, since it is registered outside of China proper. Consequently, the venture in China can enjoy all the benefits and privileges accorded a wholly foreign-owned company though, in reality, it is a joint venture.

In these exceptional cases, the venture is usually established to take advantage of lower costs in terms of labor, raw materials, component parts, or because of access to markets due to its location. Furthermore, these enterprises are required to sell 100 percent of their production outside of China unless specific agreements have been made prior to obtaining their license to establish a business venture in China.

Joint Oil Exploration

Joint oil exploration involves the exploration and development of natural resources, especially offshore oil. These projects generally proceed in two stages. The first stage centers on geophysical exploration to be carried out by foreign partners at their own risk and cost. In the second stage, both the Chinese and foreign partners share in the risk and profits. Once commercial production begins, China retains a certain proportion of the output, apart from operating expenses, and shares the remainder with the foreign partners.

The joint development arrangement contains features of both the contractual joint venture and compensation trade. It involves risk sharing and distribution of output according to agreed shares, as in the contractual joint venture. It also enables China to acquire equipment and technical assistance from foreign companies in return for a portion of the resultant output in the form of compensation trade. The Chinese apparently feel that the extremely large investment and risks that are involved in resource development necessitate the use of this special joint venture form due to the lack of capital and appropriate technology in China.

Compensation Trade

Under compensation trade arrangements, the Chinese enterprise purchases equipment and technology from foreign companies on credit and

Figure 4.6
Triangular Compensation Arrangement

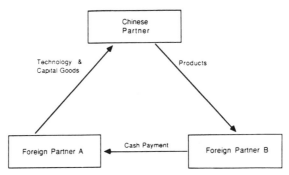

pays both principal and interest, fully or in part, with products produced using the imported equipment and technology. In some cases, payment may be made with products that are not directly produced with the imported equipment and technology. In all compensation arrangements, the foreign partner is responsible for marketing the finished products outside of China.

The obvious advantage of using this type of arrangement for the Chinese government is to save scarce foreign exchange while obtaining needed foreign technology and capital. For foreign partners, the advantage lies in much lower production costs than are possible at home, often combined with having a base closer to markets, which results in transportation cost savings. The foreign partner also may obtain needed raw materials and other products as payment. This provides a relatively safe way of becoming acquainted with and known in the Chinese marketplace. Such triangular compensation arrangements are illustrated in Figure 4.6.

However, certain problems may occur in a compensation arrangement. A common difficulty is associated with the selection of buyback products. Understandably, the foreign partner is generally interested in goods that can easily be sold internationally, while the Chinese government prefers to use only products produced directly by the imported technology and equipment as payment to the foreign partner, thus saving foreign exchange and sometimes even creating foreign exchange earnings. A problem occurs when the reject rate is high, because components or products produced do not meet international standards. Also, when a foreign partner has to take products that are unfamiliar, finding a buyer abroad may prove to be difficult. Finally, if they sell these products to an intermediary, their profits are often diminished.

The most common type of compensation arrangement is one in which the foreign partner is compensated 100 percent with products produced directly with the imported technology and equipment. Sometimes, however, the foreign partner is partly compensated with products produced directly with the imported technology and equipment and partly with other pre-arranged products. The foreign partner may also request 100 percent compensation in other goods or services that it needs for its domestic operations, thereby reducing the difficulty in marketing products in foreign markets. Still, the foreign partner may request to be compensated partly in products and partly in cash.

The final form of compensation arrangement, although not frequently used in China, is a triangular form of compensation trade (Figure 4.6). Under this arrangement, the Chinese partner imports the needed technology and equipment from foreign partner A. After goods are produced, they are sold to another foreign partner (in this case foreign partner B), who needs these goods or who has the marketing channels to sell these goods. B will then make payment to A as agreed upon (Figure 4.6).

Since China has abundant natural resources, compensation trade arrangements should have great potential. Unfortunately, this potential has not yet been fully developed. One of many reasons for slow development in compensation trade is that the Chinese are not sufficiently flexible in terms of the specific products that can be used for payment. Also, as different government departments control different products, it is difficult for the Chinese partner to exercise influence in channeling the specific products desired by the foreign partner. Therefore, coordination among these governmental departments needs to be improved to make this type of contractual agreement more effective and beneficial as a means of repaying foreign partners.

Processing and Assembling

Under processing and assembling arrangements, the foreign firm supplies raw or intermediate materials for processing, or industrial components to be assembled or manufactured according to specifications and designs provided to the Chinese partner. The finished products are turned over to the foreign firm, and the Chinese partner receives a fee for its services. Frequently the foreign partner also supplies the Chinese enterprise with machinery, equipment, and/or technology, the value of which is deducted from the processing fee payment. As in compensation trade, the Chinese treat the value of the equipment, machinery, and/or technology supplied by foreign firms under these processing and assembling arrangements as foreign funds absorbed by China.

The advantage of this arrangement is that the foreign partner may enjoy enhanced efficiency made possible, in part, by the relatively low local labor cost. For the Chinese partner, the advantage lies in earning foreign currency without much risk, while gaining some new technologies. Consequently, this type of arrangement usually involves processing and assembling operations in labor-intensive industries to produce such products as textiles, garments, footwear, and toys, as well as related industries, including electronic component assembly. Many products sold by Radio Shack in the United States are assembled in a factory in Guangdong Province under this type of arrangement.

Consequently, there is a variety of investment alternatives available in China for foreign investors. The structure selected will depend on the type of investment, needs, and desires of the joint venture partners and the specific market or markets for which the products are destined. It behooves the foreign partner, therefore, to carefully select among the alternatives available before a contract is finalized.

5

Foreign Investment Inflows

Foreign investment inflows to China have been remarkable since 1979. By the end of 1989, total inflows reached about US $19 billion. Direct investments (FDI), including equity and contractual joint ventures, oil exploration and, wholly foreign-owned enterprises (WFOEs), have accounted for over 80 percent of these inflows, while other investments such as leasing, compensation trade, and processing and assembling accounted for the remaining 20 percent. This strong performance reflects the success of the open-door policy the Chinese government has been pursuing since the late 1970s, particularly the specific policies and measures adopted to encourage foreign investment.

AGGREGATE FOREIGN INVESTMENT INFLOWS

China's efforts to encourage foreign investment inflows started in 1979; however, large foreign investment inflows did not occur until 1984. From 1979 to 1982, FDI inflows were relatively small, amounting to approximately US $1.2 billion (Table 5.1). In particular, equity investment was insignificant, accounting for less than 10 percent of total FDI inflows (Figure 5.1). Direct investment concentrated largely on contractual joint ventures and oil exploration activities (46 and 42 percent, respectively). For other investments, the bulk of inflows occurred in the form of compensation trade, which accounted for about 95 percent of total investment activities. Initially foreign investors perceived the market risk as high due to the newly opened market and economy. Therefore, investors preferred to wait for the market conditions to become more certain before making investments. Second, although the basic joint venture law on equity investment was promulgated in 1979, detailed investment regulations re-

Table 5.1
Foreign Investment Inflows, 1979–89 (In Millions of U.S. Dollars)

Types	1979-82	1983	1984	1985	1986	1987	1988	1989	1979-89¹
Direct investments²	1160	635	1258	1659	1875	2314	3194	3393	15486
Equity JVs	103	74	255	580	805	1486	1975	1610	6887
Contractual JVs	530	227	465	585	794	620	780	600	4601
Oil exploration	487	292	523	481	260	183	212	200	2637
WFOEs	40	43	15	13	16	25	226	280	658
Other investments	760	281	161	298	369	333	546	381	3129
International leasing³	--	--	--	--	48	20	161	--	--
Compensation trade	725	197	99	169	181	222	317	--	--
Processing and assembling	35	84	63	129	140	91	69	--	--
Total	1920	916	1419	1956	2243	2647	3740	3774	18615

Source: Almanac of China's Foreign Economic Relations and Trade, various issues. During the early years, several factors affected the pattern of investment inflows.

¹Disaggregated data for 1989 are estimates for the first ten months of the years as data are not available.
²The 1989 data are for the whole year.
³Data for early years are not available.

Figure 5.1
Foreign Direct Investment Inflows, 1979–88 (As a Percentage of the Total)

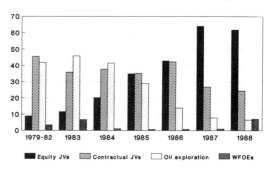

Source: Almanac of China's Foreign Economic Relations and Trade, various issues.

garding the implementation of the law were not available. Therefore, foreign investors preferred to make non-equity investment in the form of compensation trade and contractual joint ventures in order to secure a positive return on investment. Third, since the investment laws were not yet well refined, and the Chinese had little experience in equity investment, contractual joint ventures were more suitable as a means of market entry because the details of an investment agreement could be more easily arrived at through negotiations rather than through the joint venture law. Also, during the early stages of the open-door policy, a highly significant characteristic of contractual investment was the flexibility in operations and management this type of venture permitted foreign investors because the control function had not been clarified for other forms of investment. Finally, oil exploration was considered extremely promising and potentially profitable as a vast offshore area was opened to foreign oil companies.

Equity investment stepped up noticeably in 1984 and continued strongly from 1985 through 1988. Although the events of June 1989 hurt investment somewhat, the inflows for 1989 were still reasonably large for the year as a whole. Two major factors contributed to the large increase in equity investment during this period. One was the increased specification of the laws governing both joint ventures and wholly foreign-owned enterprises, as well as the laws concerning the protection of copyrights and patents. The other factor was the significant improvement in market conditions. In early 1987, the Chinese government took serious steps to instill investor confidence in the Chinese market. As a result, foreign investment grew by 30 percent in 1987 (US $3.86 billion), a dramatic change from 1986 performance, which had seen foreign investment plummet 50 percent in terms of total contract value from the 1985 level. Consequently, in 1987 the Chinese government began to listen for the first time to foreign investors' complaints concerning a variety of issues, including inadequate legislation, lack of incentives, bureaucratic complications, and foreign exchange problems.

The October 1986 "twenty-two provisions to encourage foreign investment," combined with the implementation regulations released through February 1987, provided a positive mix of investor incentives, which added to those already granted to foreign joint ventures. The package contained many strong benefits to would-be investors:

1. Legislation that reduced the bureaucracy and provided specific guarantees to foreign partners;
2. Enhanced preferential tax treatment;
3. Exemption from the payment of standard labor subsidies;
4. Exemption from most import duties on equipment and materials used in manufacturing;
5. Priority access to and controlled prices for water, power, raw materials, and necessary component parts;
6. Improvement of and priority access to the basic infrastructure facilities, including transportation and communication;
7. Improved financing from local sources for necessary working capital;

8. Reduced land-use fees and other local service charges; and

9. Greater control given to the joint ventures' top management, particularly in terms of retention, transfer, dismissal, and other matters concerning the use of local labor.

The opening of the fourteen major coastal cities to foreign investment, as noted in chapter 2, was an important move and provided foreign investors with enormous investment opportunities in these economically strong and relatively well-developed areas. The detailed regulations issued by the government in 1986 to provide additional incentives to export-oriented and import-substitution investment in these areas reinforced the effectiveness of this policy measure. The establishment of foreign exchange adjustment centers (chapter 4) addressed, at least partially, the difficult foreign exchange problem.

Toward the end of this period, the higher labor costs in the newly industrializing Asian economies, such as Korea and Taiwan, played a significant role in attracting FDI flows into China. The improved investment environment also boosted the inflows of contractual investment and compensation trade arrangements, which reflected annual increases of 25 and 50 percent, respectively.

Investment by WFOEs, however, remained weak until the mid–1980s before gaining a substantial growth in 1988–89. The major reason for the poor performance of WFOEs' investment was the reluctance of foreign investors to assume 100 percent of the risk of operating in such an unfamiliar market. Additionally, there was a lack of related laws or regulations to guide and guarantee the investors' operations and management. Oil investment also had leveled off in the latter half of the decade, reflecting the poor outcome of oil exploration activities. This situation resulted in the withdrawal of some investors and in more careful consideration of any new commitments by remaining firms.

As equity and contractual investment grew robustly, other activities, notably export processing and assembling activities, became less attractive to foreign firms; consequently, activities in these sectors declined substantially in the second half of the 1980s. The uncertainty in the aftermath of the Tiananmen Square demonstrations, combined with investor complaints concerning the high cost of doing business in China (e.g., inflated labor costs, unreliable supplies of component parts and raw materials, and bureaucratic indecision), deterred potential investors. Furthermore, the economic and political stability of a variety of South Asian countries, including Thailand, Malaysia, and Indonesia, as well as the competitive investment alternatives available in these countries, made them more attractive locations for export processing and assembly. Finally, the threat of U.S. sanctions against China during the second half of 1989 increased uncertainty and provided the impetus for firms, especially small- and medium-sized businesses, to locate elsewhere.

Even in the latter part of the period, the foreign investment boom did not continue without obstacles. In September 1988, the Chinese government launched an economic adjustment program to control rapidly rising inflation through a reduction in aggregate demand. The core of the adjustment was to halt all new large- and medium-sized investment projects and suspend or delay the approval of negotiated foreign investment agreements. Borrowing from Chinese financial institutions was either curtailed or severely restricted. The government also imposed more stringent requirements on nonessential projects in the service sector, including the construction of hotels and office buildings throughout the country. While it did not cancel the previously negotiated contracts involving foreign partners, the government nonetheless terminated many ongoing negotiations and curtailed most domestic projects under consideration.

At the same time, foreign investment also faced mounting operating problems. Due to increased inflation (more than 35 percent in 1988–89, compared with 5 percent in the early 1980s), firms were forced to pay higher prices for labor, domestic raw materials, and other production inputs. Furthermore, since local supplier companies had been unable to borrow needed funds domestically to finance their operations, they could not meet production schedules and maintain the necessary flow of products and component parts to joint venture firms. Therefore, costs rose drastically while profits declined. The financial tightening of the adjustment program also affected firms' operations by varying degrees because of the capital squeeze. The shortage of local currency forced prices up in the foreign exchange adjustment centers, further hurting firms that needed local Chinese currency financing. Infrastructural constraints worsened, due to the rapid increase in investment and the lack of credit available to Chinese firms. Power supplies became increasingly limited, often forcing firms to reduce operations. In the Shenzhen SEZ, for instance, some firms were forced to shut down three or four times a week. Similar constraints were imposed in most of the other zones and opened cities.

The economic adjustment program, nevertheless, seemed to have had little adverse impact on actual investment inflows. While equity joint venture investment declined slightly in 1989, total direct investment rose by about 6 percent, reaching US $3.4 billion for the year as a whole. Much of this increase occurred in the first half of the year and included the US $260 million Panda Motors agreement to build an automobile factory in Huizhou that was signed in March. However, after June 1989 the amount of new investment committed declined noticeably. Compared with the average 507 new contracts concluded in the first six months of 1989, only about 415 were concluded in each of the following three months,

Table 5.2
Foreign Investment Inflows by Country of Origin, 1984–89 (In Millions of U.S. Dollars)

Country	1984	1985	1986	1987	1988	1989	1984-89
Total[1]	1419	1956	1875	2314	3194	3393	14150
Hong Kong/Macao	748	956	1132	1588	2068	2037	8528
Japan	225	315	201	220	515	356	1832
U.S.A.	256	357	315	263	236	284	1712
Britain	98	71	27	5	34	29	263
Singapore	1	10	13	22	28	84	158
Italy	18	19	23	16	31	30	138
Australia	0	14	60	5	4	44	129
Germany	8	24	19	3	15	81	151
France	20	33	42	16	23	5	138
Other	45	456	42	177	241	442	1103

Source: Almanac of China's Foreign Economic Relations and Trade, various issues.
[1]Including other investment inflows.

Figure 5.2
Sources of Foreign Investment Inflows, 1984–89 (As a Percentage of the Total)

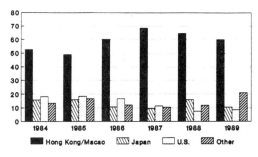

Source: Almanac of China's Foreign Economic Relations and Trade, various issues.

translating to a 20 percent decline in new investment committed in 1989, with virtually no investment flows during the last quarter.

SOURCES OF INVESTMENT

Most foreign investment in China came from other Asian countries and economies, especially Hong Kong and Japan, which accounted for 60 and 13 percent, respectively (Table 5.2 and Figure 5.2). With the exception

Figure 5.3
Trade Flows, 1984–89 (As a Percentage of the Total)

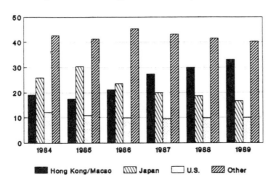

Source: IMF, Direction of Trade, 1990.

of the United States and more recently Taiwan, other countries played a
minor role. This pattern of FDI inflows is consistent with the pattern of
trade flows between China and other countries. Between 1984 and 1989,
most of China's trade took place with other Asian countries and accounted
for over 60 percent of total trade with the rest of world (Figure 5.3). Again,
Hong Kong and Japan were the largest trading partners, followed, albeit
distantly, by the United States.

It should be noted, however, that Taiwanese investment grew rapidly
in 1989 and 1990 (roughly US $1 billion each year) and is expected to
double in 1991. Already, Taiwanese investments may exceed those of
U.S. firms since it is impossible to determine the amount of Taiwanese
investment that is disguised through their subsidiary operations in Hong
Kong, the United States, Canada, and Singapore. The same is true for
South Korean investments, estimated to be US $1.5 billion as of December
1990.

The close correlation between investment and trade flows is not a surprising phenomenon. Countries that have large-scale trade activity with
China tend to be more familiar with the economic system, market environment, and business practices in China, knowledge that is undoubtedly
useful in assisting them in setting up investment operations. More importantly, significant trade flows reflect strong linkages among these economies that serve as the basis for strong investment flows.

The factors that led to Hong Kong and Macao's being the largest investors in China include:

1. Both are well connected with China in terms of geography, economy, and
trade;

2. They are closely associated with the southern part of China, particularly Guang-

dong Province, with over 80 percent of that province's investment coming from Hong Kong–Macao;

3. Hong Kong is the residence for a large segment of overseas Chinese and, during the early period of the open-door policy, it was easier for them to negotiate and operate joint ventures in China through relatives, friends, and former business ties on the mainland;

4. Hong Kong–Macao investors share the same language, culture, and family traditions, leading to a better overall understanding of the mainland Chinese; and

5. Hong Kong–Macao investors were also motivated by the desire to establish continuity and a strong base of operations to benefit the colony after it reverts to China in 1997.

During the early period (from 1979 to 1986), U.S. investment in China was strong; but after 1986, and particularly in 1988–89, the U.S. position weakened substantially and was surpassed by Japan, dropping to become only the third largest investor. In contrast to Japanese conservatism, U.S. firms were more aggressive toward the Chinese market in the first half of the decade. Their competitive advantage in technology and management, together with their eagerness to exploit new business opportunities in this vast and untapped market, led to a surge in their investment activities in these years. Poor performance was registered by the early projects, however, and deep frustration with both cumbersome bureaucracies and prolonged negotiations on joint venture deals forced many U.S. companies to adopt a more cautious approach in the latter period. Although the absolute level of investment did not decline, the U.S. share in total investment inflows decreased substantially from about 20 percent in 1984 to only 8 percent in 1989.

American investments in China from 1979 through 1989 amounted to more than US $4 billion in 952 projects, as noted in Table 5.3. The 125 contractual joint ventures accounted for the largest investment of US $1.2 billion, followed closely by the US $1.2 billion invested in 724 equity joint ventures. During the same time frame, 66 U.S. wholly foreign-owned enterprises were established. The amount committed was US $336.3 million, but that figure is understated because the Panda Motors investment was actually US $260 million, rather than US $100 million as reported in the U.S.–China Business Council study. Although the overall numbers of investments appear small, U.S.-based firms actually contributed over 12 percent of the total committed dollar inflows to the Chinese economy and showed far greater geographic distribution than those investments from Hong Kong or Japan.

The Japanese approach to investment in China was almost entirely different from that of the United States. During the early period, Japanese firms were extremely cautious and because of the uncertainty associated

Table 5.3
U.S. Investment in China by Type, 1979–89

	1979-81	1982	1983	1984	1985	1986	1987	1988	1989	Totals
EJVs										
Number of contracts	5	4	10	43	76	81	83	209	213	724
Amount committed	43.4	8.5	35.6	45.1	130.0	263.0	270.1	202.4	190.0	1,188.2
(million US dollars)										
CJVs										
Number	2	1	5	11	19	15	14	35	23	125
Amount committed	18.0	1.0	38.0	106.6	720.0	180.0	56.8	94.2	28.0	1,242.6
WFOEs										
Number	0	0	1	1	3	2	6	21	32	66
Amount committed	0.0	0.0	1.5	3.0	0.9	0.9	14.3	35.7	280.0	336.3
Offshore Oil										
Number	8	1	9	0	3	4	0	4	8	37
Amount committed	40.0	170.0	395.0	0.0	280.0	68.0	0.0	38.0	142.0	1,133.0
Other*										
Amount committed	15.0	7.0	7.5	10.5	21.1	14.1	19.3	13.9	5.4	113.9
Total US investment										
Number	15	6	25	55	101	102	103	269	276	952
Amount committed	116.4	186.5	477.6	165.2	1,152.0	526.0	360.5	384.4	645.4	4,013.9
Amount utilized**	9.0	4.2	4.5	262.6	369.9	326.2	271.3	244.4	288.2	1,780.2

Sources: MOFERT and The U.S.-China Business Council. *A Special Report on U.S. Investment in China*, 1990, p. 11. Published by the China Business Forum, The U.S.-China Business Council, Washington, D.C. Reprinted by permission.

[1]Including export processing and assembling, compensation, and leasing arrangements.
[2]Breakdown by type of contract not available.

with the newly opened market, they believed that exporting, rather than investment, was a better approach to penetrating the Chinese market. Through exporting, the Japanese firms were able to provide relatively low-priced and high-quality products with better services for their Chinese customers. Lower product prices were possible since at that time the Japanese labor cost was noticeably lower than that in the United States. Also, transportation costs between Japan and China were (and certainly still are) much lower than the costs between China and the United States. Furthermore, the Japanese saw an open window to follow up on their sales efforts by establishing lucrative joint ventures in the service sector; that is, setting up taxi firms and repair facilities, and supplying replacement parts and services. The Japanese interest in investment was strengthened as China's open-door policy continued and the market environment improved. By 1988, Japanese investment had more than doubled that of the United States and Japan became the second largest investor.

Although complete data are not available, Taiwan and South Korea have emerged as the major sources of FDI inflows to China since 1988. Economically, higher costs of production at home, particularly labor costs, have forced them to shift labor-intensive production to lower-cost countries in the region. Geographical and cultural factors have also been important in the growth of their foreign investment patterns. To encourage further infusions of Taiwanese investment, the Chinese government set up a new Taiwan Affairs Office in Beijing in mid-1990 to boost ties with Taiwan.

Trade between Taiwan and the mainland has shown a dramatic increase in the past decade. As of 1990, Taiwan is China's sixth largest trading partner while the mainland ranks as Taiwan's fifth largest. Prior to 1980, the amount of trade was insignificant and flowed indirectly through Hong Kong. However, by 1987 the unofficial volume was approximately US $1.6 billion and in 1988 it reached US $2.7 billion. Even more dramatic was the jump in bilateral trade in 1989, which more than doubled to US $3.5 billion. Official Taiwanese exports to the mainland for 1989 were roughly US $2.3 billion, with imports from the mainland accounting for the balance. In addition, indirect (illegal) trade flows are estimated to be at least a quarter of a billion U.S. dollars. Furthermore, it is estimated that more than US $1.4 billion in transfers occurred in 1989 due primarily to remittances from family members in Taiwan to the mainland, as well as from the heavy flows of tourists from Taiwan visiting their families.

The initial investments by Taiwanese industrialists began in about 1983 and were channeled primarily through firms based in Hong Kong and Macao. In mid–1988, the Beijing government openly began to court Taiwanese investors by offering them preferential treatment in establishing joint ventures and the right to withdraw profits. Two prime targets were the special economic zones of Xiamen in Fujian Province and Shenzhen in Guangdong Province. Many of the Taiwanese investors in Fujian Province have strong family linkages and speak the same dialect. In the case of Shenzhen, its location near Hong Kong, where Taiwanese firms have long had major investments, makes it an ideal investment site, not only because of its proximity, but because of the special incentives offered. The same is true of Taiwanese investments in Guangdong Province.

Production efficiencies resulting from lower labor costs are a major attraction for Taiwan-based firms to transfer operations to the mainland. One Taiwanese investor, who has placed US $4 million in a joint venture in Xiamen, notes that his workers on the mainland receive seven times less in average monthly wages than their counterparts in Taiwan. When making his relocation decision, the total incentive package offered made Xiamen the optimum choice over other possible sites in southern Asia.

While most of the Taiwanese investors are medium-sized manufacturers seeking production efficiency by moving to escape the higher cost of doing business in Taiwan, there is evidence of large industries flowing to the mainland as well. Formosa Plastics, one of Taiwan's largest conglomerates, became the focus of world attention when Y.C. Wang, Formosa's chairman, proposed the construction of a US $186 million naphtha plant

on the mainland. Although the Taiwanese government denied approval
for the proposed investment, there are indications that it may move forward gradually. Formosa Plastics is part of a strategic industry because
chemicals and downstream products account for more than a third of
Taiwan's exports by value. Furthermore, if Formosa Plastics moved to
the mainland, many other large-scale industries would follow.

Chinese officials estimate that the cumulative investment from Taiwan
amounted to about US $1 billion by the end of 1989. Unofficial estimates
place the value of Taiwanese investment somewhere in the US $3 to 5 bil-
lion range as of mid-1991. According to reports in the Taiwanese press,
recent investments exceed that of either the United States or Japan, amounting to as much as 60 percent of the investment flows to China from mid–1989
through the first quarter of 1991. If investments continue at the current rate, it
will not be long before the Taiwanese surpass Japan and the United States in
terms of total investment, ranking second only to Hong Kong, which currently accounts for almost 60 percent of total foreign investment.

Figures for Korean investment in China are even more elusive. Again,
Korean firms began their investment inroads into China in 1985 despite
the fact that neither the Korean nor Chinese Governments recognized
each other officially. Like their Taiwanese counterparts, the initial Korean
contacts were made through American, Japanese, and Hong Kong
sources. Dealing through their subsidiaries outside of Korea, these firms
gradually made inroads into the Chinese market, leading to the first joint
venture agreement signed by the Daewoo Corporation in late 1986, established to produce refrigerators for local consumption.

Unofficial estimates placed total Korean foreign investment in China
as high as US $1.2 billion as of mid–1990 and growing rapidly. Moreover,
both investment and trade flows have increased significantly since the
establishment of joint commercial offices in Beijing and Seoul in October
1990. Like their Japanese counterparts, the Korean firms have well-established trading companies and will have less difficulty than other Western firms in taking their profits out in products and raw materials that, in
turn, will be sold in world markets as well as consumed domestically.

GEOGRAPHICAL PATTERN

The geographical distribution of foreign investment inflows indicates
that foreign investment activities have been concentrated in coastal provinces and cities (Table 5.4). During the past five years, investment in
Guangdong Province alone accounted for over 40 percent of total inflows.
Together with Shanghai and Fujian Province, investment in these three
areas has accounted for about 60 percent of the total foreign investments
in China.

The strong investment inflows to the coastal areas occurred for several

Table 5.4
Foreign Investment Inflows by Province, 1984–89 (In Agreement Amount in Millions of U.S. Dollars)

Province	1984	1985	1986	1987	1988	1984-89
Total	2875	5369	2542	3254	5064	19103
Beijing	119	379	420	624	143	1684
Tianjin	106	69	94	14	110	392
Liaoning	44	254	75	106	192	672
Shanghai	431	771	303	338	333	2176
Fujian	236	377	65	118	463	1258
Shandong	105	100	49	39	260	553
Guangdong	1409	2199	869	1258	2242	7977
Other	425	1221	668	757	1321	4392

Source: Almanac of China's Foreign Economic Relations and Trade, various issues.

reasons. First, coastal provinces and cities were economically better de- veloped than other regions of the country. Hence, they were able to provide supporting infrastructural facilities, production components, and other necessary production inputs. Second, the coastal areas, particularly Guangdong and Fujian provinces, were closely linked with the overseas Chinese; thus, much of the investment into these two provinces was sponsored by the overseas Chinese business community. As mentioned earlier, investment in Fujian Province was further boosted by infusions of Taiwanese capital. Third, the flow of investment into these areas also was helped by the strong local production base and relatively well-edu- cated work force. Fourth, the opened cities had previous linkages to the West prior to World War II, particularly Shanghai, which was one of the foremost commercial and industrial centers in Asia at the time.

The share of investment in the coastal areas declined somewhat during 1984–89, however, owing to the opening up of other areas and to the strong promotion by local provincial governments to attract foreign in- vestment. The availability of raw materials, such as coal, oil, and gas, also was an advantage to foreign investors. However, infrastructural shortages, noticeably transportation and communication problems, still seriously constrain many provincial governments' ability to infuse foreign capital.

SECTORAL DISTRIBUTION

Statistics on sectoral distribution of investment inflows have been less well organized. In early years (from 1979 to 1984), the presentation of

Table 5.5

Foreign Investment Inflows by Sector, 1984–88 (In Agreement Amount as a Percentage of the Total)

Sector	1984	1985	1986	1987	1988	1984-88
Total	2875	6333	2834	3709	5297	21048
Industry	496	2384	785	1776	4022	9463
Real estate, public utilities, and services	1017	2271	1617	1471	530	6906
Building	78	133	53	55	119	436
Commerce and catering	230	527	100	29	64	950
Agriculture, forestry, fishery	79	126	62	125	209	601
Communications	84	106	33	16	91	331
Other	891	797	184	237	262	2361

Source: Almanac of China's Foreign Economic Relations and Trade, various issues.

data prepared by the Chinese government included specific industries in the manufacturing sector; however, the format was changed later into that shown in Table 5.5.

Since 1988 the pattern of sectoral distribution of investment inflows has changed substantially, shifting from real estate activities to manufacturing. Investment in real estate, including both construction and hotel industries, was hurt by the "adjustment program." There were indications that within the manufacturing sector investment was heavily concentrated on machinery and equipment, with a small portion also going to the food processing industry. Altogether, foreign investment made important contributions to the sectoral development of services, export manufacturing, and oil exploration.

Sectoral distribution of the foreign equity joint ventures is shown in Table 5.6. Hong Kong–Macao investments have been concentrated heavily in light industry, textiles, electronics, chemicals, and heavy industry. In many cases, investments represent a shift from operations in Hong Kong to the mainland for economic reasons. With Hong Kong being one of the highest cost areas for both real estate and living, combined with its rapidly rising salary and wage cost, investments on the mainland were sound business decisions. Furthermore, many of the investors sought to diversify operations to prepare for 1997 when Hong Kong reverts to Chinese authority.

American investments in equity joint ventures, as noted earlier, tend to be more widely disbursed according to economic sector. This reflects not only a wider range of interests, but also a broader spectrum of inves-

Table 5.6
Foreign Equity Joint Ventures by Economic Sector

Sector	Hong Kong Macao	USA	Japan	SE Asia	Europe	Australia Canada N Zealand	Other	Total	Percent
Agriculture	34	17	13	9	6	8	1	88	3.53
Building Materials	74	14	9	16	11	1	0	125	5.02
Chemicals	126	32	11	18	7	1	2	197	7.91
Electronics	137	49	16	6	4	5	0	217	8.71
Energy	9	10	1	0	7	0	0	27	1.08
Food	78	16	21	21	12	3	1	152	6.10
Heavy Industry	117	30	22	12	11	4	1	197	7.91
Light Industry	467	34	41	33	24	9	3	611	24.53
Medical	28	14	16	6	12	1	1	78	3.13
Miscellaneous	37	5	2	2	1	1	1	49	1.97
Packaging	48	7	1	9	2	1	0	68	2.73
Printing	14	4	4	0	0	0	0	22	0.88
Property Development	50	3	13	3	1	0	1	71	2.85
Services	64	9	9	3	4	0	0	89	3.57
Textiles	289	29	19	23	8	7	3	378	15.17
Transportation	86	17	6	2	9	2	0	122	4.90
Total	1658	290	204	163	119	43	14	2491	100.0

Source: "Foreign Investment Database." In *A Special Report on U.S. Investment in China*, 1990, p. 27. Published by The China Business Forum, The U.S.-China Business Council, Washington, D.C. Reprinted by permission.

tors. Many of the Hong Kong firms have interlocking directorates and industry is concentrated in the hands of a few major investors. On the other hand, ownership of American firms reflects not only large firms but also small- and medium-sized firms among the investor groups.

Occidental Petroleum and Atlantic Richfield were among the two largest single foreign equity joint ventures in China. Occidental's investment (the Group announced on January 14, 1991, that it would pull out of the investment to reduce its outstanding debts of US $8.5 billion) of approximately US $175 million was concentrated in an open-pit coal mine in Shanxi Province, whereas Atlantic Richfield's estimated US $170 million investment is slated for developing gas fields in the South China Sea, based on Hainan Island. A third resource investor, Texaco Inc., has a smaller (estimated US $50 million) investment in oil extraction off the South China coast.

Another major U.S. investment was begun in 1985 in Shanghai by the Portman Companies. They are building the Shanghai exhibition center in the heart of the city that will feature one of the most modern exhibition halls surrounded by a hotel, office, and residential complex and a massive shopping arcade. Initial investment was set at US $175 million; however, final completion of this complex project has been delayed by the events of 1989 and 1990 and, according to Shanghai authorities, total investment may run as high as US $200 million. Not only have costs escalated, but delays in construction have added to the overhead and projected rentals are far behind schedule. Furthermore, because of other construction projects that have been completed, there is a current glut in the Shanghai market for rentals.

EQUITY JOINT VENTURE EXPERIENCE

Most foreign equity joint ventures have suffered along with other businesses in China due to the impact of the austerity program during 1989 and 1990. However, due to external infusions of capital, foreign joint ventures have suffered less than domestic industries. Curtailment of bank credit bankrupted a larger number of China's privately owned business enterprises and brought many state-owned enterprises to a virtual standstill. Although credit was eased in the last half of 1990, both foreign and domestic companies are still feeling the pinch as of mid-1991.

The impact on foreign equity joint ventures was threefold: virtual cessation of bank loans and credits, payment lags from Chinese customers, and an inability to convert earnings to foreign exchange. Many foreign investors had determined the amount of their investments based upon their Chinese partner's ability to obtain financing from local sources. With loans from financial institutions curbed, the joint venture had to depend upon the ability of the foreign partner to source needed capital to maintain operations. Furthermore, the curtailment of loans and credits to Chinese industries impacted even more heavily on joint venture operations. Chinese firms depended upon loans from government banks to pay for their purchases of equipment or component parts from the foreign joint ventures, and without the loans payments for purchases have lagged anywhere from nine months to more than a year. In addition, suppliers to the joint ventures could not obtain loans and consequently were unable to purchase the raw materials necessary to supply end products to the joint venture companies. The result was unmet production quotas and grossly inflated per unit costs.

Even though there were guarantees on both the repatriation and use of hard currency earnings, as well as on the conversion of earnings in Chinese currency to hard currencies, the Chinese government pressured firms to utilize their hard currency earnings to pay for needed imports of component parts and equipment. The government also curtailed any conversions of Chinese currency earnings for purposes of repatriation in the form of dividends. Finally, if a joint venture was in the process of expansion, all funding had to come from external sources.

The showcase joint ventures, ranging from Beijing Jeep to Guangzhou Peugeot, were also particularly hard hit. Joint venture automobile firms were impacted because of two factors: first, all were highly dependent upon importing knock-down kits for end product assembly, which was curtailed by the reduction in import quotas as well as the severe restrictions on the use of foreign exchange; second, automobiles are considered luxury goods in China and government affiliated organizations (the major customers) stopped buying them, as did private sector consumers.

Foxboro, which perhaps received more headlines for being one of the most exemplary joint ventures in China, saw its operations come to a virtual standstill in early 1990 because of the austerity program. Foxboro was placed in a catch–22 position because by February 1990 many of its Chinese customers were more than eight months in arrears in making payments. Like many other firms, it also faced problems in getting component parts from its Chinese suppliers because these companies were unable to secure the loans necessary to purchase raw materials and other parts needed in their production processes. The shortage of foreign currency allocations prevented Foxboro from importing necessary components from abroad as well as negated its ability to repatriate dividends. To complicate matters further, the Chinese government was replacing a very efficient and well-trained Chinese director, who co-managed on equal terms with the American joint venture executive, with an individual whose expertise lay in his party connections. Although Foxboro was a joint venture producing one of the high-priority end products needed by the Chinese economy in its process of modernization, it was impacted so heavily by these factors that withdrawal from China was contemplated.

Another factor negating foreign investment is the problem of corruption among some government officials. Although the Chinese government has attempted to crack down on this activity and has given prime attention in the press to arrests and convictions, corruption still prevails in many areas. Although not unique to China—bribery is widespread throughout the developing world and also occurs in developed countries as well—the spread of bribery has been rapid in the past few years, part of it out of sheer necessity. As one investor stated during a plant interview, "the shortages of materials needed by our factory have made it virtually impossible to meet production schedules; therefore, we must pay a commission to get the goods we need or go out of business."

A significant risk negating technology transfers is that a foreign investor in a joint venture enterprise may be setting up a future competitor. A foreign firm entered into a joint venture with a Chinese pharmaceutical company in Beijing, bringing with it state-of-the-art equipment and transferring its product and production technologies. Its partner, however, worked against the best interests of the joint venture, causing heavy losses from operations. Furthermore, with knowledge of the technologies transferred, the Chinese partner became a major competitor in the Chinese marketplace. Not surprisingly, the joint venture was dissolved with heavy losses to the foreign partner. Such instances have occurred in a variety of other joint ventures in the textile, footwear, toy, and other consumer goods industries.

While there have been disappointments and frustrations, many foreign investors have been satisfied with their investments for the most part. For example, S.D. Johnson Company, a US $12 million joint venture with Shanghai Daily Chemical Industrial Development Corporation, began operations in 1987. Since then, it has upgraded production facilities in its Shanghai factory and is exporting household products to Hong Kong and other foreign markets. According to the American manager of the joint venture, what was once an inefficient plant on the verge of bankruptcy has been turned into a very profitable enterprise. Major hard currency earnings are garnered from sales to Hong Kong, while sales in the Chinese market provide funds for wages, raw materials, and local operating expenses. There are plans to build a new facility and shift production from the heart of Shanghai to one of the special economic zones, which will allow the venture to introduce more sophisticated processes and expand plant capacity. This additional capacity will, in turn, provide greater economies of scale and the opportunity for greater export earnings.

Coca-Cola has been equally successful in its investment in Shanghai, in cooperation with Shanghai Investment and Trust Company and the Food Development Center of Shanghai Light Industry. Negotiations began in August 1985, and a contract was signed in October 1986. Total registration capital was US $14 million of which Coca-Cola invested US $11 million (US $7 million in equipment and technology and US $4 million in cash), and the remaining US $3 million was divided between the two Chinese partners. Coca-Cola has a total of thirteen plants in China, two of which are located in Shanghai.

The Shanghai plant, which produces Fanta and Sprite, commands an impressive 8 percent of the Shanghai soft drink market. It operates three shifts (twenty hours per day) at full capacity and still cannot meet the market demand for its products. Profitability has been satisfactory for both Coke and its Chinese partners, and, in terms of profit repatriation, it is ahead of schedule. Consequently, there are plans to double plant capacity for the Shanghai operations if approved by the parent company in the United States.

Another example of a profitable joint venture is the Hui Xiang Precision Parts Limited plant, located in Huizhou City of Guangdong Province. This firm, which is a Chinese-Japanese joint venture, was established to supply component parts to a Phillips joint venture, also located in Guangdong Province. The end product, car radios and stereo equipment, is in turn exported to a variety of foreign markets throughout the world. In the United States, these stereo systems are sold by Radio Shack under the brand Realistic.

The Hui Xiang Precision Parts Limited is as modern a plant as one would find anywhere in the world. Production lines are operated by well-trained and hard working Chinese employees who look very much like their Japanese and Korean counterparts in their neat and well-fitted company uniforms. Operating on an incentive system, hands move rapidly on the assembly lines as they compete to exceed previous performance and quality control records. Unlike many of the state-owned factories, the equipment is of the latest technology, including robotics, and the floors and workplace appear so clean that one could eat off them. A visit to this factory quickly dispels the myth that Chinese workers cannot be as efficient or as quality control minded as their Asian competition.

The joint venture firms that have managed to succeed despite the retrenchment have been those that were designed from the onset to export a significant portion of their production. Furthermore, they were realistic in terms of their expectation from operations in China and had opted for a long-term relationship rather than for short-term profitability.

WHOLLY FOREIGN-OWNED ENTERPRISES

Wholly foreign-owned enterprises, in general, have not been impacted as heavily by the retrenchment policies that began in fall 1988. From the onset, these enterprises depended upon external sources of financing as well as generating income from exports. In most cases, 100 percent of production is exported. On the other hand, many wholly foreign-owned enterprises, like their joint venture counterparts, were affected by the chronic shortages in raw materials and supplies as well as component parts obtained from Chinese (and in some cases foreign joint venture) manufacturers. In addition, depending upon location, WFOEs had to adjust to the problems that face all firms domestic and foreign in China. For example, those ventures located in the Shenzhen SEZ and in other parts of China found that inadequate power supplies allowed them to operate only four days a week. Those enterprises that began operations in late 1988 and 1989 have been handicapped by the inability of local governments to meet commitments on infrastructure development. The construction of roads, power lines, and port facilities has lagged because of a lack of credit facilities.

On the other hand, there have been some improvements in local conditions that are favorable for wholly foreign-owned enterprises. For example, there has been a relaxation of the requirement for certain firms to export all or a majority of the goods produced in their factories. In some cases, all that is now required is a balancing of export incomes with import and profit repatriation needs. This is particularly true for firms located in Beijing and Shanghai where the bulk of their production is sold in local markets.

While most wholly foreign-owned enterprises are located in SEZs, Minnesota Mining & Manufacturing Corporation (3M Company) was one of the first to locate in one of the open cities. After three years of negotiations, the Chinese government approved the venture in 1983 and the plant began operations in 1984. Based in Shanghai, with initial equity of US $3 million, the plant primarily produces insulating tapes and electrical connectors for telecommunications users. This arrangement gave 3M the ability to protect trade secrets, respond to market changes in terms of expansion or contraction, and to maintain full control over production and sales. Other firms, whose prime concern was protecting trade secrets and controlling operations, include Motorola and Pepsico, both of which have significant sales from their operations in China.

Panda Motors Corporation is the largest wholly foreign-owned enterprise underway in China. Furthermore, it is the largest single foreign investment in China since the open-door policy began, although it may soon be superceded by Shell Oil's projected US $2.4 billion investment for a chemical complex in Guangdong Province.

The idea of establishing an automobile firm in China originated in the summer of 1988. After four years of frustratedly trying to convince several American and South Korean companies to build a plant in China to produce low-cost automobiles, a China consultant struck a responsive chord in a casual conversation with an American entrepreneur. In a matter of weeks, a firm had been incorporated and explorations were underway for a possible venture in China. Originally slated to be an equity joint venture, the decision to embark on a wholly foreign-owned enterprise was made for a variety of reasons, including autonomy in the management control of operations, recognition that funding would have to be external to China, and the need to move quickly if plans for production work were to be underway by the end of 1991.

A variety of factors influenced the selection of Huizhou as the plant site. First, there was a need to acquire land to accommodate a very large facility that would be free from polluted air. Second, there would be an immediate need for port access to bring in the plant and equipment necessary for the factory, as well as for the exportation of automobiles. Third, assurance was needed that the local government would welcome the enterprise and would guarantee providing the necessary infrastructure developments on schedule.

The Pudong Zone in Shanghai was the first site explored; however, Shanghai authorities admitted that it would be at least five years before port facilities could be developed in the zone and that infrastructure loans had not yet been allocated for development purposes. Other Shanghai sites have a major problem with air pollution, which would have created problems during the painting phase of automobile production. Although Shanghai appeared ideal otherwise, particularly with its many automobile part suppliers in the greater metropolitan area, there was another negating factor. When a firm acquires a plant site, one of the requirements is to relocate all individuals and businesses that currently reside there. In Huizhou, however, there were no businesses and very few families that needed to be relocated. As a consequence, the site in Huizhou was ideal.

A letter of intent was signed in December 1988 and initial approval was granted by Beijing in mid-March 1989 with all final approvals coming by early April. In spite of the Tiananmen Square incident, ground breaking took place on June 27, 1989, and work is proceeding virtually on schedule as of March 1991. This illustrates the expediency with which Chinese authorities can act when a project falls within the investment goals set by Chinese authorities, required documentation is explicit, and appropriate steps are followed. Much of the credit, however, goes to the innovative entrepreneur and CEO of Panda Motors, whose background and experience played a significant role in the company's success to date. If present plans materialize, by 1996 investment will have expanded to US $1 billion, approximately 300,000 cars will be rolling off the assembly line, and numerous joint ventures will have been established for component assembly. However, the firm has recently experienced financial problems and is looking for a foreign joint venture partner in the automotive business.

A REGIONAL COMPARISON

Strong foreign investment inflows to China were not unique during the 1980s. Significant inflows to other Asian countries also occurred during the same period. Compared with representative neighboring countries, investment flows into China were large in absolute amount but remained relatively small in terms of gross domestic product (GDP) and gross investment (GI). As Figures 5.4 and 5.5 indicate, foreign equity investment into Singapore between 1980 and 1989 accounted for about 15 percent of GDP and financed more than one-third of Singapore's total capital expansion. The same ratios for China were only 0.7 and 1.8 percent, respectively. Even when compared with Malaysia, Thailand, and Indonesia, the ratios for China were extremely low.

China enjoys several advantages in attracting foreign investment compared with other Asian countries. First, it has a large domestic market that provides potentially enormous opportunities for foreign investors. Second, it has abundant natural resources to attract resource-based investment activities. Finally, labor costs are much lower in China than in neighboring Asian countries and, thereby, provide a strong attraction for labor-intensive investment.

Many of these advantages, however, are offset by the disincentives prevailing in the Chinese market. These negative factors tend to discourage and limit investment activities by imposing more uncertainties,

Figure 5.4
FDI Inflows: A Regional Comparison as a Percentage of GDP

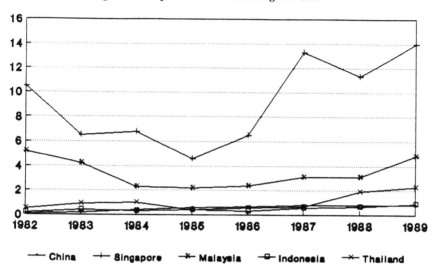

Figure 5.5
FDI Inflows: A Regional Comparison as a Percentage of Total Gross Investment

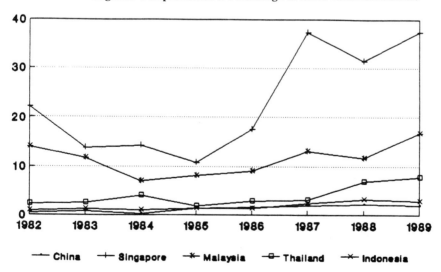

Source: IMF, *Balance of Payments Yearbook*, 1990.

and, therefore, higher risks that foreign firms must face. Major disincentives to foreign investment in China include:

1. Restrictions on capital flows and profit repatriations;
2. Restrictions on access of foreign firms to local capital markets;
3. Less productive, though cheaper, labor force;
4. Excessive bureaucracy; and
5. Above all, a centrally planned system and a highly regulated market that seriously limit the role of market forces and competition.

The events of June 1989 further destroyed market confidence, which is slowly being restored.

6

Organizations Involved in Foreign Investment

Foreign investors face a confusing array of administrative organizations and financial institutions in China, all of which have at least partial responsibility for the development and operation of foreign investment projects. Potential foreign investors should familiarize themselves with these organizations and should understand their functions in order to avoid any unnecessary delay costs and mistakes.

Central-level government organizations, in general, have local, provincial, and municipal equivalents with similar functions. For example, the Ministry of Finance, a central-level government agency, has a Bureau of Finance in each provincial and municipal government. These bureaus perform functions similar to their central-level government counterparts but bear different responsibilities. In general, the Ministry of Finance is responsible for all financial matters on a national level, while the individual bureaus are in charge of the financial matters of their respective provinces.

Whether foreign investors should approach the central-level ministries or the local bureaus for help usually depends on the scale and location of the investment project. For example, the municipal governments of Shanghai, Beijing, and Tianjin have the authority to decide on investment projects of up to US $30 million without further permission from the central government. Other cities, such as Guangzhou and Shenyang, can only decide on projects valued under US $10 million. Smaller cities have the right to decide on projects valued under US $5 million.

In order to approach the right agency from the very beginning, before negotiations begin with a Chinese partner, the foreign investor should understand whether the proposed investment project must be approved by a central government organization or by a local one. Foreign investors should recognize that local-level organizations must report to both their equivalent central government organizations and to the provincial and municipal governments of which they are a part. The provincial and municipal governments play an important role in attracting foreign investment. Consequently, local organizations can have a great deal of autonomy in approving foreign investment projects in their respective provinces and municipalities or in assisting foreign operations to gain necessary approval from central authorities in Beijing.

Foreign investors should bear in mind that different organizations in China have different responsibilities. Some have the authority to make foreign investment policies and decisions, while others are responsible for approving investment projects. There are also organizations that provide various services to foreign investors, including legal assistance, financial assistance, accounting advice, and information consulting.

Financial institutions at the central level also have their equivalents in local governments. Each financial institution, due to the different foci and limits of their business activity, provides a variety of financial services to foreign joint ventures. Some are actively involved in direct investment in projects, while others are more interested in commercial lending activities.

INVESTMENT POLICY-MAKING AGENCIES

There are about a dozen central-level organizations in charge of foreign investment. These organizations cover general foreign investment policies, investment incentive programs, and oversight of the respective authorities assigned to each provincial and municipal government. Financing, accounting, and other related policies are included in the scope of their related activity.

State Council

As shown in Figure 6.1, the State Council is the executive branch of the central government. It makes all major decisions regarding overall foreign investment policies and, in this respect, prepares or passes appropriate rules and regulations. In addition, the State Council has the final authority for approving investment projects above US $50 million.

State Council Leading Group on Foreign Investment

The State Council Leading Group on Foreign Investment (LGFI) is a supraministerial organization whose main responsibility is to coordinate foreign investment policies. It recommends policy to the State Council, drafts investment legislation, and acts as a problem solver of last resort

Figure 6.1
Organizations Involved in Investment Policy Making

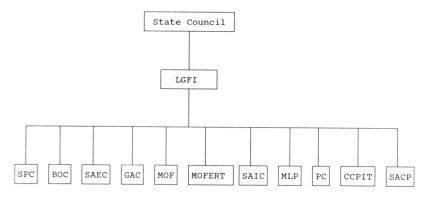

LGFI:	State Council Leading Group on Foreign Investment
SPC:	State Planning Commission
MOFERT:	Ministry of Foreign Economic Relations & Trade
BOC:	Bank of China
SAEC:	State Administration of Exchange Control
GAC:	General Administration on Customs
MOF:	Ministry of Finance
SAIC:	State Administration of Industry and Commerce
MLP:	Ministry of Labor & Personnel
PC:	People's Court
CPIT:	China's Council for the Promotion of International Trade
SACP:	State Administration of Commodity Prices

for foreign investors. The members of the LGFI include both state councilors and ministers from the various ministries that are involved in the foreign investment decision-making process.

State Planning Commission

The State Planning Commission (SPC) falls directly under the State Council. It is in charge of major economic policies and plans for China. Both the short- and long-term plans for utilizing foreign investment are prepared by the SPC and approved by the State Council. The short-term plans cover one year while the long-term plans cover periods of more than a year. Since China is still largely a planned economy, foreign investment is a part of the national economic development policy; as such, it is incorporated into the overall national economic plan. Foreign investment is particularly encouraged in those industries that are given priority by the SPC for the national economy.

Although foreign investors may not need to deal with the SPC directly, they must understand what priorities the SPC has set for different sectors of the economy. Hence, they are better able to decide whether proposed investment projects will qualify as a priority. In addition to assigning industry priorities, the SPC assists foreign investors in formulating investment policies and regulations, in granting initial project approvals (if they are beyond the authority of the local governments), and in approving feasibility studies and import-substitution applications.

Ministry of Foreign Economic Relations and Trade

The Ministry of Foreign Economic Relations and Trade (MOFERT) is perhaps the most important central-level organization in charge of external economic relations and activities, including foreign investment, in China. The primary functions of the ministry are to establish and implement foreign trade policies, as well as enforce state foreign trade plans.

With respect to foreign investment, MOFERT is responsible for formulating foreign investment policies, drafting laws, rules, and regulations for foreign investment, and approving investment contracts (if beyond the authority of the local government). The MOFERT is also responsible for issuing import and export licenses for foreign investment projects, approving the use of Chinese currency to purchase products for export by foreign investors, approving export-oriented and technologically advanced investment projects, and approving import-substitution projects.

Bank of China

The Bank of China (BOC) is a state-owned bank specializing in foreign exchange activities. Its main functions are to:

• Mobilize foreign exchange funds;
• Deal in foreign exchange businesses;
• Settle international accounts of foreign trade and nontrade transactions;
• Handle deposits and loans among international banks;
• Handle remittances from and to overseas Chinese corporations, as well as other international remittances;
• Handle foreign currency deposits and loans, and, with the permission of the People's Bank of China (central bank), handle deposits and loans in Chinese currency related to foreign exchange operations;
• Purchase and sell foreign exchange and gold bullion on international markets;
• Issue foreign currency bonds and other securities, with the authorization of the State Council; and
• Engage in trust, investment, leasing, and consultancy services.

In terms of foreign investment, the BOC is the main bank in which foreign investment projects can hold both Chinese currency deposits and foreign exchange bank account deposits. It is the major source of short-term working capital as well as long-term capital financing in Chinese and foreign currencies. The BOC is a major guarantor when investment projects are seeking to borrow from international financial markets. It also assists in arranging currency swaps for foreign investors on a commission basis. Last, but not the least, the BOC is an active investor in Sino-foreign joint ventures in various key industries.

State Administration of Exchange Control

The State Administration of Exchange Control (SAEC) is the administrative organization in charge of foreign exchange controls. Its primary functions are threefold: to administer all income and expenditures in foreign currencies for State organizations, enterprises, and individuals; to administer the issuance and circulation of bills, certificates, and bonds denoted in foreign currencies; and to administer incoming and outgoing foreign currencies, precious metals, bills, certificates, and bonds denoted in foreign currencies.

With respect to foreign investment, the SAEC is an important organization because of its involvement in the following areas:

- Approving profit repatriation for foreign investment projects;
- Approving foreign exchange and Chinese currency swaps;
- Approving domestic sales of foreign currencies for foreign investment projects; and
- Requiring that foreign investment projects report any foreign borrowings.

General Administration of Customs

The General Administration of Customs (GAC) is a state organization with administrative functions for the supervision of import and export activities. Its main functions are to ensure the effective implementation of State guidelines, policies, laws, and regulations concerning imports and exports, as well as to supervise and control postal items and luggage, transported goods, tariffs, and customs statistics. As far as foreign investment is concerned, the GAC has the authority to inspect and assess duties for imports and exports of foreign investment projects and to approve duty exemptions for foreign investment.

Ministry of Finance

The Ministry of Finance (MOF) is an administrative organization under the State Council, which controls state revenues and expenditures. Its main functions are to:

- Enforce state economic, tax, and other policies;
- Prepare the annual state budget and final fiscal report and to work out the financial management and tax systems;
- Formulate financial and accounting systems for enterprises and the system for investment allocation in capital construction projects; and
- Manage state revenues and expenditures and supervise financing and financial activities in all localities and organizations.

In addition to the other bureaus within the MOF, the following four bureaus are, to a varying degree, involved in foreign investment:

1. The General Tax Bureau is responsible for negotiating and drafting international taxation agreements with other countries;
2. The Overall Planning Department is responsible for external debt management;
3. The Department for the Financial Affairs of Industrial and Communication Enterprises participates in the examination and approval of projects using direct foreign investment and formulates the related rules and regulations; and
4. The Department of Accounting and Management exercises control over accounting at the national level and formulates decrees, rules, regulations, and plans concerning accounting with respect to foreign investment projects.

In short, the MOF handles all tax matters and sets accounting rules and procedures for foreign investment projects in China.

State Administration of Industry and Commerce

The State Administration of Industry and Commerce (SAIC) has the following responsibilities:

- Implement the government's economic policy, laws, and statutes in the supervision of industrial and commercial enterprises and market transactions;
- Protect legal business operations and ban illegal ones; and
- Promote production and stimulate the circulation of commodities.

In addition to other bureaus within the SAIC, there are two bureaus directly involved in foreign investment: the Trademark Bureau, which handles the registration of trademarks (including foreign trademarks), protects the exclusive use of registered trademarks, investigates and punishes breaches of the Trademark Law and protects consumer's interests; and the Individual Economy Management Department, which is responsible for issuing business licenses. After starting operations, foreign investment projects must apply for a license through the local offices of the SAIC.

The issue date of the approved license is the commencement date of the foreign investment project.

The SAIC also sets the requirements for debt-to-equity ratios for foreign investment and sets rules for foreign investors' capital contributions. It also helps resolve trademark disputes, if any.

Ministry of Labor and Personnel

The Ministry of Labor and Personnel (MLP) is responsible for formulating the policies, rules, and regulations on the management of labor, wage systems, personnel, and related issues. More specifically, it supervises job allocation and vocational training, administers welfare and insurance programs, sets guidelines and standards for wages and salaries, and implements health and safety standards.

The MLP sets overall labor and wage policies, with regard to foreign investment. Local-level MLP bureaus can approve labor contracts, supply labor to foreign investment projects, assist in employee transfers for investment projects, arbitrate transfer disputes, require reporting of employee dismissals on foreign investment projects, and determine the amount that foreign investment projects must pay for labor insurance, welfare, housing, and other subsidies.

People's Court

The People's Court (PC) supervises the administration of justice in China. It offers a legal means for helping foreign investment projects resolve in China patent, trademark, and other business disputes.

Council for the Promotion of International Trade

The Council for the Promotion of International Trade (CCPIT) is a people-to-people trade organization whose major function is to promote China's economic, trade, and investment relations with other countries. It grants patents and trademarks to foreign investment projects and also aids foreign investors to resolve business disputes.

State Administration of Commodity Prices

The State Administration of Commodity Prices (SACP) is responsible for determining and adjusting the price levels for all major industrial and agricultural products in the domestic market as well as determining the prices of products produced by foreign investment projects.

Table 6.1 summarizes the major responsibilities of each of the organizations discussed. It is apparent that there are significant overlaps in

Table 6.1
Responsibilities of Organizations Involved in Foreign Investment

Policies	State Council, SPC, MOF, MOFERT
Accounting	MOF
Arbitration	PC, CCPIT
Approval	MOFERT or local FERTCs
Licenses	SAIC & Local Offices
Import & Export Duties	GAC
Financing	BOC, CITIC, TICs
Swaps	SAEC, BOC, CITIC, TICs
Labor	MLP & Local Offices
Land	Land of Bureaus
Financial Guarantees	BOC, CITIC, TICs
Prices	SACP
Profit Repatriation	SAEC
Patents & Trademarks	CCPIT, PC
Taxation	MOF
Problems	LGFI, SEC, MOFERT

responsibilities within the government agencies with regard to foreign investment. Therefore, if a change in investment policies is required, several central-level government agencies must agree and approve such a change. Often, as each organization has its own interests, conflicts will emerge and will take a long time to resolve. It is for this reason that changes in China take place at a very slow pace. When a decision to change Chinese policy is made, a problem of policy coordination and implementation may develop. Prior to the establishment of the State Council Leading Group on Foreign Investment, this was a major obstacle for foreign firms. With the enactment of this group, issues concerning policy coordination and implementation have been minimized.

Local-level organizations can also complicate policy changes as they have their own interests and priorities in attracting foreign investment. Often, they can misinterpret a decision reached by central-level organizations if the decision is not in their best interest. To some extent, local organizations may even refuse to implement the policies and decisions made by the central government. For this reason, foreign investors are often understandably confused about some of the rules and regulations governing investment activities.

If foreign investors have problems in understanding the rules and reg-

Figure 6.2
The Structure of the MOFERT

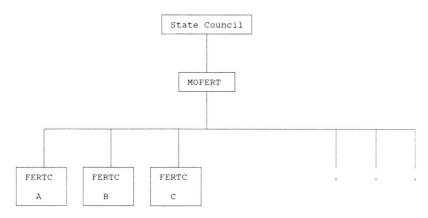

ulations governing their operations, they can contact (indirectly or directly) the LGFI for assistance. Since the LGFI consists of ministers from all the central-level organizations involved in foreign investment in China, it is easier for this group than individual ministries to reach conclusions and coordinate policy issues.

ORGANIZATIONS FOR APPROVING FOREIGN INVESTMENT

Foreign investment projects are approved either by the MOFERT directly or by the MOFERT's local-level equivalents, depending on the size and the location of the project as shown in Figure 6.1. If the size of the investment is within the authority of the local government (either provincial or municipal), the project can be approved by the local MOFERT organizations without further permission from the MOFÉRT. These local organizations are commonly referred to as Foreign Economic Relations and Trade Commissions or FERTCs (Figure 6.2).

Although the local FERTCs report directly to the MOFERT in Beijing regarding investment policies, incentives, rules, and regulations, they are subordinate to the provincial and municipal governments of which they are a part. Therefore, anything concerning foreign investment must be incorporated into local economic priorities and policies. Local conditions also must be taken into consideration when implementing foreign investment policies set by the central government (Figure 6.3) in order to facilitate approval.

There are two procedures for gaining approval of foreign investment projects (again depending on the size and location of the project). If the size of the project is within the authority limits of the local government,

Figure 6.3
The Status and Responsibilities of Local FERTCs

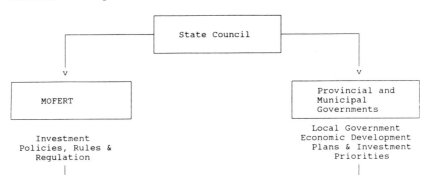

the local FERTC has the power to grant final approval. However, if the value of the investment is beyond the authority of the local government, the MOFERT in Beijing must approve the investment proposal. These two procedures are discussed in greater detail below.

The approval of a foreign investment project by a local FERTC is shown in Figure 6.4. When foreign and Chinese partners begin their discussions concerning a possible joint venture in China, it is advisable to have either one partner or both partners brief the local FERTC about the project so that the FERTC will have a record of the upcoming project. This is not legally required, but it is recommended since it may facilitate the FERTC's work in later stages.

After this stage is completed, both investment partners will begin to explore specific details of the project. Through ongoing negotiations, the parties eventually will agree on an initial investment proposal (also called an initial feasibility study) concerning the project. At this point, the project proposal will have to be examined and approved by the local FERTC. If the proposal is approved, both partners can start working on the feasibility study and the articles of the joint venture contract for the project. At a later point, the partners must submit the feasibility study and the required articles to the FERTC for examination and approval. If the FERTC finds the feasibility study and articles of the joint venture contract acceptable, it will issue a certificate of approval to the investors. At this stage, the joint venture is officially approved by the Chinese government.

If for some reason the FERTC is not satisfied with the project proposal, the feasibility study, or the articles of the contract, they must be revised and resubmitted by the joint venture partners until final approval is given.

It should be understood that this procedure has been simplified signif-

Figure 6.4
Investment Approval Procedures I (Within the Authority of a Local FERTC)

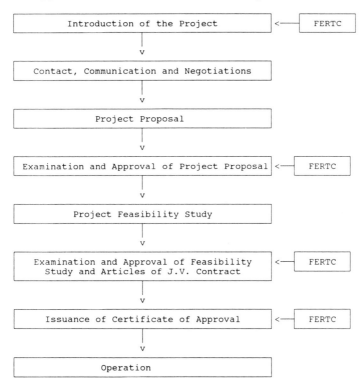

icantly for this discussion. In reality, each local FERTC must consult with the other local governmental departments during each stage of development to ensure that there are no objections to the project that could become stumbling blocks for gaining final project approval. Also, they need to be satisfied that there will be sufficient supplies and infrastructure support for the project once it is approved and operations commence. Finally, the local FERTC must make sure that the project falls in line with the local economic development plan and that it coincides with the priorities set by the Chinese government for foreign investments.

For a project whose size is beyond the approval authority of the local FERTC, the MOFERT makes the final decision about whether the project is accepted or rejected (Figure 6.5). In this case, the investing partners should keep both MOFERT and the local FERTC advised of the progress of project negotiations. In doing so, the joint venture partners can facilitate these agencies' understanding of the project. The reason why investing partners should do this is that although MOFERT gives the final approval for the project, the local FERTC is responsible for all operations of the

Figure 6.5
Investment Approval Procedures II (Above the Authority of a Local FERTC)

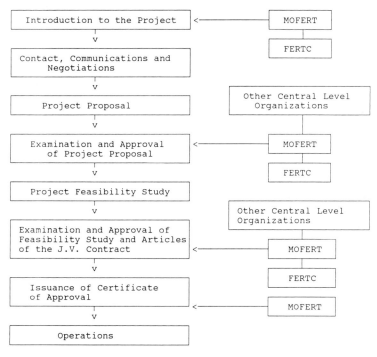

project once it is approved. Therefore, it is important for the local FERTC to be informed about the project so that it understands the nature and characteristics of the project and is thus willing and able to facilitate the implementation of the project in the operational phase.

The procedures for approving a project whose size is beyond the approval authority of the local FERTC are similar to the approval procedures for a smaller project. The investors should keep the MOFERT informed about the project and should seek approval whenever required. The MOFERT needs to coordinate with the SPC, MOF, and other governmental agencies concerning the infrastructure, financial and human resources, and other requirements of the project. The MOFERT will approve the project if it meets no objections from the other governmental organizations.

After commencing operations, the investors will need to deal with the local FERTC whenever they need assistance. Only when major problems that cannot be resolved at the local government level occur, should personnel in the MOFERT be approached for help.

FINANCIAL INSTITUTIONS

In addition to the organizations involved in instituting foreign investment policies and approving investment projects, Chinese financial institutions have an important role in assisting joint ventures. Specifically, they may interact in four major capacities:

• Acting as investment partners to investment projects;
• Acting as financial guarantors for investment projects;
• Directly lending to investment projects; and
• Facilitating financial transactions (such as currency swaps) for investment projects.

These financial institutions are all under the supervision of the State Council, with the exception of the SAEC, which is under the supervision of the People's Bank of China (China's central bank). Each financial institution has various departments that specialize in different facets of business operations. Some are involved in domestic banking, while others are responsible for international banking relationships and activities, including assistance to foreign investment projects. These financial institutions have corresponding equivalent organizations at the local level. Local branches are divided into different divisions, each of which is responsible for carrying out functions similar to those of the corresponding departments of their headquarters in Beijing, as is shown in Figure 6.6.

The first major function a financial institution undertakes in promoting foreign investment is that of a direct investor. This is particularly true of the Bank of China, which is not only actively involved in investment in the financial sector but also in private sector business operations with foreign joint venture partners. The Agricultural Bank of China (ABC) and the China Investment Bank (CIB) also are directly involved in investments with foreign investors.

A joint venture may enjoy at least two advantages in having a financial institution as an investing partner. First, financial institutions, such as the BOC, can offer financial resources in order to assist the investment project. In fact, many large manufacturing joint venture projects in China often include a Chinese financial institution as a partner specifically for this purpose. Second, financial institutions have the analytical capability to determine whether an investment project will be viable in the Chinese market. As a result, joint ventures between foreign investors and Chinese financial institutions tend to be more successful than those that do not involve investments from financial institutions.

Figure 6.6
Financial Institutions

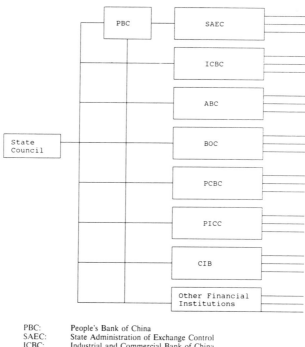

PBC:	People's Bank of China
SAEC:	State Administration of Exchange Control
ICBC:	Industrial and Commercial Bank of China
ABC:	Agricultural Bank of China
BOC:	Bank of China
PCBC:	People's Construction Bank of China
PICC:	People's Insurance Company of China
CIB:	China Investment Bank

Financial institutions also act as investing partners in foreign investment projects in many other ways. They can be the major partner in a two-party joint venture or can be the minority partner. If the joint venture is a multi-party one, the financial institution often acts as a minority partner.

The second role that financial institutions perform in assisting foreign investment in China is to act as financial guarantors for foreign investment projects. In certain cases, for example, when projects either require external borrowing before operations start, or require foreign currency financing to meet working capital requirements, guarantees may be essential. The BOC often acts as a major financial guarantor for most large investment projects. Due to the fact that this financial institution has a good credit standing internationally, its guarantee against default can ensure that investment projects will obtain external funds more easily or at lower costs.

In addition to the BOC, there are about 100 other financial institutions in China that may provide financial guarantees for foreign joint ventures.

Most of these financial institutions, which also guarantee against default, are smaller in size, weaker in financial ability, and, therefore, less well known in the international financial markets than the BOC. Their major function is to assist joint ventures in their respective provinces or municipalities to raise external financing in relatively small amounts, especially from the more familiar capital markets, such as Hong Kong and Tokyo.

FINANCIAL GUARANTEE PROCEDURES

In order to apply for a financial guarantee, foreign investors and their partners must take the following steps: In the project negotiation stage, when investing partners determine there will be a need to obtain foreign exchange by borrowing from foreign banks, a financial institution, located in the same province or municipality as the potential project, may be approached for assistance. Generally, the financial institution will examine carefully all aspects of the project, including the technical and financial viability of the project, to determine whether it will act as a guarantor and, if so, under what terms and conditions.

If the project is believed to be sound, the financial institution will issue an initial letter of agreement (usually called a letter of intent). In this letter, the institution will state that it agrees to be the financial guarantor of the project, under the condition that the final decision will be subject to the project feasibility study. This guarantee is often essential in gaining initial approval of the feasibility study from the appropriate authorities since it is recognized that the project has already been studied carefully by a bank.

After the project feasibility study has been approved by the local FERTC, the project partners are required to present a copy to the financial institution for its review and record. At this stage an official letter of guarantee will be issued. A typical letter of guarantee includes the name of the guarantor, the name of the project (or the foreign partner), the amount of funding guaranteed, and the valid date of the letter of guarantee.

With such a financial guarantee from a Chinese financial institution, the project partners can either raise external funding for the project through their own efforts or through the same financial institution. Normally, the latter approach is taken since it is both easier for the project partners and relatively cheaper for the project, given the financial status of the guarantor as well as the latter's presence in the international financial markets.

There are several factors that project partners should keep in mind when they seek guarantees from Chinese financial institutions. First, the guarantee from a financial institution will be granted depending on the debt-to-equity ratio of the project. The debt-to-equity ratio requirement will vary, according to the size and nature of the investment project. The

Table 6.2
Debt-to-Equity Ratio Required by Foreign Investment

TOTAL INVESTMENT	APPLICABLE EQUITY/ TOTAL INVESTMENT RATIO
US $3 million or less	7:10
Between US $3-10 million	5:10
Between US $10-30 million	2:5
About US $30 million or more	1:3

larger the project, the larger the debt-to-equity ratio that is permitted by the Chinese government (Table 6.2).

In general, financial guarantees are not provided for the equity portion of an investment. For the debt portion, financial institutions rarely provide a full guarantee for the entire debt financing required. The remaining portion of the debt, which is not guaranteed, is the sole responsibility of the investing partners. For example, if the size of an investment project is US $50 million, the total registered equity capital contributed by the investing partners should not be less than US $16.5 million—leaving a debt portion of US $33.5 million. In most cases, the financial guarantee may only cover between 50 and 70 percent of the US $33.5 million debt. If the project receives a 70 percent guarantee, the investing partners must secure the additional 30 percent of the debt financing from other sources, including their own resources.

A second factor that investors must keep in mind when seeking financial guarantees is the need for collateral as backing for the external borrowings. If joint venture partners fail to repay a loan due to cash flow problems associated with the project, the financial guarantor will assume responsibility for repaying the loan. In return for their guarantee, financial institutions desire collateral that can be used to offset any losses incurred if the joint venture defaults on the loan.

Quite often, finding suitable assets for use as collateral can be difficult for the investing project partners. If the project is situated on land, the land may be used as collateral; such other tangible assets as machinery and buildings may also be used. In certain cases, financial institutions may agree to take a certain share of the project as collateral, although this practice is not customary.

Foreign investors must also be aware of the fee that the guarantor receives as compensation for the guarantee. The size of the fee depends on the amount of potential borrowing and the nature of the project. Normally, it is 0.5 percent of the amount guaranteed and is usually required to be paid in advance of the loan or, at the latest, on receipt of the funds.

Obtaining a financial guarantee has been difficult for many investment

Figure 6.7
Financial Guarantee Application Procedures

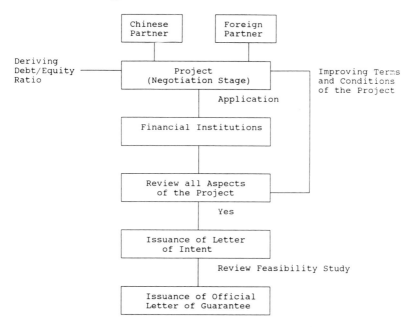

projects, particularly small ones, because of these three factors. Due to these difficulties, many investment projects have invited financial institutions as partners so that the financing needs for the project could be covered. As a result, the project partners would not need to worry about financing problems in the project negotiation and operational stages.

The procedures to be followed in obtaining a financial guarantee in China are illustrated in Figure 6.7. Careful work at each stage of approval is essential to expedite the approval process.

Along with the growth of foreign investment activities in China, the demand for financial guarantees has increased rapidly. This expansion has minimized the financial ability of many financial institutions in providing guarantees. As a result, project partners have experienced increasing difficulty in obtaining guarantees to meet financing requirements. In addition to the normal requirements for applying for guarantees, financial institutions today are paying more attention to the potential cash flows of a project, particularly the project's export potential.

LENDING ISSUES AND TYPES OF LOANS

Due to the negative impact of the austerity program on both foreign joint ventures and Chinese firms in the 1988–90 period, many companies experienced repayment difficulties. As a consequence, the Chinese government has been reluctant to honor loan guarantees issued to these troubled enterprises. The foreign banks that made the loans have sought repayment from the guarantor's parent organizations at both the provincial and central government levels. However, no one appears willing to accept responsibility and make good on the bad debts.

The arguments made by officials in the central government vary. Some officials maintain that the guarantees are invalid if the guarantee did not have central government approval; of course, many guarantees were made without central government approval because they were within the limits established for approval at the municipal or provincial levels. Other officials, citing the revisions of the foreign investment law of 1987, state that enterprises are responsible for their own profits and losses.

At the end of 1989, China's total foreign debt totaled US $41.3 billion, most of which was covered by government guarantees. Of this figure, about US $1.3 billion was guaranteed by various financial institutions on loans to foreign joint ventures. To complicate the matter further, many guarantees were issued by various financial institutions in the early 1980s to encourage foreign investment at a time when registration of loan guarantees with the central government was not required. This came at a time when the country's foreign exchange reserves had dropped dramatically, particularly in 1989, increasing the government's inability to service its foreign debt.

In most cases, loan guarantees specified the applicability of Hong Kong law to assure both the foreign investor and the lending bank that the commitments would be honored. In reality, when foreign banks have sought repayment from the Chinese guarantors through Hong Kong courts, they have found to their dismay that these decisions are not enforceable in China.

Consequently, the role played by foreign guarantees in providing financial guarantees has declined. Furthermore, since the latter part of 1989, the Chinese government has restricted severely the categories for which a guarantee can be given. For projects that do not produce for the export market, receiving a guarantee from a well-known financial institution such as the BOC seems to be virtually impossible. Increasingly, foreign investors are finding their own ways to fund their projects before discussing these projects with potential Chinese partners.

Another important role that Chinese financial institutions play in promoting foreign investment is to lend directly to foreign joint ventures. Basically, there are four types of loans provided by these financial institutions: fixed-asset loans, including short and medium term loans, buyer's credit, syndicated loans, and project loans; working capital financing; mortgage loans; and reserve loans. These loans can be denominated in both Chinese currency as well as foreign currencies. The fixed-asset loans

Figure 6.8
Process of Obtaining Financing from Chinese Financial Institutions

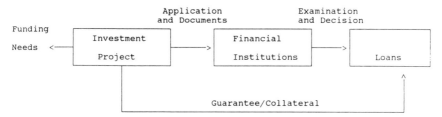

generally do not exceed seven years. The time period for extending working capital loans is a maximum of twelve months. The time limits for specific loans can be extended but in all cases maturities cannot exceed the life of the project minus one year.

INTEREST RATES AND LOAN PROCEDURES

Methods for charging interest rates on Chinese and foreign currency loans differ substantially. For the Chinese currency loans, interest rates tend to be the same as for those charged on loans to Chinese domestic state-owned enterprises. For the foreign currency loans, however, interest rates fluctuate according to the international market rate, specifically the London Interbank Offered Rate (LIBOR). In these cases, the final interest rate charged at the current LIBOR plus a spread will depend on the nature of the project and the significance of the joint venture to meeting China's needs.

The procedure for applying for financing through Chinese financial institutions is not complicated, as is shown in Figure 6.8. The joint venture submits an application, together with other required supporting documents indicating the nature, operations, and financial performance of the project, to a financial institution. The financial institution examines this information carefully. A decision is then made as to whether the application should be approved and, if so, under what conditions. If the financial performance of the project is sound, a loan may be provided without any guarantees for repayment. However, if the project is not very attractive, the financial institution may deny the request or may require certain types of securities or guarantees from the joint venture before the funds are released.

The final role financial institutions may play with respect to foreign joint venture projects is aiding the project partners to carry out their currency swap transactions. As will be discussed later, the most difficult problem for a majority of the foreign joint ventures in China is the shortage of foreign currency earnings. Currency swaps provide joint ventures, which

Figure 6.9
Major Trust and Investment Corporations

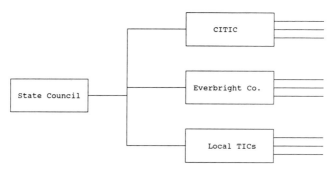

CITIC: China International Trust and Investment Corporation

TICs: Trust and Investment Corporations

have surplus Chinese currency earnings but lack foreign currency financing, with a means of obtaining their needed foreign currency financing from other joint ventures. One joint venture will swap its excess Chinese currency earnings for another joint venture's foreign exchange earnings. In most cases, the second joint venture project will have excess foreign exchange earnings but may need Chinese currency for financing its day-to-day operations. Hence, both joint ventures benefit from currency swaps. Generally, these currency swaps are facilitated by the financial institutions located in each province and municipality.

TRUST AND INVESTMENT CORPORATIONS

China's banking system is a universal one under which all financial institutions can freely engage in both commercial and investment banking businesses. However, there are some differences between commercial banks and the trust and investment corporations (TICs) in China (Figure 6.9). Similar to Japanese banks, Chinese financial institutions may take an equity position in enterprises, including those to which they have extended loans.

Commercial banks in China are engaged primarily in the deposit-taking and loan-providing businesses. Many of the larger commercial banks also have trust and investment departments to carry out investment banking related activities. The major functions of TICs are to help organize foreign joint ventures, to act as a major equity investment partner in joint venture projects, and to provide investment consulting services to project partners. In general, commercial banks specialize in commercial banking activities, while TICs tend to focus primarily on investment banking services.

There are several large TICs active in both commercial and investment banking business. The most well-known TIC is the China International Trust and Investment Corporation (CITIC), which was established in 1979 under the direct leadership of the State Council. Its main functions are to:

- Organize equity and contractual joint ventures, compensation trade, and other forms of business with foreign companies;
- Invest both in China and abroad;
- Develop technical cooperation with foreign companies;
- Operate foreign exchange banking and international financing activities;
- Deal with international and domestic leasing;
- Engage in the real estate business;
- Provide insurance for foreign investment in China; and,
- Provide consulting services to both international and domestic clients.

Recently, the CITIC established a separate bank specializing in commercial banking activities providing services similar to those of the Bank of China. Thus, it has became an important source of financing for joint venture operations.

SUMMARY

China, like most countries, has a variety of financial institutions that play a significant role in foreign investment activities and operations. While understanding the organizational structure and each organization's function may be difficult, this understanding is essential for foreign investors who desire to operate businesses successfully in China. It is particularly true for those foreign investment projects that must deal with various Chinese governmental agencies on an almost daily basis.

While this chapter may serve as a basis for a general understanding of China's governmental organizations that are involved in foreign investment, a more thorough understanding can only be achieved through the experience gained by the foreign investor's operations in that marketplace. Furthermore, the role of financial institutions in China is changing as the leadership gains experience in moving toward a more market oriented economy. However, by understanding how these organizations work, foreign investors can avoid unnecessary delays and costs in their Chinese operations from the initial stages of project approval through the later stages of operation and expansion.

7

Investment Negotiation and Approval Procedures

China's complex bureaucracy can pose formidable problems for foreign companies attempting to make successful investments even within the SEZs and open cities. First, foreign investors face problems including how to make initial contacts with the Chinese and how and where to find potential joint venture partners. Second, they must start their investment with a Chinese partner unless they plan to initiate a wholly foreign-owned enterprise.

Often it may take months or even years to produce an investment proposal and feasibility study for a project. An investor needs to obtain all necessary approvals for a project from the Chinese authorities, so that the investor can officially start operations as soon as the other preparatory work is completed. The channels and procedures to follow in setting up a foreign joint venture are shown in Figure 7.1. For wholly foreign-owned ventures, see Figure 7.2.

The time period required for this approval process depends on the size and complexity of the investment project, the skill and efficiency of the Chinese partner, and the interest shown by the Chinese authorities responsible for foreign investment. Equally significant are the reputation, preparation, willingness, and degree of commitment by the foreign investor. In general, the smaller the size and complexity of the project, as well as the degree to which it meets one of China's major development goals, the shorter this process tends to be. Also, this process may be expedited with an efficient and well-recognized Chinese partner and if the foreign investor has a strong international reputation that is easily recognized by the Chinese officials.

In the past few years, foreign investors have often complained about

Figure 7.1
Channels and Procedures of Examination and Approval to the Establishment of Joint Ventures Using Chinese and Foreign Investment

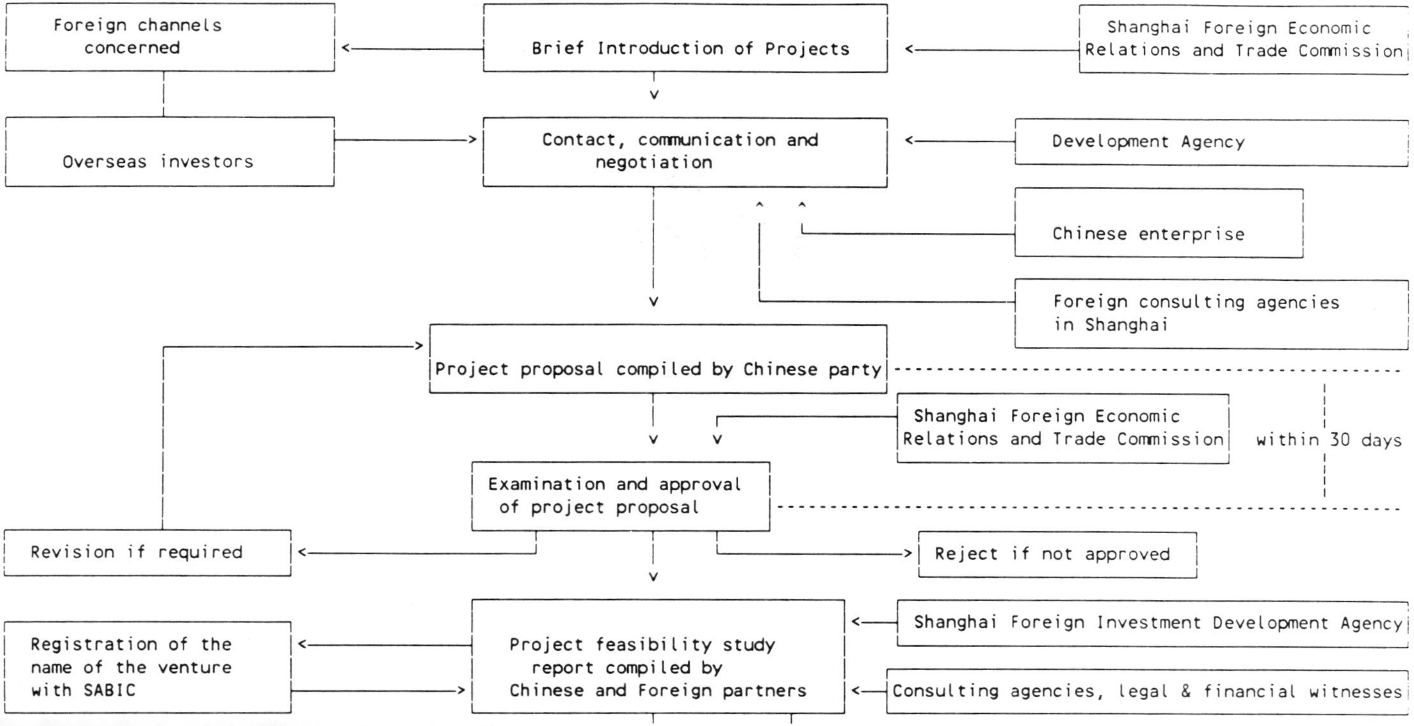

Foreign channels concerned

Overseas investors

Shanghai Foreign Economic Relations and Trade Commission

Development Agency

Chinese enterprise

Foreign consulting agencies in Shanghai

Brief Introduction of Projects

Contact, communication and negotiation

Project proposal compiled by Chinese party

Shanghai Foreign Economic Relations and Trade Commission   within 30 days

Examination and approval of project proposal

Reject if not approved

Revision if required

Project feasibility study report compiled by Chinese and Foreign partners

Shanghai Foreign Investment Development Agency

Consulting agencies, legal & financial witnesses

Registration of the name of the venture with SABIC

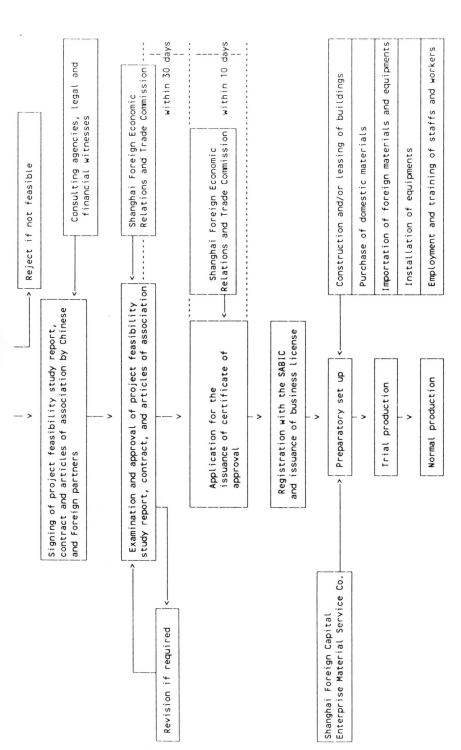

Reject if not feasible

Consulting agencies, legal and financial witnesses

Shanghai Foreign Economic Relations and Trade Commission --- within 30 days

Shanghai Foreign Economic Relations and Trade Commission --- within 10 days

Construction and/or leasing of buildings

Purchase of domestic materials

Importation of foreign materials and equipments

Installation of equipments

Employment and training of staffs and workers

Signing of project feasibility study report, contract and articles of association by Chinese and Foreign partners

Examination and approval of project feasibility study report, contract, and articles of association

Application for the issuance of certificate of approval

Registration with the SABIC and issuance of business license

Preparatory set up

Trial production

Normal production

Revision if required

Shanghai Foreign Capital Enterprise Material Service Co.

SABIC = Shanghai Administrative Bureau for Industry and Commerce

123

Figure 7.2
Channels and Procedures of Examination and Approval to Establish Wholly Foreign-Owned Enterprises

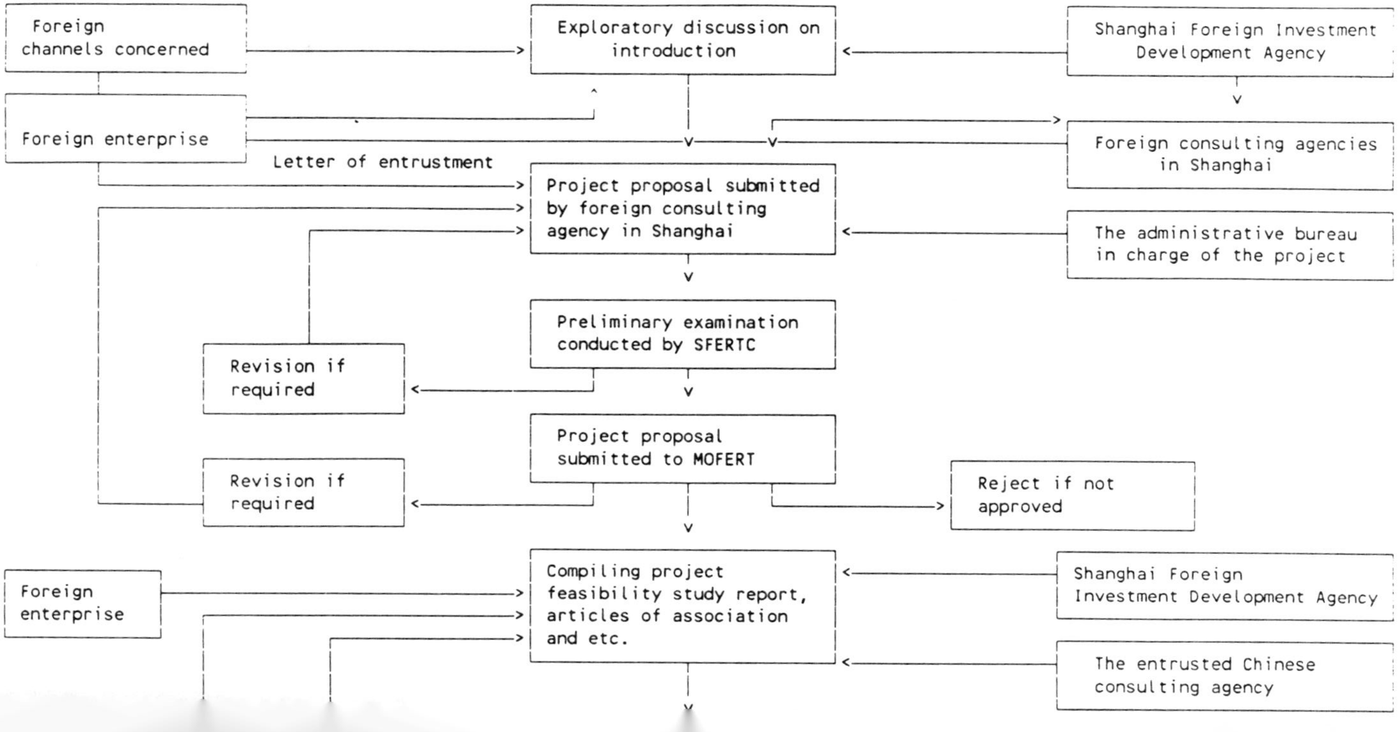

124

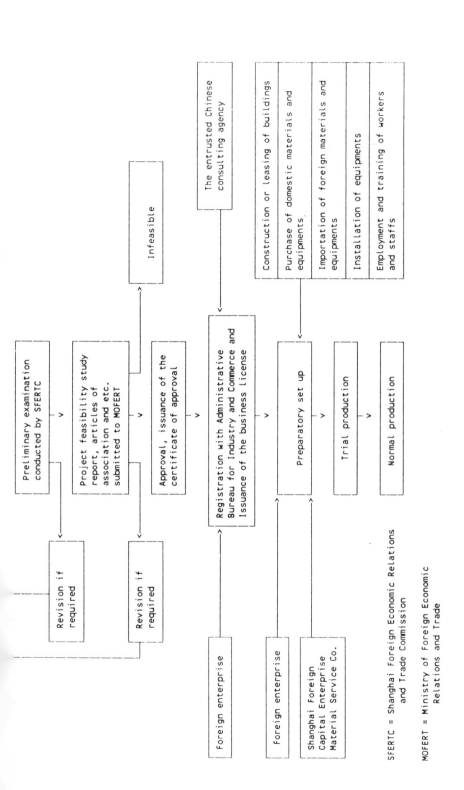

Preliminary examination conducted by SFERTC

Revision if required

Project feasibility study report, articles of association and etc. submitted to MOFERT

Revision if required

Infeasible

Approval, issuance of the certificate of approval

The entrusted Chinese consulting agency

Foreign enterprise

Registration with Administrative Bureau for Industry and Commerce and Issuance of the business license

Construction or leasing of buildings

Purchase of domestic materials and equipments.

Importation of foreign materials and equipments

Installation of equipments

Employment and training of workers and staffs

Foreign enterprise

Preparatory set up

Shanghai Foreign Capital Enterprise Material Service Co.

Trial production

Normal production

SFERTC = Shanghai Foreign Economic Relations and Trade Commission

MOFERT = Ministry of Foreign Economic Relations and Trade

125

the length of investment negotiations and the confusion involved in this process. These complaints led to the issuance of new regulations by the Chinese government in 1987, which specified the time requirements for each type of investment approval. The local Chinese government authorities have taken similar measures to simplify the approval procedures and have set deadlines for approvals in order to encourage foreign investment in their respective areas. In practice, however, these time commitments are more often a goal than a reality.

MAKING INITIAL CONTACTS

There are many ways foreign investors can learn about the Chinese market before making an initial business contact either through their own visits to the country, introductions by their friends and business associates, or through the assistance of their governments, including the various commercial attachés based in China. Prospective investors also may become acquainted with investment opportunities in China through Chinese embassies as well as though various Chinese trade missions stationed in their respective countries. Often there are semiofficial trade and investment organizations in investors' home countries to assist them in understanding how to approach the Chinese market. In the United States, for example, the National Council on U.S.-China Business provides extremely effective service to U.S. firms in dealing with Chinese counterparts in the areas of trade and investment. All major accounting and law firms that have representative offices in China can also provide sound advice and service to prospective investors.

With the insights gained through these sources, foreign investors may either directly contact a source in China for investment opportunities or indirectly seek assistance through one of the Chinese financial institutions or trust and investment corporations. The former channel is called the direct approach and the latter is referred to as the indirect approach, which is used more often than the direct one. Another indirect approach is to contact an expert on China who has been successful in guiding a foreign firm through the investment process and who is well known and respected in China.

The use of the direct approach is simple: the foreign investor identifies a potential Chinese company, contacts it directly, and determines whether or not the Chinese company wants to become an investment partner in a potential joint venture. If the response is positive, both sides begin more detailed discussions about the project. If the response is negative, the foreign investor may contact another Chinese company and the process continues until a receptive partner is identified.

The mechanism for the indirect approach, however, is more complicated. First, the foreign investor must select a person or business entity as its "agent" in China. In most cases, this business entity is a consulting firm or an affiliate of a major financial institution. This agent acts on behalf of the foreign investor in selecting potential Chinese partners, conducting business negotiations, and concluding joint venture agreements. Selecting a good agent is a rather difficult task. The agent must be sufficiently influential and well respected by the Chinese authorities so that he can work effectively through the appropriate channels. The agent also must be experienced so that the business negotiations and required follow up may be performed quickly. The agent, of course, will charge a consulting fee for the services provided to the foreign investor.

Normally, there are several criteria for choosing an agent, which would include the agent's:

- knowledge about investment procedures in China
- reputation with foreign investors
- relations with the Chinese government
- record of consulting performance in China
- financial strength/credit rating
- overall experience
- knowledge of English, Chinese, or other relevant language
- lines of business specialization
- size of firm and support staff skills
- willingness to cooperate with foreign investors, if a Chinese organization

Information on a prospective agent in China may be obtained from various sources: government agencies in China; banks that have business relations with China; trade associations; trade publications, such as the *China Business Review* and *Intertrade*; trade fairs; advertising agencies; directories; chambers of commerce; unsolicited inquiries; contacts made on personal visits; and personal referrals. When using these sources to identify agents, the foreign investor should look for prospects that appear to fulfill the above criteria.

After the investor has developed a prospective list of potential agents, it is essential to obtain more information for a second screening. The most direct way to do this is by writing a letter to each prospective agent, asking about the agent's interest in acting on the investor's behalf and for information relating to the items in the agent criteria developed in the proceeding step. Most important is to obtain information on the prospective agent's experience and a list of valid references.

There are many horror stories about selecting the wrong agent that have been recounted by foreign investors in China. As in any other business, there are disreputable individuals looking for gullible clients who are willing to rely solely on the agent's judgment. In one case, a novice American investor selected a Hong Kong–based agent who did, indeed, have contacts in China. However, he told his client that he needed advances for the entertainment of Chinese officials as well as for appropriate gifts to pave the way for the project. An initial advance of US $50,000 was spent very quickly and few, if any, receipts were provided. Through this agent, the foreign investor did meet many Chinese, including officials from several industries in various locations in China. On these occasions, however, it was the foreign investor who picked up the tab for the entertainment and other expenses. After spending almost US $200,000, and still not having identified a strong joint venture partner for what was a very desirable project for China, the investor dismissed the agent. He then turned to the consultative division of a branch of the China International Trust and Investment Company and quickly found a viable partner. In a matter of months, an agreement had been reached and the project approved. However, in the interim the former agent sought legal recourse for what he termed a breach of contract. When the case came to court in Hong Kong, bank records showed that he had deposited the advanced funds in his account and could not show appropriate expenditures. It was also proven that funds had been used for private deals, and many of the Chinese the investor had met were relatives of the agent and had no business connections at all. Although the foreign investor won the case, a considerable amount of time expended and money spent could have been saved by doing the appropriate research in advance of selecting an agent.

An investor should make the choice of an agent only after a round of personal interviews with the most promising prospects. Apart from providing answers to specific questions and laying the ground for contract negotiations, personal interviews are perhaps the best way for the investor to judge the ability of the agent, combined with a reference check of former reputable clients.

Too many firms have made the mistake of selecting a very promising but inappropriate agent to work on their behalf. In some cases, the agent may be a Chinese based in Hong Kong, the United States, or elsewhere, who has little familiarity with the environment in China apart from being Chinese. Furthermore, some may purport to have "great contacts" when in reality they do not. Others may have spent time in China and have established good relationships in academic institutions but have little familiarity with how to deal with Chinese enterprises or the government. Worst yet is to select an agent who has a negative reputation among various Chinese authorities because of previous dealings that were either illegal or not in conformity with Chinese procedures. Finally, the agent should either possess the appropriate Chinese dialect or have personnel available to act as interpreters because of the language differences that exist in the various provinces.

Once an agent is selected, it is essential that a legally binding contract be developed to ensure performance of the agent on behalf of the foreign investor. The agent contract, sometimes also called the letter of intent, should be a written contract and include the following items:

1. General Provisions
    Identification of parties to the contract (foreign investor and agent)
    Duration of the contract
    Conditions of cancellation
    Arbitration of disputes
2. Rights and Obligations of Foreign Investors
    Conditions of termination
    Supply of information to the agent
    Payment of a consulting fee
3. Rights and Obligations of Agent
    Safeguarding the investor's interest
    Payment arrangements
    Information to be supplied to the investor
    Provision of services
    Confidentiality clause

All major banks, as well as trust and investment corporations in China and numerous specialized consulting companies, may be contacted for assistance in drawing up the agent contract. Preferably, foreign investors should utilize an organization in the specific location where the potential investment project is to be located to further insure the agent's ability to work on the foreign firm's behalf.

SELECTING A CHINESE PARTNER

For a foreign investor, selecting a proper Chinese investment partner is more difficult than selecting a consulting agent. If foreign investors try to identify the partner through their own efforts without the assistance of an agent, the work will be more complicated unless introductions have been made by a reliable source.

The steps for selecting a local partner are as follows. First, the foreign investor needs to become acquainted with the Chinese industries and the major companies in similar lines of business unless the investor dealt with China previously. Second, the foreign investor must focus on a few companies that have the potential to be an investment partner. The investor must try to obtain information about these companies from different sources, as well as from the agent, if one is used. Third, the foreign investor must visit China and meet personally with these prospective partners before making a final choice. These steps take time and effort.

In addition, information regarding Chinese industries and companies may not be readily available to foreign investors. As such, it is almost impossible for an investor who possesses little knowledge about the country to contact the local Chinese companies directly for a partnership agreement. One of the pitfalls in dealing with China is that many local companies seek foreign investment partners because of their lack of technology, managerial expertise, and capital. When these Chinese companies learn that someone is looking for a joint venture partner, they quickly seek to obtain a joint venture agreement regardless of whether they have the expertise or not because they see the opportunity to become involved in a profitable enterprise. Consequently, a more realistic approach is to utilize an experienced consulting agent to select the Chinese company. Although the foreign investor must pay for this service, it has proven to be more efficient and cheaper when compared to the direct contact approach.

The selection of a Chinese partner is one of the most important decisions of the foreign investment process. A good partner can assist the potential joint venture in many ways, while a poor choice of a partner may hinder the development of an investment project. Unfortunately, many foreign investors neglect this extremely important step. Many simply accept the joint venture partners recommended by their agent, or some other intermediary, without personal meetings and interviews or without investigating other potential joint venture partners. Others only pay attention to the size and/or connections of the potential partner, without carefully considering other qualities or doing appropriate reference checks.

Foreign investors always should remember that, even though the Chinese consulting agent will help make a selection, the investors themselves should make the final decision. To facilitate the agent's work, the investor should provide as much information as possible regarding the potential investment project as well as the specific requirements for an investment partner. This information should include:

1. Information about the Foreign Investor
   Headquarters location
   Line of business
   Scope of current operations
   International business activities
   Basic objectives in the Chinese market
2. Information about the Potential Project
   Scope of production
   Products

   Market to be serviced
   Financing requirements
   Technology transfers
3. Requirements for the Chinese Partner
   Line of business
   Size and scope of current business operations
   Location
   Operational experience
   Technical expertise
   Financial performance
   Marketing experience
   International activities

After this information is obtained, the Chinese agent will provide the
foreign investor with a list of potential partners. The foreign investor may
then decide to make further contacts with some of the firms on the list.
During this stage, the foreign investor usually sends representatives to
have personal meetings and discussions with the potential partners, as
well as with the appropriate governmental investment authorities. The
following factors should be considered during this process:

1. *Authority of the partner.* Not all Chinese companies are allowed to engage in
   joint venture activities with foreign companies. Therefore, in choosing a
   Chinese partner, it is essential to confirm the degree of the partner's authority.
   The foreign investor should expect full cooperation from the agent in investigating the limits of the Chinese partner's authority.
2. *Location of the partner.* Location also plays a critical role in choosing an
   appropriate partner. On the one hand, some provinces may provide better
   investment incentives and more liberalized policies and, therefore, a better
   environment for foreign investment projects. On the other hand, other provinces and municipalities may have better infrastructure facilities such as
   transportation, communication, electricity, and other important facilities.
   Therefore, the foreign investor must weigh the value of these conditions in
   each location.
3. *Size of the partner.* In general, the larger the partner, the more influential and
   experienced the partner should be. This will help the potential joint venture
   resolve operational problems more easily should they arise. An influential
   partner is able to approach Chinese authorities for assistance if needed. However, the reverse may be true and the larger the partner, the less efficient the
   firm may be. This can cause potential problems for the venture. Foreign investors, therefore, should compare the size of the partner with the size of their
   own company. If the Chinese partner is much larger than the foreign investor,
   the Chinese partner may look down upon or take advantage of the foreign
   investor.

4. *Production and managerial ability of the partner.* The partner should be efficient in production and management and understand the ways a venture is to be managed. Companies differ greatly in this respect in China. Some are managed rather efficiently while others are poorly managed. There are several sources through which a foreign investor can learn whether the partner is efficient or not: the partner's financial statements; personal visits to get first-hand impressions; the help of an agent, and such other sources as trade associations or knowledgeable Chinese officials at the local level.

5. *Experience in dealing with foreign business.* It is also important that the Chinese partner has previous experience in dealing with foreign businessmen. This will make it easier for both partners to cooperate in forming a joint venture and operating it successfully.

In short, choosing a partner is just like choosing a spouse. In the process, both partners should get to know each other and evaluate their common interests and objectives. The extent of trust and understanding between the two partners can determine the degree of success of the venture. Experience has shown that successful joint ventures have a loyal, efficient, and experienced Chinese partner who is willing and able to deal with the complex bureaucracy, obtain favorable treatment on labor, capital, raw materials, taxation, the market, and other terms for the joint venture, and help resolve in an effective manner any operational problems that may arise.

Vast differences in political, economic, and sociocultural traditions between China and Western countries make identifying a satisfactory local Chinese joint venture partner difficult. However, a foreign investor should make every effort possible to find a good partner so that the venture cannot only avoid unnecessary difficulties and problems in the future but also can produce a successful and profitable "marriage." In fact, in all cases finding a good partner is more than half of the key to success. The time and effort expended in the selection process is never wasted.

JOINT VENTURE NEGOTIATIONS

Once the partner is identified, the foreign investor begins the official business negotiations process. These meetings can be arranged either in China or the investor's home country. However, as noted earlier, this process usually will involve multiple visits to both locations.

Joint venture negotiations can be divided into three stages. The initial stage involves discussions between the two partners, with or without the assistance of the agent, to outline the basic structure of the joint venture. Sometimes, discussions at this stage can be pursued through letters, telex, and facsimile messages, or through other indirect means.

At the end of this stage, a letter of intent usually is signed between the two (or more) partners indicating the willingness of both sides to continue joint venture discussions. This agreement is not a legally binding document and generally contains the following information: the names of the two (or more) partners, the name of the potential joint venture, where it will be located, production capacity, total investment, percentage of investment for each party, and the form of investment. All these terms are subject to change during future discussions. In general, the Chinese partner sends a copy of the letter of intent to the local FERTC (or the MOFERT in Beijing, depending upon the authority of the local government) for its records. If possible, both partners should visit the appropriate FERTC during the briefing in the initial negotiation stage.

Business negotiations at the second stage are more serious. At this stage, details of the potential joint venture agreement should be outlined. Foreign investors should travel to China frequently and the Chinese partner should be invited to visit the foreign investor's production facilities. For a large joint venture, a preliminary feasibility study is required at the end of this stage. In the preliminary feasibility study, rough estimates should be used to forecast the capital requirements of the projected investment, scope of production, requirements for and sources of raw materials, energy consumption, and expected rate of return on investment. The Chinese partner usually bears sole responsibility for the preparation of a preliminary feasibility study, although the foreign partner's assistance may be requested and required.

At the final stage of negotiations, both partners must work out a detailed feasibility study for the joint venture. This feasibility study, if approved by the Chinese government, will become the basis of the official joint venture contract or agreement. Therefore, foreign investors should make sure that every item contained in the study is clearly understood and agreed upon by both partners. Major problems could occur due to cultural misunderstanding of terms and/or terminology, as well as the foreign partner's taking for granted that problem areas or unresolved issues would be worked out at a later date.

During the entire negotiation process, the foreign investor may or may not need the assistance of an agent, depending on the complexity of the project and the fee charged by the agent. It is advisable for new investors in China, however, to seek such assistance. In doing so, they benefit from the experience of the agent and avoid unnecessary mistakes and delays due to their inexperience or lack of procedural/technical knowledge in the Chinese market.

FEASIBILITY STUDY

After the two investment parties have agreed on the major aspects of the project, they should prepare a formal feasibility study. This is required by Chinese law for all joint ventures and usually takes place after the project proposal has been approved but prior to the signing of the official joint venture agreement. This study is a major effort to be undertaken by both the Chinese and foreign investors, as it covers all aspects of the proposed agreement.

The importance of the feasibility study can never be overstated. A good feasibility study will minimize the potential for misunderstandings and problems between the two partners, while an ill-prepared study will almost surely create confusion, if not cause a total collapse of the joint venture project. Versions in both Chinese and the language of the foreign investor (usually English) are required, but it is the Chinese version that will become the official and legally binding document.

The feasibility study can be conducted by the partners themselves, if they have in-house counselors, or it can be performed by an outside consulting firm specializing in investments in China. The cost should be shared by both partners. If the study is conducted by an outside consulting firm, the partners should carefully examine and understand the assumptions, analyses, and calculations for the project, ensuring that they are realistic in terms of the political, economic, financial, technical, and sociocultural environments in China.

The contents of a feasibility study may differ, depending on the scope and nature of the joint venture. The feasibility study for a manufacturing joint venture usually is more complicated than for a service joint venture; the feasibility study for a large-size joint venture also tends to be more complicated than for a small one, as does one that involves three or more partners. However, some common elements that should be incorporated into all feasibility studies are as follows:

1. General Data

    Joint venture name, location, objective

    Description of partners (include agent in China and name of person with primary responsibility for the project)

    Business scope, legal format (limited liability company), and duration

    Joint venture administrative structure (include name and number of positions to be filled)

    Summary of total investment

    • Proportion, value, and form of each partner's contribution
    • Loan details, if applicable

2. Market Analysis

    Current and future market for product

    • Sales estimate (aggregate and by price category)
    • Projected foreign and domestic distribution
    • Local industry conditions and prospects

Past product imports and projected trends

Role of the industry in the national economy

Anticipated competition (local and foreign)

3. Location and Site

Land-use arrangement (include land-use fee and local department in charge if land not part of equity contribution)

Complete layout of joint venture plant/buildings and capacity

Infrastructure improvements required

4. Production/Operations Plan

Quality of product/service (include international technical standards if appropriate)

Estimated annual output/turnover (both before project reaches full capacity and each year thereafter)

Transport and local storage requirements

Product testing and quality control

Trial production procedures and equipment

Products, by-products, and waste (include estimated annual cost of waste disposal)

Environmental protection plan (include projected pollution problems and treatment)

Details on separate work locations, if applicable (input/output of each location, amount processed annually, value added at each facility, labor costs)

5. Material Inputs

Approximate input requirements for all materials

Present and potential sources of supply

Availability of utilities, especially power

Transport routes planned

Rough estimate of annual cost of local and foreign inputs

6. Project Engineering

Description of technology and equipment to be used

Cost estimate (include, if applicable, technology transfer fees, royalty rate, and terms of payment)

Layout of proposed equipment and costs

Layout of civil engineering works and costs

7. Organization and Overhead Costs

Planned organizational structure (production, sales administration, management)

Estimated overhead (factory/operations, administrative, financial)

8. Manpower

Estimated manpower requirements (local/foreign staff by major category of skills)

Work units where employees will come from and positions they will fill

Estimated wage scales, including overhead

Personnel training plan

9. Financial and Economic Evaluation

Estimated total investment cost (include working capital, fixed assets, and amortization)

Project financing

- Proposed capital structure
- Proportion and value of each partner's contribution
- Terms of proposed financing, if applicable

Production cost

- Initial establishment/installation cost
- Annual operation cost analyzed by work location, if applicable
- Cost of technology, training, material inputs, transport, utilities, and overhead

Levy of taxes, duties, and insurance (include expected rebates, reductions, and exemptions)

Financial evaluation based on above-cost estimates (factoring in inflation)

Projected annual profits (RMB and foreign currency)

Profit distribution plan

Cost analysis for products to be introduced later on, if applicable

Statement of plan for balancing foreign exchange income and expenditure (must be separately approved by the MOFERT or the local FERTC depending on the size and nature of project)

Evaluation of project impact on the national economy

10. Joint Venture Implementation Schedule

Overall time schedule proposed

Schedule for preliminary operations and estimated cost

Subcontractors and consultants involved (Chinese and foreign)

11. Accompanying Documentation

Indicate documents to be prepared, by whom, and specific responsibilities

- Market studies, technical studies, economic studies, as applicable
- Accounting statements
- Financial plan
- Written guarantees granted to investors, if applicable

- Written statements of opinion from relevant government organizations
- Formulation of Joint Venture agreement and/or contract
- Formulation of the Joint Venture articles of incorporation
- Other relevant documents, understandings, and agreements

12. Work Plan Preceding Establishment of the Joint Venture

Detailed plan for each stage of feasibility study, work flow chart[1]

Upon completion of the feasibility study, the Chinese partner is required to present it to the local FERTC for appraisal and approval if the total investment is within the approval authority of the local government. If the FERTC is not satisfied with the study, the partner may have to revise it according to the requirements of the FERTC. After the feasibility study is approved, the partners can start working on the joint venture agreement.

JOINT VENTURE AGREEMENT

The joint venture agreement is the most important legal document for both the Chinese and foreign investors. It determines the nature of the venture, the scope of operations, and most important of all, the rights and responsibilities of each partner throughout the entire investment period (see Appendix I for a sample joint venture agreement). A good contract can help avoid unnecessary confusion, misunderstanding, and even mistrust between partners at a later date and, therefore, lead to successful cooperation between partners. An ill-prepared agreement, however, can cause the failure of the investment project. Again, it should be remembered that it is always the Chinese version that is official.

Preparing a good joint venture agreement is not an easy job. Both partners may seek assistance from an agent who has extensive experience in drafting such documents. The agreement also must be examined and approved by the FERTC in the final approval stage. After the agreement is approved, the joint venture must be registered and an application must be filed for a business license at the local SAIC office. Once the license is issued, the joint venture can start official operations.

NEGOTIATIONS AND APPROVALS

The negotiation process in any nonmarket country is characterized by the conflicts that may arise between the foreign private investor and the host government partner. These conflicts may be reduced substantially if the foreign joint venture partner is cognizant of the issues that have been

Table 7.1

Main Negotiation Points in Establishing a Joint Venture

Point in contention	Chinese demand	Foreign demand
Type of product	Limited (several types)	Not limited (possibly of future expansion)
Ratio of exports to overall production	Large (70 percent or more)	Medium to small (depending on product)
Foreign currency	Foreign currency surplus	Balance
Investment	Investment in kind and in RMB loans	Foreign currency and investment of own funds
Equity ratio	50 percent or more	50 percent or more
Total investment	As small as possible	Expand if necessary
Procurement of loans	Depend on foreign capital	Joint venture to procure funds by itself
Recovery of funds	Short-term (3 years)	Long-term (10 years)
Depreciation and internal holdings	As low as possible	As high as legally allowed
Profit-to-sales ratio (before taxes)	High (35 percent or more)	Low
Dividends	High dividends, in foreign currency	Suitable dividends according to monetary investment
Purchase of equipment	Low price and priority on domestic makes	Performance and priority on imports
Technical transfer	Advanced, and detailed in content	Suitable, and general in content
Technical royalties	As low as possible	International levels
Term of joint venture, cooperation	10 to 20 years	As long as possible or independent investment
End of term settlement	Liquidation by book value	Liquidation by market price
Arbitration of contract disputes	Arbitration commission of China International Trade Promotion Organization	Arbitration commission of the host country
Prices of materials and parts	Imported items low, domestic ones high	Imported items high, domestic ones low
Price of products	Exports high, domestic low	Exports low, domestic high
Exchange rate	Variable, US $1 = RMB 6.0	As much as possible US $1 = RMB 5.3 (official rate)
Number of employees	Many Chinese and few foreigners	As few as possible of either
Salary to executives	Equal work, equal pay	Based on salary of company dispatching
Housing for executives	Borne by company dispatching same (foreigner)	Borne by joint venture
Position on land cost (including development costs)	Suitable (according regulations)	"Too high"
Position on factory costs (including construction costs)	Suitable	"Too high and quality poor"
Status of proposal and feasibility study	Official, with binding force	Unofficial, and with no binding force
Overall negotiations	Following Chinese procedures	"Too complicated and time consuming"
State of legal regulations	Being worked out	Not yet in place, not standardized, too many "internal" (not public) documents

Source: Reproduced from *Jetro China Newsletter*, No. 79 (March-April 1989), p. 16.

Table 7.2

Problems after the Start-up of Joint Ventures and Means of Resolution

Field	Problem	Example of resolution
Systems and policies	Arbitrary decisions and actions by Chinese directors	Thorough discussions (with party involved and superior organization)
		Change of members
	Delay in various permits and approvals	Publication of "internal" circulars
		Appointment of person with ability to be aggressive
		Strengthening of "relations" with related sector
	Opposing opinions within Chinese	Arbitration by higher organization
Infrastructure and transport	Failure to connect telephones or facsimile equipment	Virtually nothing can be done
	Unscheduled, unintentional blackouts	Installation of private generators or other backup power sources
	Large fluctuations in voltage	Installation of power stabilizers
	Supply of poor-quality water	Installation of cleaning equipment
	Insufficient truck transport	Purchase of private trucks
		Special contracts with trucking companies and strengthening of "relations"
	Ship delays	Modification of route or containerization
Raw materials and parts	Delay in receipt of materials and parts of Chinese make	Increased inventories
		Strengthening of "relations" with suppliers of materials and parts
	Sudden price hikes or terminations of contracts	Partial payment in foreign currency
		Diversification of sources of supply
	Low quality	Technical guidance
Sales of products	Poor domestic sales	Advertisements, PR, agency system
		Adjustment of prices
	Poor exports	Re-evaluation of prime costs of export products
		Diversification of export routes
		Application for sale domestically, in foreign currency, as import substitute
Personnel management	Poor working attitude of Chinese workers	Scaled bonuses
		Warnings and, in the case of failure to improve, dismissal
	Drop in morale of foreign staff	Improvement of living environment (housing)
		Establishment of domestic salary system
		System of periodic return home
	Delay in improvement of productivity	System of periodic training domestically and overseas
		Introduction of quality circle activities
		Bonus system reflecting productivity
Operations and funds	Shortage of foreign currency	Acquisition of foreign currency by exchange with RMB at "foreign currency adjustment center"
		Loans from Bank of China
	Shortage of Renminbi	RMB loans, with foreign currency as collateral
		Conversion of foreign currency to RMB at "foreign currency adjustment center"
	Fall in Renminbi exchange rate	Nothing can be done

Source: Reproduced from *Jetro China Newsletter*, No. 79 (March-April 1989), p. 17.

Table 7.3

Overall Problems for Foreign Joint Ventures in China

1. Problems Up to the Time of Establishment
   - o Difficulty in acquiring necessary documents and information. Without full information, feasibility studies are difficult to implement and only a mediocre business plan can be drawn up, so there are inevitably delays in decision making inside companies. Moreover, there is frequent trouble after the commencement of the business, necessitating additional expenditures.
   - o Complications stemming from the existence of "internal" (non public) regulations.
   - o Too many government offices involved in negotiations over the establishment of ventures and applications for permits. These are vertically organized, often with no lateral communication. Such a situation prolongs negotiations. Furthermore, the negotiations are sometimes changed midway, with insufficient transitional instruction, so the negotiations have to be started all over.
   - o Laws are arbitrarily enforced, with different conditions for different projects.
2. Extreme Demands on Foreign Investors
   - o Strict foreign currency balance
   - o High export ratios
   - o Overvaluation of land-use rights and investment in kind (factories and facilities)
   - o Responsibility for workers at pre-existing factories
   - o Overly high salaries for higher-level Chinese executives
   - o Strong demands for technical transfer and low valuations of software
3. Problems During Construction
   - o Troubles regarding contracts stemming from differences in perception about their meaning and a lack of sense of responsibility
   - o Too many additional expenses (unanticipated work, etc.)
   - o Difficulty in acquiring construction materials, pricing disputes
   - o Delays in construction work
   - o Poor quality construction and outright negligence
   - o Interference by administrative sector in such areas as the designation of contractors
4. Lack of Infrastructure
   - o Insufficient power due to the need for additional outlays to purchase power usage rights and power bonds; power interruptions without prior notice rendering operation difficult
   - o Inadequate communications facilities (telephones, telexes, facsimiles, etc.), particularly in local regions
   - o Poor water quality
   - o Insufficient transport capacity and inadequate cargo handling equipment, resulting in delays in delivery, mistaken deliveries, and other problems; rough handling of cargo
5. Problems in the Procurement of Materials and Parts
   - o Large price hikes for materials and parts due to the effects of inflation
   - o Problems in quantity, delivery, and quality
   - o Strict import controls
   - o Irrational double pricing system: large difference in prices for goods from state-run enterprises
   - o Lack of development of the parts industry and other related industries
6. Problems in Fund Procurement
   - o Insufficient foreign currency
   - o Insufficient RMB
   - o Falling exchange rate
7. Problems in Operations and Management
   - o Large shifts in policies
   - o Sudden amendments to laws and lack of information about current rules and practices (adequate advance notification and standard means of notification are required)
   - o Arbitrary decisions and actions by Chinese managers, particularly frequent short sighted choices (e.g., too hurried in trying to recover funds)
   - o Delays in granting various permits
   - o Discrepancies in perception between top and lower-level organizations, lack of communication of ideas from top to bottom, and failure to report negative aspects of operations to top (not only inside companies but also among central government, local governments, other companies, and factories)
   - o Non observance of laws (same tendency found in workers)
   - o Poor quality control
   - o Poor attitude of workers (lack of determination to work hard)

Source: Reproduced from *Jetro China Newsletter*, No. 79 (March-April 1989), p. 15.

noted in negotiating prior agreements. While no list of issues will address all potential problems, the points summarized in Tables 7.1, 7.2, and 7.3 may be helpful to investors prior to and during their contract negotiations.

The sequence to follow, from initial contact through receiving a business license to commence business operations in China, is outlined in the following six steps. While the sequence is based on joint venture procedures in Shanghai, the process would be similar in any other open city or special economic zone. For a graphic illustration, refer to Figures 7.1 and 7.2.

1. On the basis of Shanghai's current projects or other projects considered desirable to meet actual needs of Shanghai, investors may be recommended to prospective partners either through the medium of the Shanghai Foreign Investment Development Agency or through direct contacts with enterprises or corporations.

2. Negotiations on the terms and conditions of cooperation are held once initial talks prove that the establishment of a joint venture is feasible.

3. The Chinese party drafts a project proposal and submits it to the Shanghai Foreign Economic Relations and Trade Commission for approval. It receives the latter's decision within one month of the date of submission.

4. Upon project proposal approval from the Shanghai Foreign Economic Relations and Trade Commission, both parties enter into detailed negotiations and jointly develop a feasibility report. They then sign an agreement, a contract, and the articles of the association.

5. The authorities in charge of the Chinese enterprise apply to the Shanghai Foreign Economic Relations and Trade Commission for approval, and they receive its decision within one month. If the application is approved, a certificate of approval will be issued.

6. The joint venture then registers with the Shanghai Administration for Industry and Commerce and receives a business license (Figures 7.1 and 7.2).

NOTE

1. Sue-Jean Lee and Andrew Ness, "Investment Approval," pp. 17–18. This article first appeared in the May/June 1986 issue of *The China Business Review* and has been reprinted with permission of the US-China Business Council.

8

Joint Venture Feasibility Studies: An Example of a Construction Industry Project

Preparing a joint venture feasibility study is perhaps one of the most important and challenging tasks for both the Chinese and foreign joint venture partners. Under normal circumstances, joint venture partners have two ways of preparing the feasibility study; they can either hire an independent management consulting firm specializing in investment projects in China to do the job for them, or they may prepare the feasibility study themselves. If the feasibility study is prepared by an outside consulting firm, the partners would have to understand whether the assumptions in the study are reasonable in terms of the political, social, economic, and financial environment in China. They would also have to understand whether the market analyses and financial projections set forth are accurate and realistic. If the study is to be prepared by the partners themselves, they have to know what channels they should follow and what factors should be included in the study, as well as how these analyses should be undertaken and documented.

Although feasibility studies for joint ventures in other industries than construction may differ somewhat, the basic principles for preparing a feasibility study remain the same. Therefore, this case study should provide useful insights for the preparation, research, and analyses of data, thereby facilitating the process of undertaking a feasibility study.

Each feasibility study should include the following sections:

1. Summary of the project
2. Country environment analysis (omitted in this study as it has already been discussed in chapters 1 through 3)
3. Industry analysis

4. Specific locational environment analysis

5. Market analysis

6. Project financing

7. Financial projections and analyses

PROJECT SUMMARY

Project Name. This proposed project is a high-rise multi-purpose residential and commercial complex to be built in a metropolitan city (hereinafter referred to as the City) in China. The project is an equity joint venture between the China Commercial Development Corporation (hereinafter referred to as Party A) and the Pan Am Construction Company of the United States (hereinafter referred to as Party B). The official name of the joint venture is the Metropolitan Plaza (hereinafter referred to as the Project).

Project Objective. The objective of the Project is to meet the needs of the increasing number of foreign travelers, business executives, and residents of the City. There is currently a great shortage of both office and residential facilities for foreign business executives, particularly people involved in joint venture operations in the area, as well as those who maintain resident trade offices. Most foreigners are presently renting hotel rooms for both their offices and place of residence. Since rental space is at a premium on the market, the prices charged are extremely high and become a major cost factor for all foreign firms located there.

Partners. Both the Chinese and U.S. partners of the project have had extensive experience in the construction industry. Party A was incorporated in 1952, soon after the establishment of the People's Republic of China. It has been engaged in hotel construction and land development ever since. Currently, the company has more than 4,000 workers and technicians, making it one of largest construction companies in the country. It is equally important that the company is financially strong.

In addition to the profit potential, there are several motivations for the Chinese partner in this project: to acquire advanced technology and equipment, to gain valuable construction knowledge from the American partner, and to gain experience in cooperating with foreign developers, which may provide them entry into the international construction market at a future date.

Party B is also a well-established construction company in the United States and overseas. Its business has focused mainly on the eastern part of the United States, particularly in the greater New York and Boston areas. The company also has enjoyed a very successful growth record in the construction business. In recent years, the company has been actively involved in overseas construction, especially in the Far Eastern market, including both Hong Kong and Thailand. The company is interested in the Chinese market, mainly because it regards this market as one of the potentially strong construction markets in the 1990s.

The company is currently planning a two-step strategy for entry into the Chinese market: first, it will cooperate with a local Chinese construction company in building hotels or other types of commercial facilities designed solely and specifically for foreign visitors and resident business executives; second, as the company gains experience, it will gradually tap the Chinese domestic market by building housing facilities for the local residents through its own efforts. Therefore, the company regards this project as an important step in gaining experience in the Chinese market. The company is highly rated in the construction industry in the United States, ranking among the top fifty firms in size, and is well positioned financially to undertake the project in China.

Project Structure. Both parties have agreed that Party A will invest the equivalent of US $1.5 million in Chinese currency as its contribution to the Project, while Party B will contribute US $8.5 million. The remaining capital requirements will be financed through borrowing. According to the joint venture law governing equity investment, both partners will share the risks and profits of the Project based on their respective capital contributions.

The duration of the Project will be seventeen years, including two years of construction and fifteen years of the actual operation. Construction is expected to start at the beginning of 1991 and will be completed by the end of 1992. The official start of operations will be in early 1993 just prior to the Chinese New Year. At the time of the expiration date (2007), the project will be sold to Party A at a price of US $10 million in cash and will become solely Chinese owned.

Based on the capital contribution structure, Party B will chair the board of directors of the project while Party A will have a vice-chairman on the board. The board will consist of five members, three from Party B and two from Party A. Party B will also be responsible for selecting the management team to manage the Project once it is completed. If there is an impasse on the board of directors that cannot be resolved through consultation and negotiation, the final decision will then be made by the chairman.

Project Facilities and Services. The Project is designed to provide the following main facilities and services: i) The office and business center will provide office space, equipped offices for temporary and short-term business people, and supporting facilities such as conference and meeting rooms. There will be a total 150 office units that, together with business function rooms, will occupy about 200,000 square meters with a floor area of 22,500 square meters. ii) The apartment, service, and leisure facilities will provide 150 residential apartments of one to three bedrooms, fully serviced apartments for temporary and short-term business people, shops, restaurants and coffee shops, bars, function rooms, and a variety of health facilities. Altogether, these will occupy an additional 200,000 square meters with a floor area of 22,500 square meters.

Project Cost. The total cost of the Project is estimated to be approximately US $40 million, including predevelopment expenses, which will be divided further into professional fees, construction costs, management and administrative expenses, as well as design and engineering fees. Also, it is estimated that there will be a substantial marketing cost during this period. The specific breakdown of the forecasted project cost is as follows:

Professional fees	US $ 1,500,000
Construction cost	29,500,000
Design and engineering cost	500,000
Management cost	1,500,000
Marketing cost	2,000,000
Financing expenses	4,500,000
Other expenses	500,000
TOTAL	US $ 40,000,000

Among the projected costs, the professional fees will include feasibility studies, consulting and research, travel, business negotiations, legal, communications, and other related expenses. The construction costs would include all expenses necessary for the leveling of land for construction and the relocation costs of any residents currently on the property to be acquired. Management costs include administrative expenses during the construction phase. Marketing costs include expenditures for advertising, promotional, and all other related work. Financing expenses include interest payments on the loans borrowed in both years one and two for building construction.

Project Financing. Project financing will contain both equity and debt financing. Equity financing will be 25 percent of the total capital needed, of which 15 percent is to be contributed by Party A and 85 percent will be contributed by Party B. The remaining 75 percent of the necessary financing will be arranged by the China International Trust & Investment Corporation (CITIC) through international syndicated loans. The repayment of the loan will be guaranteed by CITIC based on the expected cash flow of the project. It is expected that the interest rate will be about 10 percent per annum.

Party A	US $ 1,500,000
Party B	8,500,000

Financing arranged through CITIC	<u>30,000,000</u>
Total capital required	US $ 40,000,000

Project Financial Projection and Analyses. The profitability of the project will depend on many factors that will be discussed in detail in the following sections. However, under the assumptions given below, the project will generate positive rates of return. Therefore, the project should be accepted without any difficulty.

CONSTRUCTION INDUSTRY ANALYSIS

General. The present standards of housing construction in China are low as well as very inadequate. At the present time, more than one-quarter of the population has insufficient housing facilities. New residential buildings do not meet Western safety standard codes, in both design and quality, and lack quality in both the materials used as well as in the layout and design. Hence, China needs to build as well as upgrade its housing sector since the demand for housing is surging and will continue to grow during the 1990s for both foreigners and the local population.

Foreign construction companies are not yet heavily involved in the construction business for Chinese residents for two principal reasons: Chinese construction companies are trying to build all the housing facilities by themselves, and by doing so, government authorities believe that they can help the country save on foreign exchange spending that otherwise would be needed if foreign companies became involved. However, since Chinese construction technology is increasingly falling behind the state-of-art technology available in the West, and as Chinese firms have to acquire foreign capital to finance their needs in the housing construction industry, it is expected that China will soon open its domestic housing industry to foreign competition.

Present Housing Conditions. Data regarding the housing and construction industries are not readily available in China. Therefore, it is difficult to collect the latest information for an accurate industry analysis. Furthermore, most studies are published only in Chinese and are not readily made available to the public.

According to a recent survey conducted by the State Council, the living area of the average urban household is about 38 square meters, which is equivalent to about 10 square meters per person. Apartments with kitchen and toilet facilities are in short supply. More than 70 percent of the households have to share either kitchen or toilet facilities or both with their neighbors. In some cases, eight or more families share the same common facilities. In rural areas, the living space for the average household is somewhat larger, estimated to be around 62 square meters per household.

However, the infrastructure supporting current housing facilities is extremely poor. For example, only 54 percent of the villages have electric lights, 14 percent of farmers have running water, and 40 percent of the population has access to purified water. This indicates how serious the housing problem is for both urban and rural residents.

Traditionally, the central government has been the main sponsor of all housing construction, including office and residential buildings. From 1950 to 1985, for example, the central government provided more than 90 percent of the total financing needed for housing construction. Since 1985, individuals have been encouraged to build and buy their own houses. This is particularly true in coastal areas and the southern areas near Hong Kong. In 1980, for example, only 3 percent of urban housing was owned by individuals. In 1989, however, the figure rose to about 15 percent. The central government is gradually decreasing its investment in housing; instead, more financing is being provided by the local governments, enterprises, and private individuals.

In order to improve housing conditions, the government has taken three policy measures in recent years:

1. *Increasing investment in housing construction.* Before 1980, an average of about 100 million square meters of new housing was built in the rural areas each year. Between 1981 and 1985, however, an estimated 3.2 billion square meters of new housing facilities were constructed. The government projects that another 650 million square meters of urban housing were expected to be completed by the end of 1990, as well as 3 billion square meters of housing in rural areas. It is also expected that, between 1991 and 2000, emphasis will be placed on improving the quality of average housing, that is, to improve the basic structure and supporting facilities of the buildings to be constructed. Foreign capital and technology will be needed if China is to accomplish its goal of doubling available housing during this period.

2. *Reforming the urban housing system.* The present housing system in China is a low-rent one. A typical rent accounts for only about 5 percent of total household spending. This low-rent policy has created at least two problems: excessive demand for housing and a large government budget subsidy for the housing sector. In order to resolve these problems, the government is now encouraging the personal building and purchase of houses, as well as introducing a new housing rent policy that will increase rents to more accurately reflect costs and thereby reduce government subsidy spending. The money thus saved will be used for other high-priority needs, including communication systems, port facilities, and transportation projects in which foreign construction involvement will also be essential.

3. *Setting new housing standards.* The government has recently set new standards for urban housing, which state that all new apartments should have a separate sitting room, bedroom, kitchen, toilet, and storage area. With these new guidelines being put into practice, it is expected that housing conditions will move

closer to present standards in the West. In order to achieve this goal, Western construction technology and experience will be needed.

Construction Industry with Foreign Involvement. Construction activities can be divided into the following six segments:

1. *Domestic housing segment.* As mentioned above, this type of housing is designed for domestic use and includes domestic residential housing, hospitals, schools, and shopping centers. The financing required comes basically from domestic sources and is provided by government budgets at the state, provincial, or municipal levels, or through treasury bond issues. Foreign construction companies have no access to this segment of the construction industry as existing domestic resources are sufficient and the government is not prepared to spend the foreign exchange necessary to attract foreign construction companies.

2. *High-technology construction segment.* This type of construction is designed either wholly or partially for domestic use. It includes such projects as nuclear power plants, private hospitals, and international airports. The financing of construction may come from equity investment or official loans provided by foreign governments and international agencies. Usually, the Chinese retain most construction undertaken for these projects for local firms and suppliers, and they only utilize imported supplies and foreign contractors when needed.

3. *Low-technology construction segment.* This type of construction is designed particularly for domestic use. It may include roads, bridges, port facilities, and domestic airports. Financing mainly comes from international financial institutions and regional development banks, such as the World Bank, Asian Development Bank, or World Development Fund. The funds obtained from these sources are used to supplement domestic financing. In this segment of construction projects, there is a possibility of foreign involvement as long as the project is partially financed by an international financial institution. However, if the project is financed 100 percent by the Chinese, there is no such possibility.

4. *Domestically financed construction for foreign use.* This type of construction is designed for foreign use but is financed either wholly or partially by domestic sources. It includes offices, hotels, and residential housing. Financing may come from the Bank of China, CITIC, or other domestic financial institutions. These projects are particularly popular in the southern part of China, where houses are built for overseas Chinese. However, there is limited foreign access to this segment.

5. *Construction for foreign use by foreign developers.* This category includes offices, hotels, and residential housing. These projects are designed basically for use by foreigners in China, although space may be rented by private domestic enterprises and export-oriented companies that need to be near their customers and that can pay rent in hard currency from their earnings. Full turn-key financing is arranged for building design, construction, fitting out, and commissioning. Usually, foreign funding organizations will contract out the most difficult parts of the project to foreign contractors.

6. *Joint venture construction.* This type of construction may include two groups of facilities: industrial facilities with both low-technology and high-technology construction and commercial facilities, which include international hotels, residential buildings, and offices built to meet international standards. These facilities are basically designed for foreign residents in China and are usually financed jointly by both local and foreign investors. This presents the most likely opportunity for foreign contractors to gain access to China's construction market, although the Chinese may insist on having local Chinese design and construction companies involved, but this participation is subject to negotiation.

Similar to the boom in the domestic construction industry is the significant growth experienced in recent years by the construction sector's using foreign involvement. These activities are focused mainly on hotels, luxury housing designed for the overseas Chinese, apartments for corporate expatriates, and office buildings. The reason for this rapid development is simple: these projects are self-liquidating because rental fees are paid in foreign currencies and, therefore, there are few foreign exchange problems.

Starting in 1989, China began to control construction projects joint ventured with foreign companies. There is and will be, however, a considerable amount of construction activity throughout China in the next decade and the capital shortage will require foreign involvement. Most importantly, the project in this illustration has already received initial approval from the City's government, indicating that the project will proceed unless the feasibility study suggests that the project is not a worthwhile undertaking.

Construction Problems. Despite the fact that foreign-sponsored construction mushroomed in the 1980–88 period, foreign construction companies must consider several construction constraints before entering into the Chinese market. A major problem in China is the shortage of basic quality building materials—lumber, cement, steel, and fasteners. This shortage is the result of inadequate investment by the Chinese government in the past to upgrade inefficient industries compounded by poor transportation systems. For example, there is an inability to transport such materials as logs and timber products from the northern part of the country to the more industrialized eastern areas. Steel plants are remote from markets, and both the rail and water systems are inadequate for the deployment of goods. As a result, many essential materials must be imported in large quantities each year. In fact, transportation is less expensive and more efficient from the West Coast of the United States than from the north of China to the south. Closer markets, such as Japan, South Korea, and Taiwan, can also out compete most domestic Chinese firms in terms of quality, price, and ability to meet delivery schedules.

Coupled with the shortage problem is the nonstandardization of local materials and semibuilding products. Consequently, when a joint venture project is constructed using imported equipment and materials, it is often difficult to find local products that are compatible. Due mostly to transportation and production deliveries, there are often delays in supply when local materials are ordered. The result is an extension of the construction phase, causing cost overruns. Therefore, joint venture projects prefer to import most of the materials needed rather than to purchase them partially in the local market. In this project, however, the Chinese partner is a very influential construction company in China and can guarantee that the equipment and material the project needs will be supplied without delays and will meet all quality standards.

China's construction industry, like most other industries, is very labor intensive. A majority of the construction work force is made up of either farmers or people from rural areas with little or no training and experience. Technical personnel are only an estimated 4 percent of the work force. Intensive training has to be provided for workers hired by any joint venture project. However, in the coastal areas, and particularly in the City where this project is to be located, there is an increasing number of construction workers who either have had experience in working on a joint venture construction project in China or in working overseas, particularly in the Middle East.

The average productivity of construction workers in China is estimated to be about 50 percent of their counterparts in industrialized countries. In order to make up this difference in productivity, long hours (usually ten hours per day and six days per week) are needed. Shift time schedules are often extended to meet production deadlines.

As mentioned previously, projects in China may often experience delays in construction. Major delays are likely to occur in both the design and construction phases. Designs have to meet many local regulations. In all major projects, the Chinese try to have a local construction design company at least partially involved in the project so that they can learn Western design technology. If a local Chinese contractor is hired for a high-standard project, modern finishes and construction technology can also be a problem. This is why, in this joint venture, both parties agreed that the project will use the designs provided by Party B.

LOCATIONAL ENVIRONMENT ANALYSIS

The City is one of the largest in China. Situated in the southern part of the country, it has a population of over 10 million. It is rich in culture and tradition. Its people are well known for their creativity and innovations. In fact, most of China's scientific and technical innovations have originated here. This is also true of the construction industry. The City has the largest number of major construction companies in the nation and the best quality construction work force. Some of the buildings constructed since 1985 are comparable to those in the West in terms of design, quality, and style.

The City is well known for its high standards of education. There are approximately fifty universities and colleges within the greater metropolitan area, with some ranking among the best in the country. In addition, the local government provides a well-received television education program for its citizens several times a week. Its purpose is to raise the overall educational level of the local residents. As a result, the City has the highest literacy rate in the country (92 percent), and its work force is believed to be among the best educated and well trained in the nation.

Most importantly, the City was one of a few open port cities in China before 1949. Most foreign investment projects were located here, including ventures in manufacturing, banking, insurance, and transportation. Therefore, the City has a relatively long history of being engaged in foreign trade investment and of dealing with foreigners. This gives the City a valuable asset that few other areas of China enjoy: the environment, and the ways in which the people think, work, and live are more Westernized than in other parts of the country.

Economy

The City is one of the most important industrial bases in China. It has some 9,000 enterprises, including metallurgical, electrical power, construction materials, housewares, petroleum, chemicals, electronics, machinery, foodstuffs, textiles, tailoring, leather, papermaking, arts, and handicrafts. Their industrial output accounts for more than 10 percent of the total for the country. Also, 15 percent of the state-owned enterprises and 10 percent of the collective-owned enterprises are located in this area. In terms of industrial output per capita, the City is comparable to the newly industrialized economies of Hong Kong, Singapore, South Korea, and Taiwan.

The City is also one of the most important foreign trade ports for China. Between 1950 and 1979, the total annual foreign trade by the City accounted for more than 30 percent of the total foreign trade of the country. After 1979, as other parts of China became more actively engaged in foreign trade and investment, the City's share in trade declined somewhat; however, it still ranks as one of the world's largest and busiest ports.

Infrastructure

The City has more than 100 berths that handle over 100 million tons of cargo annually, or more than one-third of the tonnage of China's main ports. It has an ambitious program to expand the port's loading, unloading, and storage capacities in the current five-year plan, the 1990–95 period.

There are currently three tunnels linking the southern part of the City to the northern part. There is also a plan to build two bridges over the river so the two parts of the City can be more closely and efficiently linked. However, building these two bridges requires a substantial amount of investment (estimated at about US $2 billion). Numerous foreign companies are conducting feasibility studies for the bridge projects; however, funding for one of these projects has not yet been provided. It is believed that the bridges will take at least ten years to complete once work is begun.

The City's highway system is very congested and outmoded. This is one of the major problems the City government has to resolve in order to attract more foreign investment into the area. Furthermore, transportation between the City and the neighboring cities and towns is not very efficient, nor is port access. For example, nonrush-hour travel between the City and a nearby town (which is about thirty miles away) often takes two hours. Improvement of the highways around the City has been discussed as well; however, due to lack of funding, highway improvement is only in the planning phase.

The City's street conditions are not good and are very crowded, particularly on weekends and in the evening; however, the public transportation system is highly efficient. As in other parts of the country, a majority of workers use the public transportation system to go to work. Some of them also use underground railways as a mode of transportation, and the heavy use of bicycles and handcarts adds to the downtown congestion.

The air transportation system is relatively well developed. There is a direct line linking the City to Japan, the United States, and Canada, as well as to Hong Kong and most seaside capitals. Domestically, the City is well connected by air with other parts of the country, and airport facilities are continually being upgraded.

The telecommunication system has been updated significantly with the help of firms from several Western countries. Most of the joint ventures are using fibre optics as well as digital and satellite systems. There are direct lines between the City and most major countries in the world, including the United States. This is particularly important for the hotel industry since customers have to use telephones, telexes, and facsimile machines for their daily business activities.

However, the City has other problems. For example, there is serious air and water pollution that is compounded by a lack of sewage disposal, as well as power and water supply problems. Due to these problems, a project such as a hotel must get permission first from the City government during the feasibility study stage in order to assure adequate and constant water and power as well as sewage disposal services.

Business and Investment Environment

The City has an ambitious plan of regaining its position as one of the most important financial and commercial centers in the Far East. Therefore, the local government updates its laws and regulations periodically in order to encourage foreign investment and trade. Over the past ten years, it has attracted more than US $3.0 billion in foreign capital, which is about 10 percent of the total foreign investment in China. There are also more than 100 wholly foreign-owned enterprises located within the metropolitan area, representing a wide range of industries. It is estimated that over 5,000 foreign personnel are working for these ventures and, if families are included, the number of foreigners residing in the City was approximately 8,000 at the end of 1990.

However, there are also problems that impact negatively on foreign business and investment in the City, namely bureaucracy and the relatively high costs of having personnel and their families based there. The cost of living, for example, is a major complaint of many foreign joint venture partners. A modest apartment can cost US $40,000 per year or more. A firm with an expatriate general manager and engineer on site must budget at least a minimum of US $80,000 per year for their accommodations—a substantial dent in operating expenses.

In addition, arrangements for the families of expatriate managers stationed in the City are also problematic. Since schooling arrangements can be difficult and costly, Western firms prefer to send staff whose children have finished high school. Some Western managers believe that their families would be happier if they could live in the downtown area, near the cultural and shopping centers, but suitable housing in that area is expensive and extremely scarce.

To help resolve some of these problems, the City government recently issued a new set of regulations for foreign investment. These new regulations have further simplified the procedures for setting up foreign ventures. Also, there will be further reductions in income tax for these ventures. In light of its needs and of future developments, the City government announced that it would encourage foreign investment in the following areas:

1. *Energy*. Raising the efficiency of boilers, internal combustion engines, pumps, compressors, and power-driven machines, improving the design and manufacturing technology of thermal power plants, and introducing new technology and techniques for energy conservation.

2. *Raw materials*. Increasing the varieties of metal products produced, more intensive processing of petroleum and coal, developing new technologies for the production of elementary chemicals, chemical fibers, plastics, synthetic rubber, polymerized resin, solvents, and dyestuffs.

3. *Mechanical engineering.* Drilling rigs and vessels for offshore oil operations, high-precision, multi-purpose machine tools, high-efficiency forging presses, equipment for producing cement and other building materials, textiles, frozen food, and technology for printing, packaging, forging and casting, welding, hot treatment, and electroplating.

4. *Electronics.* Production of large-scale integrated circuits, electronic computers, communication and navigation equipment, electronic monitoring equipment, and development of technology for producing software and auxiliaries.

5. *Building materials.* Products for construction, builders' machinery and hand tools, cement, plate glass, new lightweight building materials, and prefabricated parts.

6. *Consumer goods and pharmaceuticals.* Prepared food, children's food, beverages, instant food and nutriments, new fabrics for household decoration and textile finishing, semisynthetic antibiotics, new-type antibiotics, vitamin compounds, hormones, prepared herbal medicines, apparatus and instruments, wristwatches, clocks, household electrical appliances, bicycles, sewing machines, cosmetics, detergents, essences, recreational goods, plastic and leather products, and packaging and decorating materials.

7. *Transportation and telecommunication.* Construction of highways and railways, harbors and wharves, stations and piling yards, as well as postal and telecommunication facilities.

8. *Urban construction.* Modern hotels, residential and office buildings, trade centers, transformation and renovation of old areas and development of new ones, and construction of satellite towns.

9. *Environmental protection.* Moving old factories that cannot meet environmental standards out of the City, enforcing strict codes on all new construction, and requiring the use of emission control devices on vehicles and heating systems.

MARKET ANALYSIS

Based on past developments, as well as on the City's plans and incentives for foreign investment, there is great potential that more foreign investment will flow into the City during the 1990s. Therefore, the demand for housing—both offices and residences—will remain high. The market for the Project will target foreigners living and working in the City, as well as those visiting on a short-term basis for business purposes. Foreign residents can be divided into permanent and temporary ones. Permanent residents are those who have been granted resident status by the Chinese authorities and are registered as such. Temporary residents are those who visit, either on a regular basis or for short periods of time during negotiations and project operations, but who are not registered as permanent residents.

There are approximately 5,000 permanent foreign residents in the City at the present time, with the majority being American and Japanese company representatives. However, many are also from Hong Kong and Europe. Although no statistics are available concerning the number of temporary foreign business visitors to the City each year, it is believed that the number is increasing rapidly and has exceeded the number of permanent residents. In recent years, the City has become more and more attractive in terms of foreign trade and other international business opportunities. Also, as the City is trying to become a financial and banking center, the number of foreign banks and other financial institutions with branch or representative offices in the City has increased dramatically since 1988.

Current Apartment Demand and Projection

The shortage of suitable accommodations at reasonable prices is considered one of the most significant obstacles faced by foreign companies doing business in China in general and in this City in particular. Although the City government has tried hard to build hotels and apartment buildings to accommodate foreigners, it takes time to do so. It is estimated that the foreign community is growing by a minimum of about fifty offices and forty joint ventures each year (five foreign workers per each office and joint venture). This will increase the potential demand for offices by about 100 and for apartments by about 450 each year.

It is also estimated that there are currently several foreign-sponsored buildings either in the planning stage or under construction. These buildings will be ready between 1991 and 1993. By then, the housing market will have become very competitive. In order to successfully compete in this market, that is, to retain a good occupancy rate for offices and apartments, the proposed Project will contain the following special features:

Well-Designed and High-Quality Construction. Much of the construction underway for foreign residents in the City is of a lower standard than that to which foreign residents are accustomed. Construction must be of a high standard to ensure the comfort of residents during the hot, humid summers and the cold, damp winters. The current housing accommodations in the City, whether provided by previous foreign joint ventures or by the Chinese, lack the amenities that will be provided by this Project, which will include:

- Adequate storage space for both clothing and food. Much of the food consumed by foreign residents in the City is imported and needs to be stored or frozen. Therefore, a large storage space is needed.
- Adequate cooking facilities and kitchen space for entertaining in the Western style.
- Western-style furniture for offices and apartments. There is no opportunity for foreign residents to buy furniture suited to their own taste in the local markets.

Competitive Support Services. As a result of language and cultural differences, expatriates often find that what they can do easily at home may not be as easily accomplished when living in China. Therefore, the Project will provide a good management team to manage the buildings. This management team will work closely with residents and will respond quickly to the residents' needs and assist them in resolving problems. It is hoped that this will make foreign residents feel more comfortable in their new environment. In addition, the Project will give the highest privacy and security to its residents and will provide first-class recreational facilities.

Both parties agree that there is a great need to stress the marketing efforts of the Project. A specialized marketing team, consisting of both Chinese and foreign individuals, will work on this particularly important issue. The Project is planning to hire a specialized advertising company in the City to publicize the Project on its behalf during the construction stage.

Marketing work will start as soon as the agreement on the Project is signed and approved by the City government. An adequate budget will be available for this particular effort. During the construction period, the marketing budget will be set at US $2 million. During the operation period, yearly marketing budgets will be 1 percent of the total projected revenues. This will help ensure that the Project maintains a high occupancy rate.

PROJECT FINANCING

The total project cost is estimated at US $40 million, which will be divided into the following segments:

Professional fees	US $ 1,500,000
Construction cost	29,500,000
Management cost	1,500,000
Design and engineering	500,000
Marketing expenses	2,000,000
Financing expense	4,500,000
Other expenses	500,000
Total	US $ 40,000,000

Professional fees include expenses for the feasibility studies, Party B's visits to the City, and both parties' consulting work with other companies in the City and in the United States. Construction costs include the purchases of necessary building materials, furniture, and expenses paid to the construction company. Management and administrative expenses are forecast for planning and managing the Project during the construction period. The projection for design and engineering, as well as for marketing expenses, is based on estimates. Financial expenses include the potential interest payment on the funds borrowed through the CITIC (a more detailed discussion is set forth in the following section).

Of the proposed US $40 million project cost, US $10 million will be contributed by Parties A and B as their capital shares in the Project. Therefore, the remainder (US $30 million), will be borrowed through the CITIC from foreign banks. The estimated terms and conditions will be as follows:

Loan amount = US $30,000,000

Maturity = Seventeen years

Grace period = Five years

Interest rate = 10% fixed rate, plus a 0.5% spread

Interest payment = yearly

Principal repayment = Twelve equal installment payments

Loan drawdown = Two of equal amounts at the beginning of the first and second years

Commitment fee = 0.5% of the undrawn portion of the loan

CITIC guarantee fee = 0.5% of the total loan (up front)

(*Note*: In reality, either a foreign bond or Eurobond is more suitable than international syndicated loans to raise such long-term financing. Also, a floating interest rate is more often preferred by lenders or investors in this kind of case than a fixed one. Also, it is common for interest to be paid semiannually rather than annually.)

Once the Project becomes operational (starting after the third year), the financing required for operations, as well as for servicing the interest and principal repayment of the loan, will come from operating revenues. No additional equity or loan financing should be required. The repayment schedule is shown in Table 8.1.

Commitment fee: year 1 = US $75,000
                year 2 = 0
Guarantee fee: US $150,000 (up front)

FINANCIAL PROJECTIONS AND ANALYSES

This section provides the financial projections and analyses for the Project. The financial analyses for a proposed project are a key part of the feasibility study. If these financial analyses produce a positive rate of return for the project, it is likely that the project will be accepted. If,

Table 8.1
Repayment Schedule

Year	Interest payment	Principal payment	Total payment	Principal outstanding
		(In Millions of U.S. Dollars)		
1991	1.50	--	1.50	30.00
1992	3.00	--	3.00	30.00
1993	3.00	--	3.00	30.00
1994	3.00	--	3.00	30.00
1995	3.00	--	3.00	30.00
1996	3.00	2.50	5.25	27.50
1997	2.75	2.50	5.00	25.00
1998	2.50	2.50	4.75	22.50
1999	2.25	2.50	4.50	20.00
2000	2.00	2.50	4.25	17.50
2001	1.75	2.50	4.00	15.00
2002	1.50	2.50	3.75	12.50
2003	1.25	2.50	3.50	10.00
2004	1.00	2.50	3.25	7.50
2005	0.75	2.50	3.00	5.00
2006	0.50	2.50	2.75	2.50
2007	0.25	2.50	2.75	--
Total	33.00	30.00	63.00	--

however, the project tends to have a negative rate of return, the project should be rejected.

In order to conduct a good financial analysis, all factors involved in a project should reflect realistic, not optimistic, assumptions. Computer simulation is quite often required to produce financial projections under different scenarios. Currently, the most commonly used computer software for a project feasibility study is Lotus 1-2-3.

The financial projections in this section are based on information provided by both parties. It is believed that the information used in this report is an accurate reflection of market conditions. The following assumptions are made:

1. Number of apartments provided: 150;

2. Area of each apartment: 150 square meters;

3. Monthly apartment rental charge per square meter in the first year will be US $29; the annual rental charge will be US $350 per square meter;

4. Number of offices provided: 150;

5. Area of each office: same as assumption 2;

6. Monthly office rental charge: same as assumption 3;

7. Area of shops: 500 square meters;

8. Shop rental charge: same as assumption 3;

9. Expected shop rental occupancy rate: 100%;

10. Area of restaurants: 1,000 square meters;

11. Restaurant rental charge: same as assumption 3;

12. Expected restaurant occupancy rate: 100%;

13. Operating cost: 10% of the total revenues;

14. Repairs and maintenance: 1% of the total revenues;

15. Management fee: 2% of the total revenues;

16. Marketing fee: 1% of the total revenues;

17. Land-use fee: 3% of the total revenues;

18. Property tax to the City government: 1% of the Project cost (US $40 million);

19. Property insurance: 0.5% of the Project cost;

20. Depreciation: straight line over fifteen years;

21. Building residual value: US $10 million (will be paid to Party B by Party A at the end of the project life);

22. Income tax rate: 30%;

23. Reserve funds: 0.5% of the net income (to be used for emergency purposes. In this study, it is assumed that all reserve funds are used up.);

24. Profit share for Party A: 15% of the net profit of the Project;

25. Profit share for Party B: 85% of the net profit of the Project;

26. Foreign remittance tax: 10% of the total profit being remitted out of China;

27. Other taxes: A tax treaty between China and the United States will avoid double taxation for Party B.

In addition to these assumptions, two additional variables deserve more detailed analysis: expected yearly rental charge increases and expected occupancy rates for the apartments and offices. Clearly, these two variables will be among the most important in the entire financial analysis. Any expected change in either of these variables will directly affect the profitability of the Project. Therefore, five scenarios are prepared for these two variables as shown in Table 8.2.

Among the five scenarios presented, the financial results for scenario I are displayed in Tables 8.3 and 8.4, while only selected items (revenues, expenses, gross income, and net income) are shown for other scenarios. Under scenario I, the Project will have a positive net present value; the internal rate of return for the year 2007 will be 29 percent, a reasonable rate of return given the relatively high degree of risk for undertaking such a project in China. It should be noted that for the 1993–97 period, the internal rate of return is negative and, therefore, is not displayed in the computer output. The project generates a positive net present value (NPV) for Party A, with an internal rate of return (IRR) similar to that of the Project. Therefore, the Project should be accepted from the Chinese partner's point of view. The net profit for Party B is also very positive. The NPV is positive, with the IRR being about the same level as that of the Project and of Party A. Therefore, the Project also is acceptable from the foreign partner's point of view.

Table 8.2

Financial Projections under Different Scenarios (In Millions of U.S. Dollars)

	1993	1994	1995	1996	1997	1998	1999	2000	2001	2002	2003	2004	2005	2006	2007
SCENARIO I															
Assumptions															
Annual rental increase (%)	5	5	5	5	5	5	5	5	5	5	5	5	5	5	5
Expected occupancy rate (%)	50	50	60	60	70	70	70	70	70	70	70	70	70	70	70
Total revenue	8.4	8.8	11.0	11.5	14.0	14.7	15.5	16.3	17.1	17.9	18.8	19.8	20.7	21.8	22.9
Total expenses	7.3	7.1	7.5	9.8	10.0	9.9	9.7	9.6	9.5	9.4	9.3	9.2	9.1	9.1	9.0
Gross income	1.1	1.7	3.5	1.7	4.1	4.9	5.7	6.6	7.6	8.5	9.5	10.5	11.6	12.7	13.9
Net income	0.8	1.2	2.5	1.2	2.8	3.4	4.0	4.6	5.3	6.0	6.7	7.4	8.1	8.9	9.7
SCENARIO II															
Assumptions															
Annual rental increase (%)	3	3	3	3	3	3	3	3	3	3	3	3	3	3	3
Expected occupancy rate (%)	50	50	60	60	70	70	70	70	70	70	70	70	70	70	70
Total revenue	8.4	8.7	10.6	10.9	13.0	13.4	13.8	14.2	14.6	15.1	15.5	16.0	16.5	17.0	17.5
Total expenses	7.3	7.1	7.4	9.7	9.8	9.6	9.4	9.3	9.1	8.9	8.7	8.6	8.4	8.2	8.1
Gross income	1.1	1.6	3.2	1.2	3.2	3.8	4.3	4.9	5.5	6.2	6.8	7.4	8.1	8.7	9.4
Net income	0.8	1.1	2.2	0.8	2.2	2.6	3.0	3.5	3.9	4.3	4.7	5.2	5.6	6.1	6.6
SCENARIO III															
Assumptions															
Annual rental increase (%)	5	5	5	5	5	5	5	5	5	5	5	5	5	5	5
Expected occupancy rate (%)	50	50	65	65	80	80	80	80	80	80	80	80	80	80	80
Total revenue	8.4	8.8	11.9	12.5	15.0	16.8	17.6	18.5	19.4	20.4	21.4	22.4	23.6	24.7	26.0
Total expenses	7.3	7.1	7.6	10.0	10.1	10.2	10.1	10.0	9.9	9.8	9.7	9.7	9.6	9.6	9.5
Gross income	1.1	1.7	4.2	2.5	4.8	6.6	7.5	8.5	9.5	10.5	11.6	12.8	14.0	15.2	16.5
Net income	0.8	1.2	3.0	1.7	3.4	4.6	5.2	5.9	6.6	7.4	8.2	8.9	9.8	10.6	11.5
SCENARIO IV															
Assumptions															
Annual rental increase (%)	6	6	6	6	6	6	6	6	6	6	6	6	6	6	6
Expected occupancy rate (%)	50	50	70	70	80	80	80	80	80	80	80	80	80	80	80
Total revenue	8.4	6.9	13.0	16.8	15.6	17.6	18.6	19.7	20.9	22.2	23.5	24.9	26.4	28.0	29.7
Total expenses	7.3	7.1	7.8	10.2	10.2	10.3	10.3	10.2	10.2	10.1	10.1	10.1	10.1	10.1	10.1
Gross income	1.1	1.8	5.2	3.6	5.3	7.2	8.4	9.5	10.8	12.1	13.4	14.8	16.3	17.9	19.5
Net income	0.8	1.3	3.6	2.5	3.7	5.1	5.8	6.7	7.5	8.4	9.4	10.4	11.4	12.5	13.7
SCENARIO V															
Assumptions															
Annual rental increase (%)	8	8	8	8	8	8	8	8	8	8	8	8	8	8	8
Expected occupancy rate (%)	50	50	70	70	80	80	80	80	80	80	80	80	80	80	80
Total revenue	8.4	9.1	13.5	14.5	16.8	19.3	20.8	22.5	24.3	26.2	28.3	30.6	33.1	35.7	38.6
Total expenses	7.3	7.1	7.9	10.3	10.5	10.6	10.6	10.7	10.7	10.8	10.9	11.1	11.2	11.4	11.7
Gross income	1.1	1.9	5.6	4.2	6.3	8.7	10.2	11.8	13.6	15.4	17.4	19.5	21.8	24.3	26.9
Net income	0.8	1.4	3.9	3.0	4.4	6.1	7.1	8.3	9.5	10.6	12.2	13.7	15.3	17.0	18.8

It is interesting to note that both party's internal rates of return tend to be the same. This is designed, of course, by the authors to demonstrate that profit is fairly distributed between the two partners. In reality, however, it is possible that one partner may gain more than another based on the capital contribution and the different costs of capital for each partner. This should not pose a problem as long as both partners agree initially. In fact, this is quite often the case for contractual construction joint ventures.

SUMMARY

The outcome of a project, like the one discussed in this chapter, depends on two key assumptions: expected occupancy rates and yearly rental charge increases. The expected occupancy rate depends on local housing market conditions and the management of the Project. The local housing

Table 8.3
Financial Pro Forma Analysis (In Millions of U.S. Dollars)

	1993	1994	1995	1996	1997	1998	1999	2000	2001	2002	2003	2004	2005	2006	2007
Total revenues	8.4	8.8	11.0	11.5	14.0	14.7	15.5	16.3	17.1	17.9	18.8	19.8	20.7	21.8	22.9
Apartment rental	3.9	4.1	5.2	5.5	6.7	7.0	7.4	7.8	8.1	8.6	9.0	9.4	9.9	10.4	10.9
Office rental	3.9	4.1	5.2	5.5	6.7	7.0	7.4	7.8	8.1	8.6	9.0	9.4	9.9	10.4	10.9
Shop rental	0.2	0.2	0.2	0.2	0.2	0.2	0.2	0.2	0.3	0.3	0.3	0.3	0.3	0.3	0.3
Restaurant rental	0.4	0.4	0.4	0.4	0.4	0.4	0.5	0.5	0.5	0.5	0.6	0.6	0.6	0.7	0.7
Total expenses	7.3	7.1	7.5	9.8	10.0	9.9	9.7	9.6	9.5	9.4	9.3	9.2	9.1	9.1	9.0
Operating cost	0.8	0.9	1.1	1.2	1.4	1.5	1.5	1.6	1.7	1.8	1.9	2.0	2.1	2.2	2.3
Repairing & maintenance	0.1	0.1	0.1	0.1	0.1	0.1	0.2	0.2	0.2	0.2	0.2	0.2	0.2	0.2	0.2
Management fee	0.2	0.2	0.2	0.2	0.3	0.3	0.3	0.3	0.3	0.4	0.4	0.4	0.4	0.4	0.5
Marketing fee	0.1	0.1	0.1	0.1	0.1	0.1	0.2	0.2	0.2	0.2	0.2	0.2	0.2	0.2	0.2
Land use fee	0.3	0.3	0.3	0.3	0.4	0.4	0.5	0.5	0.5	0.5	0.6	0.6	0.6	0.7	0.7
Property tax	0.4	0.4	0.4	0.4	0.4	0.4	0.4	0.4	0.4	0.4	0.4	0.4	0.4	0.4	0.4
Property insurance	0.2	0.2	0.2	0.2	0.2	0.2	0.2	0.2	0.2	0.2	0.2	0.2	0.2	0.2	0.2
Principal repayments	0.0	0.0	0.0	2.5	2.5	2.5	2.5	2.5	2.5	2.5	2.5	2.5	2.5	2.5	2.5
Interest payment	3.0	3.0	3.0	2.8	2.5	2.3	2.0	1.8	1.5	1.3	1.0	0.8	0.5	0.3	0.0
Loan commitment fee	0.1														
Loan guarantee fee	0.2														
Depreciation	2.0	2.0	2.0	2.0	2.0	2.0	2.0	2.0	2.0	2.0	2.0	2.0	2.0	2.0	2.0
Gross income	1.1	1.7	3.5	1.7	4.1	4.9	5.7	6.6	7.6	8.5	9.5	10.5	11.6	12.7	13.9
Income tax	0.3	0.5	1.1	0.5	1.2	1.5	1.7	2.0	2.3	2.6	2.9	3.2	3.5	3.8	4.2
Net income	0.8	1.2	2.5	1.2	2.8	3.4	4.0	4.6	5.3	6.0	6.7	7.4	8.1	8.9	9.7
Property insurance	0.2	0.2	0.2	0.2	0.2	0.2	0.2	0.2	0.2	0.2	0.2	0.2	0.2	0.2	0.2
Total operating cost	2.0	2.1	0.5	2.6	3.0	3.1	3.2	3.4	3.5	3.6	3.8	4.0	4.1	4.3	4.5
Loan amount	30.0														
Principal repayment	0.0	0.0	0.0	2.5	2.5	2.5	2.5	2.5	2.5	2.5	2.5	2.5	2.5	2.5	2.5
Loan outstanding	30.0	30.0	30.0	27.5	25.0	22.5	20.0	17.5	15.0	12.5	10.0	7.5	5.0	2.5	0.0
Interest rate (%)	10.0	10.0	10.0	10.0	10.0	10.0	10.0	10.0	10.0	10.0	10.0	10.0	10.0	10.0	10.0
Interest payment	3.0	3.0	3.0	2.8	2.5	2.3	2.0	1.8	1.5	1.3	1.0	0.8	0.5	0.3	0.0
Commitment fee	0.1														
Guarantee fee	0.2														
Total financing cost	3.2	3.0	3.0	5.3	5.0	4.8	4.5	4.3	4.0	3.8	3.5	3.3	3.0	2.8	2.5
Depreciation	2.0	2.0	2.0	2.0	2.0	2.0	2.0	2.0	2.0	2.0	2.0	2.0	2.0	2.0	2.0
Total operating expenses	7.3	7.1	7.5	9.8	10.0	9.9	9.7	9.6	9.5	9.4	9.3	9.2	9.1	9.1	9.0
Income before tax	1.1	1.7	3.5	1.7	4.1	4.9	5.7	6.6	7.6	8.5	9.5	10.5	11.6	12.7	13.9
Income tax rate (%)	30.0	30.0	30.0	30.0	30.0	30.0	30.0	30.0	30.0	30.0	30.0	30.0	30.0	30.0	30.0
Net income	0.8	1.2	2.5	1.2	2.8	3.4	4.0	4.6	5.3	6.0	6.7	7.4	8.1	8.9	9.7
Reserve funds	0.0	0.1	0.1	0.1	0.1	0.2	0.2	0.2	0.3	0.3	0.3	0.4	0.4	0.4	0.5
Net profit	0.8	1.2	2.5	1.2	2.6	3.4	4.0	4.6	5.3	6.0	6.7	7.4	8.1	8.9	9.7
Equity investment	10.0														
Discount rate (%)	10.0	10.0	10.0	10.0	10.0	10.0	10.0	10.0	10.0	10.0	10.0	10.0	10.0	10.0	10.0
NPV	-9.3	-8.3	-6.4	-5.6	-3.9	-1.9	0.1	2.3	4.5	6.8	9.1	11.5	13.8	16.1	18.5
IRR (%)						4.0	10.0	15.0	18.0	20.0	22.0	22.0	24.0	25.0	25.0
Profit distribution															
Party A															
Equity investment	1.5														
Net profit	0.1	0.2	0.4	0.2	0.4	0.5	0.6	0.7	0.8	0.9	1.0	1.1	1.2	0.3	1.5
Party B															
Equity investment	8.5														
Net profit	0.7	1.0	2.1	1.0	2.4	2.9	3.4	4.0	4.5	5.1	5.7	6.3	6.9	7.6	8.3

market is an independent variable over which the Project partners can exert little influence. However, much can be done on the management side. It is extremely important that the management team for the Project be both experienced and dedicated, as well as flexible in working together. Also, a good marketing team must be developed to sell the Project's facilities and services to the foreign communities in the local market.

The assumption for an annual rental charge increase depends on two factors: the rate of inflation and the degree of competition in the local market. The higher the inflation rate, the higher the rental charge increase should be each year. In the Chinese market, it is believed that the expected rate of inflation in the coming years will be well above 5 percent. In fact,

Table 8.4
Project Assumptions and Financial Projections (In Millions of U.S. Dollars)

	1993	1994	1995	1996	1997	1998	1999	2000	2001	2002	2003	2004	2005	2006	2007
Total revenues	8.4	8.8	11.0	11.5	14.0	14.7	15.5	16.3	17.1	17.9	18.8	19.8	20.7	21.8	22.9
Number of apartments (units)	150	150	150	150	150	150	150	150	150	150	150	150	150	150	150
Area per apartment (sq. m.)	150	150	150	150	150	150	150	150	150	150	150	150	150	150	150
Rental (annual/per sq. m.)	350	368	386	405	425	447	469	492	517	543	570	599	629	660	693
Expected occupancy rate (%)	50	50	60	60	70	70	70	70	70	70	70	70	70	70	70
Total apartment rental	3.9	4.1	5.2	5.5	6.7	7.0	7.4	7.8	8.1	8.6	9.0	9.4	9.9	10.4	10.9
Number of offices (units)	150	150	150	150	150	150	150	150	150	150	150	150	150	150	150
Area per office (sq. m.)	150	150	150	150	150	150	150	150	150	150	150	150	150	150	150
Rental (annual/per sq. m.)	350	368	386	405	425	447	469	492	517	543	570	599	629	660	693
Expected occupancy rate (%)	50	50	60	60	70	70	70	70	70	70	70	70	70	70	70
Total office rental	3.9	4.1	5.2	5.5	6.7	7.0	7.4	7.8	8.1	8.6	9.0	9.4	9.9	10.4	10.9
Area of shops (units)	500	500	500	500	500	500	500	500	500	500	500	500	500	500	500
Rental (annual/per sq. m.)	350	368	386	405	425	447	469	492	517	543	570	599	629	660	693
Expected occupancy rate (%)	100	100	100	100	100	100	100	100	100	100	100	100	100	100	100
Total shop rental	0.2	2.0	0.2	0.2	0.2	0.2	0.2	0.2	0.3	0.3	0.3	0.3	0.3	0.3	0.3
Area of restaurant (units)	1000	1000	1000	1000	1000	1000	1000	1000	1000	1000	1000	1000	1000	1000	1000
Rental (annual/per sq. m.)	350	368	386	405	425	447	469	492	517	543	570	599	629	660	693
Expected occupancy rate (%)	100	100	100	100	100	100	100	100	100	100	100	100	100	100	100
Total restaurant rental	0.4	0.4	0.4	0.4	0.4	0.4	0.5	0.5	0.5	0.5	0.6	0.6	0.6	0.7	0.7
Project and operating costs															
Professional fee	1.5														
Construction cost	29.5														
Management	1.5														
Design and engineering	0.5														
Marketing	2.0														
Financing expenses	1.5	3.0													
Other expenses	0.5														
Total project cost	37.0	3.0													
Operating cost	0.8	0.9	1.1	1.2	1.4	1.5	1.5	1.6	1.7	1.8	1.9	2.0	2.1	2.2	2.3
Repairing and maintenance	0.1	0.1	0.1	0.1	0.1	0.1	0.2	0.2	0.2	0.2	0.2	0.2	0.2	0.2	0.2
Management fee	0.2	0.2	0.2	0.2	0.3	0.3	0.3	0.3	0.3	0.4	0.4	0.4	0.4	0.4	0.5
Marketing fee	0.1	0.1	0.1	0.1	0.1	0.1	0.2	0.2	0.2	0.2	0.2	0.2	0.2	0.2	0.2
Land use fee	0.3	0.3	0.3	0.3	0.4	0.4	0.5	0.5	0.5	0.5	0.6	0.6	0.6	0.7	0.7
Property tax	0.4	0.4	0.4	0.4	0.4	0.4	0.4	0.4	0.4	0.4	0.4	0.4	0.4	0.4	0.4

the annual inflation rates during the 1986–89 period averaged more than 20 percent. Although the inflation rate dropped to about 5 percent in 1990, there are strong indications that it will creep upward in the near future. Therefore, the assumptions in this case are reasonably conservative.

9

Selected Case Studies

The following case studies illustrate three different types of operations within China. The first case focuses on the Beijing Tokyo Photographic Art Company Ltd., a Chinese-Japanese joint venture, and the problems it faced concerning local labor relations, foreign exchange deficits, and negotiations. The second case also highlights a Chinese-Japanese venture, the Beijing New Century Hotel Company Ltd., and examines the unexpected problems encountered by the foreign partner due to inflationary and other macroeconomic conditions within China. Finally, the third case examines a Sino-American venture, the Babcock & Wilcox Beijing Company Ltd., and offers insight into the Chinese bureaucratic involvement in business, especially the role of the Chinese government in negotiations. All three cases portray difficulties involving labor relations, government regulations, joint venture negotiations, and unanticipated costs that are typical issues faced by foreign joint venture firms in China.

In reviewing these cases, one must recognize that no set of cases can fully illustrate all the problems and successes of foreign investment operations in China. Moreover, one must be cognizant of the time frame in which the joint ventures were initiated and recognize that each case portrays the initial experience of a foreign company in establishing a joint venture operation in China. After eleven years of the open-door policy, firms embarking on new ventures in China during the 1990s are able to benefit from the experiences of their predecessors.

CASE ONE: THE BEIJING TOKYO PHOTOGRAPHIC ART COMPANY LTD.[1]

Motivation and Background of Investment

The Japanese partner, the Tokyo Group, did not previously have a base in China and invested in this venture to gain a foothold in the Chinese market.

The subject of a joint venture in photography was revised in Tokyo in October 1981. At the time, discussion was made only of a joint venture with the Chinese Ministry of Railways, and no discussion took place concerning the Beijing Municipality. In January 1982, the Tokyo Group's president, the current joint venture's president, and a director visited China to investigate the photographic situation. At the time China was just shifting from black and white photography to the use of color.

According to the agency in charge of foreign relations for the Chinese Ministry of Railways, the China Railroad Foreign Service Corporation, a related railroad publishing company, had negatives of scenic photographs from all over the country, as well as photographs of minorities. It wanted to establish a joint venture to make more use of them and had the idea of using the negatives to earn foreign currency in Japan so as to purchase new processing equipment.

Processing outlets were set up, although the joint venture determined that these alone would not be profitable. It was decided, therefore, to also establish shops on busy streets in the major cities. By May 1983, it was clear that the business would not be sufficiently profitable with just the Ministry of Railways involved, so the Tokyo Group proposed that the Beijing Municipality participate in the venture as well. Thus, two Chinese partners and one Japanese partner would participate in the venture.

The Beijing Food, Drink, and Service Corporation (under the Beijing Municipality) and the China Railroad Foreign Service Corporation, however, could not agree on an equity split, and the Ministry of Railways decided to pull out. The Ministry of Railways apparently wanted to invest only in the negatives, so the talks broke down.

Application was eventually made for a permit at the end of 1985, and a temporary permit was granted by the Beijing municipal government in January 1986. The contracts were signed on April 28, 1986.

Under the economic retrenchment program, which got underway in the spring of 1985, the photography business was designated as an "unnecessary" or "non-urgent" business and fell under investment restraints. Tremendous difficulty was experienced in setting up the enterprise, taking over a year to obtain a consensus to proceed.

At the time, there were fifteen divisions and bureaus in Beijing in one way or another related to the enterprise, and of these over half reportedly opposed the project. It took over a year to receive fifteen seals of approval. On September 26, 1986, the State Administration for Industry and Commerce issued the business permit, and the joint venture commenced operations in May 1987.

The Chinese partner, Beijing Food, Drink, and Service Corporation, is a local state-run corporation under the Beijing Municipal Commerce Committee and operates restaurants, barbershops, domestic hotels for the Chinese, public bathhouses, bicycle repair shops, photographic shops, and cleaning establishments. The corporation supplied the land and buildings, and its directly run Pulande Washing Factory provided the building and infrastructure (sewerage, electricity, boilers, etc.) for the processing lab, so both firms were deputized members as directors of the joint venture.

Prior Surveys and Feasibility Studies

At the time of the Japanese investors' visit to China in 1982, 120 single and twinlens reflex cameras were the fashion, and 70 percent of the processing was black and white. A study was made, based on a survey by the Japanese partner and data provided by the Beijing Food, Drink, and Service Corporation, to obtain a grasp of overall market conditions. The photographic field was advancing rapidly, however, and as the negotiations continued for over four years, the Chinese photographic market was changing considerably. Corrective measures had to be taken. In July 1986, there was the 16 percent devaluation of RMB currency. It was not feasible to increase the amount of investment; thus plants and equipment not immediately required were cut—with concomitant problems.

In considering land costs, no standard for land-use fees had been announced, so there was no material on which to base a judgment of appropriate value. (Standard prices for land use in Beijing had still not been released.)

Another problem was what to do with the foreign currency balance. Since there were no longer any negatives for leasing, it was decided to balance the foreign currency ledger by exporting other photography-related items to Japan.

Another unknown was how much it would cost to lay power lines into the processing laboratory. Fortunately, the washing factory was able to provide the electric power.

Negotiations

All in all, there were no major disputes during the negotiations because the Japanese partners did not understand the situation in China. The main points contested were only the method of calculating wages, the appropriateness of the land-use rights, and the infrastructure requirements.

When a question arose as to whether the venture contract was legitimate, because the document was very short compared to similar venture contracts with, say, the United States, the Chinese partners convinced the Japanese partner to sign the contract as it was.

During the negotiations, the Chinese partners came up with outright extravagant conditions. They first asked for RMB 180 per square meter per year for the land-use right for the processing lab, but they finally settled for RMB 120. They also demanded that only new equipment be brought in, not second-hand equipment. In response, the Japanese partner said it would be willing to bring in new equipment if necessary, but it questioned if the volume of business would justify it. Ultimately the Japanese partner was able to persuade the Chinese partners on this point.

The charge for the land-use rights, provided as investment in kind, was RMB 300 per square meter per year for the store in downtown Beijing and the previously mentioned RMB 120 per square meter per year for the processing lab in another location. It would have been possible to acquire the land-use rights for the laboratory for RMB 30 had the venture borne the cost of the sewerage disposal connections and the laying of power lines, but when calculations were made, it was found this would have meant higher costs than acquiring land in a downtown location.

The depreciation period for the building and equipment was ten years and five for the vehicles. At liquidation, depreciated assets would be turned over to the Chinese free of charge, while nondepreciated assets would be credited to the investors at the remaining book price, according to their equity ratios.

Buildings

The venture's store was the old Friendship Photo Center of the Dongcheng Food, Drink, and Service Corporation. The exterior was left as it was, while the interior was completely renovated. The processing lab was to be located on the second floor of a plant under construction. The construction did not go as scheduled; yet the venture managed to start up business without too many delays.

Much of the construction work was poor. The concrete used was of a lower grade than designated, and the walls soon began to crumble, and the paint began to peel off in just a little over a year after completion. The fuses would often blow and the boiler did not operate well due to poor circulation planning. It recently had to be reinstalled and the renovations added to both costs and delays.

Infrastructure and Transport

The downtown store was supposed to do without power every Thursday, but in actuality it was never cut off during the winter and the store was blacked out only twice a month in the summer. The store is on the busiest street of the city, Beijing's "Ginza," or "5th Avenue," and is open year-round. At the start of operations, when the power was cut off, it had to operate by candlelight. The Chinese authorities subsequently prohibited business by candlelight, so the store now uses pocket flashlights or manages with only window light when the electricity is off.

The official power allocation for the washing factory was 400 kWh per month, but it was lowered to 116 kWh per month on March 1, 1987. As a result, the processing lab, which was supposed to get its power from the washing factory, found its power supply plans thwarted. The lab initially demanded 100 kWh per month, but later it had to agree to 50 kWh.

As the lab was now to receive only half the electricity it required, it was decided to purchase another 30 kWh worth of power rights at RMB 2,500 per kWh for a total of RMB 75,000. Under the agreement, the lab is supposed to receive the power for twenty years at the price set in government plans. The problem of power rights had not come up in the negotiations concerning establishment of the venture.

When the power allocation from the Power Supply Bureau is exceeded, a surcharge must be paid. There are different rates for amounts over 10 kWh, 120 kWh, 150 kWh, and so on. The charge is said to be as high as tenfold on amounts over 150 kWh, so the venture decided to purchase the power usage rights.

Gasoline is also under an allocation system. The venture can only purchase 500 liters per quarter from the Beijing Food, Drink, and Service Corporation. At the onset, this was sufficient as there were only two cars, but when the number was raised to three, the 500 liters became inadequate. Therefore, the venture could no longer pick up and take home the Japanese president and technician. If it had continued, it would have become necessary to pick up supplies and make deliveries by bicycle.

Procurement of Parts and Materials

The Japanese initially brought in one set of spare parts for the equipment to provide for possible breakdowns. When parts ran out, at first they were able only to obtain replacements from Hong Kong or Japan, but they can now procure imported parts in Beijing as well.

Of the materials needed, the only items being imported that could be procured on the domestic market are basic film and paper. Chemicals and special papers are Japanese products procured from Hong Kong. The domestic products are poor in quality and cannot be used. The imports have depleted the foreign currency originally brought in as cash investment. At the present time, the venture is borrowing foreign currency from Japan.

Production and Sales

The processing laboratory currently handles the processing of general commercial portraits and special photographs. In the future, it plans to exert more effort on commercial portraits. China does not yet have advanced technology, and unfortunately the necessary materials are still not available, and the technical level is also still low.

The store, located beside the Wangfujing Department Store, includes the store proper, a studio, and offices. The first-floor store offers four-hour processing of photographs and sells cameras and photographic materials and equipment, while wedding photographs and general portraits are taken on the second floor.

Sales are in cash. The approach to selling in the store lacks even the basic courtesies common in Japan. The clerks do not bother to welcome or thank their customers; in fact, they take a condescending attitude toward clients. The president is trying to personally train the clerks, but not much improvement has been seen.

Funds Procurement

Currently, the joint venture is able to make do with its own funds for local currency expenditures. It is making preparations for local currency loans and borrowed once from the Bank of China in April 1987. It has already paid back half of the loan. At the time loan procedures were simple.

Foreign currency, however, is lacking, so the venture has borrowed twice from its Japanese parent companies. In such cases the Bank of China is notified of the loan. When foreign currency is remitted from abroad, the State Foreign Currency Management Bureau, which is part of the Bank of China, enters it in a foreign debt registration certificate. It has not been difficult to raise funds until recently.

Management

The Chinese partners initially demanded that there be four Chinese directors and three Japanese directors so as to secure a hold over the management, but finally the two sides settled on four directors each. The president is supposed to be a Japanese for the first five years, then a Chinese for five years. The reverse is to be the case for the vice-president.

In the beginning, the Chinese vice-president would not listen to the chairman of the board (Chinese), saying that he had his own way of doing things. He apparently believed that he was doing the actual work and that his superior was lazy. The situation has been improved now, however, with the vice-president often going to the chairman for advice and discussing issues with the president on an almost daily basis.

The vice-president, who is thirty-nine years old, only graduated from high school, so he was taking courses at a university twice a week in the daytime. He graduated last year. In China, it is seemingly permissible to take time off during the workday if it is for study.

Labor

The joint venture took over 80 employees from the old photo center (the Friendship Photo Center). There was a request to do so during the negotiations to establish the venture. Judging from the scale of operations, eighty workers were unnecessary, so it was decided to reduce the number to fifty. The Chinese side drew up standards for the layoffs, and in the end female workers over forty-three and males over fifty-five were dismissed. With normal retirements and transfers to other jobs, there is a total of forty of those inherited workers left.

Training is provided on the job. There were sixty workers in total at of the end of 1988, of which two, the president and a technician, were Japanese.

Wages

The wages of the employees (take-home pay) were RMB 120 to 150 per month as of 1987, but the nominal wages were RMB 350 per worker. Broken down, this RMB 350 includes, in addition to the take-home pay of the workers, RMB 70 to 90 in taxes to the state and 20 percent for a retirement fund, anti-inflation subsidies, housing allowances, and so on. The real per capita wages were RMB 185—an average RMB 120 in basic pay plus bonuses. In the Labor Management Provisions of Beijing Municipality, payment to the state, reserves, and so forth are supposed to total 49 percent of the real wages.

In the past, wage levels have been decided by the Beijing Food, Drink, and Service Corporation. In October 1988, the board of directors decided to raise the base pay but at the same time to also assess individual workers and give differential raises. It was decided to generally raise the base pay by 10 percent at first, with 10 percent assumed as the inflation rate, but later the decision was made to pay a separate RMB 15 as an inflation allowance, so the total raise would be 17 to 18 percent. (The inflation allowance had to be RMB 10 or more according to a directive from Beijing authorities.) As a result, the nominal wages of general workers rose to RMB 385, and the real wages rose to RMB 205 (47 percent of the nominal figure). Of this, the base pay comes to about RMB 130, and the remainder consists of incentives.

The raise in nominal wages averaged RMB 35 per worker, but of this 47 percent went to the state, so the workers would be left with some RMB 20 more. The range of base pay raises for general workers was from RMB 4 to 16, with the difference retained for use as incentives.

Individuals were assessed in three stages. First, the individuals were asked to make self-assessments. Next, their group leaders made an evaluation and, finally, the executives (seven people from the vice-presidental level up) made one. The general workers were assessed according to twenty criteria, with three to twenty points given for each item. The criteria were set by the Chinese, and the employees accepted the findings because of the method used.

Evaluation Criteria:

1. Enthusiasm for work
2. Positive attitude
3. Sense of responsibility
4. Completion of work in terms of quality, volume, and time
5. Wearing of work clothes and proper name badge
6. Prework preparations
7. Observance of financial regulations
8. Service attitude
9. Observance of operating regulations
10. Visiting neighboring work groups or leaving workplace
11. Personal telephone calls during working hours
12. Visits by friends during working hours
13. Causing disturbances during work
14. Early arrival for tidying up
15. Clean work clothes, worn neatly
16. Turning off light switches and locking up for safety
17. Reporting voluntarily to superiors
18. Customer opinions
19. Rules violations
20. Mistakes
21. Pioneering spirit, creativeness, contribution to the company
22. Enforcement of rules by group leader
23. Good job by group leader

24. Good arrangement of work by group leader

25. Liaison between groups

(Items 21–25 are for the assessment of group leaders.)

The president and vice-president receive the same salary according to the province of the venture, so the Chinese partners at first agreed that the amount should indeed be equal. But since the venture was not making a profit, the president (Japanese) ended up receiving RMB 4,300 paid in foreign currency certificates and the vice-president (Chinese) received RMB 3,000 paid in local currency. The Japanese technician received RMB 3,000. The rent for the housing (hotel) for the Japanese president and technician was borne by the joint venture in local currency.

Performance

The joint venture anticipated sales in the first fiscal year (1987) of RMB 2.2 million and RMB 3 million in 1988, for a deficit in the first year and a slight surplus in the second, but it was prepared either to break even or sustain a slight deficit. In actuality, sales reached RMB 4 million in 1987 and RMB 7 million in 1988.

The reasons for the unexpected growth in sales were the increase in the number of items on display in the store and the bargain sales in the spring, summer, and fall, both of which increased sales of durable goods; the increase in wedding pictures due to advertisements on television and in the newspapers; and the strengthened desire of the people to purchase in order to beat inflation.

Recently, sales have been running RMB 0.5 to 0.6 million a month. In 1988, the company was able to eliminate accumulated debts with its surplus. Of course, the venture is still running a deficit when head office expenses are considered.

Operating Problems

The biggest headache is the inability to balance the inflow and outflow of foreign currency. Ninety-five percent of sales are in the local currency and only 5 percent in foreign currency, so it is difficult to maintain a positive foreign currency balance. For this reason, the Japanese president is allowed to pay for his housing (hotel) in Chinese currency. If the photography library had been started four to five years earlier, negatives would have been circulated to Japan, the business would be going well by now, and the foreign exchange would be available, but there have been difficulties due to the delay.

There is no need to achieve a foreign exchange balance for the first two years after the contract is signed, but a balance is required from the third year on. The deficit in the foreign currency account represents future dividends that would have been sent to Japan. When the permits were applied for, the Chinese partners proposed a figure at which a foreign currency balance could be achieved, but the Japanese partner stated that achievement would be difficult. As it turns out, a balance has not been achieved.

As a balance will not be possible with photographs alone, there are plans for the venture to have its parent companies in Japan instead take albums, camera bags, giveaway toys, and other products that could be handled by the Tokyo Group. Experience now shows that the small stuffed panda giveaway toys were not well received and the cloth camera bags were not suitable merchandise and could not be sold. Whatever the case, the only choice is to improve such products or develop new ones.

At the present time, the range of business is supposed to be limited to photography-related items, so the venture is in the process of applying for permission to deal in other exportable products to achieve a foreign currency balance.

Further, the venture is searching for places in foreign affiliated hotels and office buildings frequented by foreigners to set up stores. By doing so, it could make sales in foreign currency certificates, which would help alleviate the foreign currency problem.

Pointers and Proposals

The following points and suggestions derive from the Tokyo Group's experience:

- Establishing a joint venture in China is like playing poker according to a new set of rules. The Chinese play with their cards face down while the foreigners are required to play with them face up. When the Chinese win a hand, they take the whole pot, but when the foreigners win, they get only a few chips.

- Patience and more patience is needed. Japanese who have headed other joint ventures in China state that any foreigner sent to a joint venture in China must be a stolid type, not ruffled by anything. High-strung individuals will not survive. Patience is required in everything.

- It is important to serve as a model. There is a large gap between the real and nominal wages of the Chinese, and there are some among them who are of the opinion that the salaries paid to the foreigners are too high. There are also differences in national characteristics. To lead Chinese workers, one must be consistent in both word and deed. For this reason the president comes to work early every morning and wipes all the desks in the office clean. In the beginning, the toilets were filthy, and the Chinese workers were unwilling to clean them. Unable to stand the sight of them, the president cleaned them himself. After a while the workers began cleaning them too. The president commutes to work on the same crowded buses as the Chinese.

- There is a big difference between what one dreams is possible in China and what one can actually attempt and do. Methods thought through in Japan may not work in China.
- Much happens below the surface in China. One must live day by day, tackling problems that develop unexpectedly, one after the other.
- Terms resulting from negotiations differ widely depending on the venture and the degree of Chinese interest in it. In the future, such terms must be standardized.
- The Chinese are impetuous. They are definitely not the kind of people who work methodically and precisely. For one reason or another negotiations take place slowly, but once concluded the Chinese become hasty in their efforts. They pay scant attention to quality, so in the long run difficulties often arise. When exporting products, the products of the venture are known to be of poor quality. When the products are sold domestically, the workers wonder why the quality is low despite the products' being produced by a joint venture, and they conclude that the foreign guidance is at fault.
- The water in Beijing is hard and of low quality. The company introduced filters from Japan to filter the water, but when a slight difference in color appeared on the photographs, the Chinese claimed that the chemicals were at fault. When they learned that the chemicals were good, they maintained that the method of training by the Japanese management was poor. When they discovered that the method of instruction could not be faulted, they maintained that the equipment was defective.
- The president carefully notes down all the negative remarks made about the Japanese technical staff and orders the truth to be ascertained for each point. He maintains an operations chart that shows the state of the chemicals. As for the equipment, the Chinese operators are often at fault, but they will seldom ask for help when they do not know or understand something, as they are very proud and often difficult to work with. It is therefore necessary to spend a little time with them every day.
- In Japan, workers think of their wages as coming from their customers, but in China they think of them as coming from the State, and quarrels with the customers seem almost to be a source of pride. There is a strong attitude of condescension by clerks and a lack of humility.
- There is nothing to do about the problems except to advance step by step. In the beginning, the president would often become irritated and got embroiled in arguments daily, but recently he has become more relaxed.
- The president believes that foreigners should not interfere in personnel matters but should leave everything to the Chinese. One should make use of good local people. If the Chinese vice-president is a good man, it is only necessary to train the vice-president. The president developed a good working relationship with the vice-president after a year and a half.
- In regards to money, the monthly accounts were apparently falsified once, so the president now keeps a close watch. The president's seal was also affixed to something without his knowledge, and checks were arbitrarily issued. These

practices were quickly stopped. There are problems concerning responsibility in China, so payments are often not made. Generally, payment is by check.

• The Chinese often ask to simply be trusted, but if one does this, one may have to pay for it later. People have been hired without the president's knowledge and have quit without him knowing about it.

• During the negotiations to establish the venture, some of those in the head office in Japan suspected that the future president was "on the side of the Chinese." He had his superior come to Beijing to see matters for himself and was able to convince his supervisor of the difficulties of doing business in China.

Requests to the Chinese Side

From the experiences of the Japanese president, the following points might be key ones to be considered by the Chinese side:

• No matter how hard the foreign side tries, those on the Chinese side must also try or else problems will not be solved or difficult situations will not improve beyond a certain point.

• One should really listen to what others (including those on the foreign side) say.

CASE TWO: THE BEIJING NEW CENTURY HOTEL COMPANY LTD.[2]

The Beijing New Century Hotel, located directly in front of Beijing's Capital Gymnasium, in Haidian District, is a 60/40 equity joint venture among Xiyuan Hotel, the Bank of China, All-Nippon Airways (ANA), and C. Itoh. The venture was set up on January 24, 1987. The joint project involves the building and managing of an international hotel for foreign tourists plus an office building for rental purposes. The construction was completed in the summer of 1990, prior to the opening of the 1990 Beijing Asian Games.

Initial investment capital was set at US $19.25 million, of which US $7.7 million (40 percent) was to come from Xiyuan in the form of land, other nonmonetary contributions, and US $1 million in RMB cash; US $3.8 million (20 percent) from the Bank of China; and the US $7.7 million (40 percent) from the Japanese partners split between ANA and C. Itoh at a four-to-one ratio. Total investment was set at US $92 million, including a US $72.75 million loan. The period of the joint venture was set at eighteen years, including a four-year construction period. The current payroll stands at forty-six people, including two Japanese. The board of directors has five members, three Chinese and two Japanese.

The 24,000 square meter compound contains a 33-story, 740-room hotel complex (including two underground floors), and a 17-story office complex with two basement floors and 13,000 square meters of office space for rent. It offers a full range of shopping and catering facilities for both foreigners and local Chinese and also includes a discothèque, an indoor swimming pool, a bowling alley, tennis courts, a sports club, sauna, barber and hairdressing facilities, convention halls, conference rooms, business service centers, a supermarket for foreigners, and underground parking.

History of the Venture

As early as 1984, three years before the All-Nippon Airways Beijing-Dalian-Narita service was inaugurated in 1987, the Japanese carrier began looking into possible investment opportunities in China. A study mission was sent to Hangzhou in 1984, followed by some fifteen similar missions to various Chinese cities in the ensuing two years. But conditions were judged to be difficult, and for a long time no firm investment decision was reached. In May 1986, Chinese authorities made known their interest in finding possible partners to provide parking and other facilities around the Metropolitan Stadium, the chosen location for the 1990 Asian Games. C. Itoh, which had been involved in other joint projects, was asked by the Chinese side to approach ANA. A consultation meeting was held, resulting in a first round of concrete negotiations between the two sides.

From this point on, the pace of development accelerated. By August 1986, a basic understanding was reached and a joint venture contract was signed the following October. The quick tempo was partly attributed to the expertise of the negotiators and partly to Japanese concessions over some points.

In any case, the new company was registered with the State Administration for Industry and Commerce in January 1987, and a joint construction design contract was subsequently signed with a Hong Kong architects' office and the Beijing Architecture Institute.

In April 1987, the Japanese partners assigned a permanent staff to Beijing, and the entire amount of capital committed by the Japanese partners was paid in May. In December, the board of directors decided to take out a US \$72.75 million loan (larger than was first anticipated) and raise the amount of initial investment to US \$92 million. In the same month, a Chinese construction company was chosen as building contractor, and actual work started the following February. (Bids by foreign companies lost out to Chinese firms due to higher costs and other considerations.)

Though the foundation work was finished in September 1988 as scheduled, a shortage of both raw materials (cement and steel) and workers (due to lack of accommodation) in autumn 1988 delayed work by about a month and a half. By February 1989, construction had reached only the fourth floor of the office complex and only the third floor of the hotel building.

Japanese Reasons for the Choice of Chinese Partners

The Japanese partners did not make a firm decision on what type of project to undertake until the choice of partners was finalized. According to the Japanese side, there were several advantages to cooperating with Xiyuan and the Bank of China. Xiyuan not only runs an international hotel of its own, but that hotel is itself a joint venture with foreign partners, built only a few years back. The experience and available personnel are expected to be useful in the current project. The Bank of China is well versed in international business methods. It has played a useful role in resolving deadlocks (by convincing Xiyuan of the importance of following international business practices), and the fact that there are two Chinese partners is expected to generally help reduce direct conflicts with the Japanese partners.

Both Chinese partners have strong ties with the Beijing municipal government, and this can help smooth the way for the project, especially when it comes to concrete practical problems.

Main Points of the Joint Venture Contract

1. *Total investment capital.* The initial capital of US $19.25 million, including US $6.7 million in the form of land and other nonmonetary contributions, is equivalent to 21 percent of the estimated gross investment of US $92 million (as opposed to the 25 percent it would have been of the initially estimated US $77 million).

   The value of the nonmonetary contribution by Xiyuan—including land-use rights, land-leveling costs, compensation to former users, and fees to the municipal government for the enhanced infrastructure—was formally established and certified by a local Chinese accounting firm, thereby resolving a bone of contention frequent in such ventures.

   The annual payment for use of the land amounts to RMB 1.8 million, which is equivalent to RMB 75 per square meter. The contract covering the land-use arrangement has been registered with the central government's Land Management Office. Payment of rent started in the second half of 1988, but at the rate of only 50 percent until the complex was completed and ready for opening. (General land-use cost for hotels runs between RMB 50 to 100 per square meter, so RMB 75 is deemed to be in line.)

   The Japanese partners are not completely satisfied with the brevity of the joint venture contract, especially the section dealing with capital contributions, in which no clear specifications have been made regarding Xiyuan's nonmonetary contributions. But they are satisfied that the amounts stipulated for compensation and infrastructural upgrading were arrived at according to prevailing rates.

   Though the Japanese partners initially took the position that the Bank of China should provide the guarantees for the entire syndicated loan (from the

Japanese banks), agreement was ultimately reached for the Japanese partners to arrange collateral of their own in proportion to their respective equity holdings.

2. *Composition of the board of directors.* The board of directors is composed of five members, including a Chinese chairman, two deputy chairmen (one Japanese and one Chinese), and two ordinary directors (again, one from each side). Unanimous agreements are preferred, but it is stipulated that any motion can be adopted by a simple majority as long as it includes at least one non-Chinese vote.

3. *Management structure.* Top management consists of a general manager, two deputy general managers, and a chief and a deputy accountant. The general manager's post will go to a Japanese during the first half of the joint venture period, after which a Chinese will take over. All top department managers will be sent from Japan, including the business manager, room service manager, and catering manager.

4. *Profit sharing.* Dividend payment will start two years after business begins and will be in proportion to the equity contribution. Chinese expectations of immediate profit return are seen as not very practical by the Japanese partners.

5. *Duration of the joint venture.* In accordance with the practice in the Beijing Municipality, the period is set at eighteen years from the establishment of the joint venture (not from completion of construction as was sometimes the case with joint venture deals concluded before 1986). In fact, the eighteen-year period is currently the maximum allowed by Beijing.

6. *Other stipulations.* The joint venture contract specifies the following points:

   - Outside directors have no say in management matters;
   - Employment contracts of top management personnel may be terminated in the case of abuse or inadequate performance; and
   - Investing partners have the right to audit the accounts.

The Preparations Office

1. *Organization.* The top management is made up of five members: one director; two deputies; and one chief assistant, three of the five being Chinese and two Japanese. They will oversee a staff divided into six departments: general administration, accounting, planning and personnel, procurement, construction work, and opening preparations.

2. *Operation.* Management decisions are generally made at a weekly management meeting attended by the top management (five people) and nine department managers. Prior notification is given regarding matters to be discussed, and minutes are kept so that decisions reached cannot be reversed at will (a not uncommon Chinese practice that also affected the New Century Preparation Office in its early period).

3. *Payroll.* Currently there are forty-six employees on the payroll, but the number

is expected to increase shortly. Some 500 service staff members, cashiers, and cooking staff members are currently receiving training at special schools.

Employees and Work Conditions

1. *Number of employees.* New Century plans to employ a regular staff of 1,350 members (including fifty foreigners) and another 200 workers on a part-time basis.

2. *Recruitment.* The hotel management will recruit all nonmanagement staff directly, without using governmental personnel agencies. A total of 240 service staff members were selected from about 3,500 applicants when the new company first advertised for employees in 1987. These people are now undergoing training. The management has chosen to recruit in several separate drafts in order to choose from a large pool and be able to weed out unsuitable people in a timely way. It also believes that it will be necessary to recruit new staff members every year.

   Most recruits will be junior high school graduates. Once selected, they will be sent to some thirty vocational schools within Beijing. These vocational schools are part of the secondary school system and provide three years of vocational training in hotel service, bookkeeping, cooking, and other subjects. Students have to pass a qualifying examination at the end of the three years of study.

   Apart from donating language teaching materials and equipment and providing some teaching staff, the joint venture also contributes RMB 2,500 a year for each hotel staff member enrolled in such schools. It has signed advanced contracts for several classes on a fifty-student-per-class basis.

   Those recruited for posts in the banks included in the project, or as accountants for shops and other facilities, are trained at accounting schools. Another sixty people are undergoing three years of English language training and English language typing.

   All New Century employees are hired under contracts of two to three years' duration. These contracts will be renewed at the discretion of the management. The social security problems involved in the case of termination of employment have not been resolved, but New Century intends to study the matter in conjunction with other joint venture businesses operating in Beijing.

   Cleaning staff members (dishwashers, car park attendants, sanitation staff, etc.) will be employed on a two-hour shift, part-time basis.

3. *Regulations.* Management is still working out rules regarding categories of work, wages, recruitment, and holidays.

4. *Terms of employment.* Specific terms of employment differ between local Chinese staff and expatriates and between regular staff and preopening staff.

   - Joint venture staff will enjoy the same number of holidays as other workers in Beijing.
   - The joint venture intends to adopt a six-day work week with the daily shift lasting from 8:00 to 5:30, including a ninety-minute lunch break

from 11:30 to 1:00. The long lunch break is a concession to the Chinese custom of going home to prepare lunch for children and other dependents. (These hours will be applicable to both local and expatriate staff.)

• Apart from national holidays, the local Chinese staff enjoys a limited number of paid leaves. In the case of sick leaves exceeding the allocated periods, the workers will continue to receive their entire basic salary, but a fixed amount will be deducted from their bonuses. Expatriates will have annual leaves according to individual terms of contract.

• Salaries of the New Century staff will be calculated according to three different scales, including the local pay scale, and Japanese domestic and expatriate pay scales. Local Chinese staff will be paid on the same scale as Xiyuan employees. New Century is expected to work out its own pay scale for expatriates and senior staff, with due consideration being paid to parity with other similar establishments in Beijing. The Japanese expatriates will be paid on different scales, depending on the type of work, rank, and their original employers.

• Local Chinese staff members will enjoy all usual allowances given to workers in Beijing. Expatriates will be given bonuses and various kinds of special allowances for food, cleaning, and so on.

• At present, the joint venture staff is using the staff canteen facilities at the Xiyuan Hotel, but they will have their own canteen when New Century is completed.

Credit Matters. A total of credit amounting to US $72.75 million has been agreed upon by a syndicate of ten Japanese banks, with the Bank of Tokyo, Daiichi, and Fuji acting as lead managers. Loans will mature in ten years, and repayment will not commence until four and a half years after they are drawn.

The loan contract was signed in Beijing on March 14, 1989, and a first installment was paid out in April. Collateral was provided separately by the Chinese and Japanese partners in proportion to their equity holdings.

Problems. So far, the joint venture has found itself facing several unanticipated problems, such as added costs. When the joint venture contract was negotiated in mid–1986, the partners had no hints of several changes in the investment situation and government policies that would add greatly to the cost to the project.

In October 1986, the State Council issued a circular requiring major electricity users to purchase electricity bonds at RMB 1,000 per kilowatt in proportion to the number of kilowatts consumed per day. In the case of New Century, the share worked out to RMB 8 million (US $2.16 million). The bond issue, it was argued, was needed to pay for installing a transmission station and network linking the users with the generating plant. Another State Council circular, issued the following October, stipulated that electricity users who failed to comply with the October 1986 requirement would be required to pay for their electricity at double the rate for bond buyers.

Government repayment of the bonds is to start after ten years, and they are to be paid off in full within a subsequent five-year period. Since the question did not arise at all during contract negotiations, it is not clear what will happen to the bonds should the Japanese partners decide to pull out of the venture before the bonds mature. After negotiation, it was decided that 25 percent of the RMB 8 million cost of the bonds must be paid at the time of purchase and the remainder paid in two equal installments, one prior to the hotel's opening and the other immediately afterward.

The difficulties arising from the bond purchasing demand underline a major problem facing Japanese investors: there is no way for the Japanese partners to accurately determine inflationary and other macroeconomic conditions in China. Furthermore, the circumstances faced by different types of projects can vary widely, and interpretations of terms can bring on serious conflicts between joint venture partners when operations start.

The next most significant item in added costs stems from a Beijing Municipality notification issued in November 1986 (approved by the State Council in September 1986) that users of the four utilities (cold and hot water, gas, and sewers) should shoulder the development costs. In the case of New Century, the bill plus the electricity bond purchase will come to a hefty US $3 million, consuming 4 percent of the initial investment of US $77 million.

It is necessary to pay the municipal construction committee a construction plan fee when registering the plans as required. In the case of New Century, this fee amounted to RMB 150,000. The municipal construction committee has under it a "quality supervisory bureau." Even after New Century managed to halve the fee for construction quality certification from 0.3 percent of the construction costs to 0.15 percent, the company still owes the bureau another US $400,000 or US $500,000, depending on final construction costs.

A new rule introduced in October 1988 requires that borrowers of funds pay 0.0003 percent of the amount borrowed as a stamp tax. For US $70 million, the stamp bill comes to US $210,000. In contravention of the original arrangement, the joint venture is in fact being made to shoulder part of the burden of residents for converting residential land into parking space. Municipal authorities have also asked New Century to provide bus parking space and to pay for various infrastructural work—roads, transportation, and water supply among them.

Though each item may not seem large when viewed individually, the accumulated amount cuts deeply into the amount available to be spent on the project itself. And since the Chinese partners do not have the financial resources to endlessly raise capital, the added costs can mean an unanticipated and unwanted greater contribution (and equity holding) by the foreign partner.

In the case of New Century, raising the investment capital from US $77 million to US $92 million cannot but upset targets anticipated in the initial feasibility study and depress profitability. Moreover, the Chinese authorities (in this case the Beijing municipal government) do not always approve capital changes of more than 10 percent if these involve loans, insisting that the ratio of committed investment capital to borrowed capital should be kept within certain limits.

Finally, administrative fiat of the municipal authorities has also cost the joint venture over US $1 million as they insisted that the more expensive local interior decorator (bid: US $5 million) be chosen over Hong Kong competitors (bid: US $3.5 million to US $3.8 million).

Conflicts within the Chinese Side

The Beijing municipal government has been an active party in the project all along, as it was anxious to see that the necessary infrastructure— car park, telephone network, sewerage, and electricity network—be put in place in the area around the Capital Gymnasium in preparation for the 1990 Asian Games.

By comparison, Xiyuan is less enthusiastic about the project. It cannot but worry about competition from this new joint venture hotel so similar to its own. There is evidence, for example, that workers from Xiyuan are treated differently from others.

Another problem concerns the fourteen college graduates joining the staff. They are not given full cooperation by the rest of the staff.

Interference by the Local Government

The interfering behavior of Beijing municipal officials indicates that they see the New Century project as a "national" project, even though it is the joint venture partners who are footing the bills. While such interference sometimes stems from personal bureaucratic abuse, at other times it is clearly the result of government policy. The selection of a local construction company for the work is one such case. The municipal government obviously sees the job as an opportunity to promote local industrial development.

Sometimes the interference involves petty matters. Certain people insisted that non-Japanese-made elevators be brought in, clearly because there are already many Japanese-made elevators in use in Beijing, and they want to try something different. Conflicts have also occurred over whether to use Chinese electrical parts or foreign ones. The preference seems to lie with Chinese products, since adoption for use by a foreign-related outfit like New Century can lead to export opportunities. On the other hand, some merit is also seen in using imports: their use can provide opportunities for overseas training of maintenance people, thus raising Chinese technical standards. In general, however, Chinese officials are always anxious to promote Chinese-made items, particularly those manufactured by other joint ventures.

The attitude of the Chinese staff of the preopening preparation office also leaves something to be desired. They come from an assortment of Chinese and joint venture hotels like the Xiyuan, Minzu, and Great Wall and tend to give higher priority to remaining within the budget than to anything else. In opting for the cheapest supplies on the market, little thought is given to quality or suitability. This leads to waste and will also leave a residue of problems for the New Century staff, which has to use these supplies in the future.

Bureaucratism

The Chinese authorities have a myriad of regulations and rules for virtually all contingencies. Unfortunately such rules are liable to divergent interpretations, depending on the official in charge. This state of affairs is causing many problems for the New Century project.

Though materials imported for joint venture use are supposed to be exempt from import duty, this is not always the case in practice. An imported generator might enter duty free, but parts and peripheral equipment may be taxed. (On occasion, a portion of imported shipments simply gets lost when going through customs.) In one case, a shipment of Japanese restaurant uniforms imported for use by the students of the catering class was subjected to import duty because they could also be worn "outside of work."

Conflicts of opinion and differences in interpretation have also arisen over such minor matters as where to locate a bus stop.

One simple reason for the abundance of red tape is that Chinese authorities are used to dealing with Chinese companies whose managers have learned to be just as ingenious in trying to circumvent regulations. They simply are not prepared to deal with foreigners who tend to take government regulations at face value.

Another problem—much more serious—is corruption. Almost invariably some sort of payment is necessary when the joint venture tries to acquire articles in short supply.

Conflicts Arising from Cultural and Organizational Differences

From a Japanese point of view, Chinese work morale suffers from the tendency to avoid responsibility, an inability to distinguish between private and public prerogatives, and a lack of company loyalty.

Difficulties Concerning the Use of Expatriate Workers

The standard of living of the average Chinese is still very low compared to standards in foreign countries. Trying to maintain a resemblance of the lifestyle one is used to in the home country is bound to make the foreigner look extremely extravagant in Chinese eyes.

Paychecks of Japanese expatriates working in joint venture hotels can also be a heavy burden on the company. For this reason, some hotels opt to use Hong Kong or Singapore executives, instead of more efficient Japanese personnel, to cut costs while remaining competitive. This choice often causes conflicts between Japanese and non-Japanese expatriate staff. A thirty-year-old Hong Kong executive can be obtained at a salary of under US $2,000 a month, with a three-year contract, while his Japanese counterpart will cost much more. Indeed, in highly competitive Beijing, assembling an adequate number of Japanese management personnel can be extremely costly. After all, the average Japanese hotel spends up to 35 percent of its funds on wages, compared to 2 to 3 percent for Chinese-owned hotels such as the Beijing Hotel.

Relations with the Building Contractor

Chinese contractors, unlike their Japanese counterparts, are not general contractors. They depend on the client company to ensure the supply of such building materials as cement, timber, and steel. Nor does the contractor pay any attention to work schedules or quality. It is not "their job," apparently, to consider the effects of their work on future operations. The joint venture company must take responsibility for everything. In making procurements, cost is often the only consideration, quality and delivery schedules being simply irrelevant. The pricing system is also very confusing. For inexplicable reasons, joint venture companies have to pay two different prices for the cement they use.

Chinese workers also seem to interpret their role and responsibility in a different way. They are not use to considering the larger perspective in terms of ultimate benefit for the company. For instance, a buyer will have no inhibition in procuring inferior products from manufacturers, so long as the prices fit the budget he has been given. He gives little thought to whether the procured items can be used.

Personnel Policy Problems

The common practice in the Chinese hotel industry is not to rehire the people who help in preparing the hotel for opening after the hotel starts normal operation. The regular staff is recruited separately, and it is not easy to adopt the Japanese practice of offering employment to all preopening staff. On the one hand, there are people who work better when their future is assured, but then there are also others who slack off. On the other hand, those who have to search for new jobs cannot, in fact, commit their entire attention to current tasks.

Dealing with Problems

There is no fixed solution for all these problems, but it helps if foreign partners in joint ventures pay constant attention to the following points:

1. *Building human ties*. It is necessary for the foreign staff to take the initiative to promote ties with their local counterparts after work. Efforts should be made to understand how the Chinese think and work, their customs, and points of view.

   It helps to join in social activities and pastimes like mahjong and bridge. Every effort must be made to ensure that no individuals or groups are seen as being given special preference.

   Language is a constant source of difficulty. While one may manage with English or a mixture of Japanese and English in the workplace, it always helps to understand the local speech, at least enough to convey good will.

   Making an effort to build human ties will help stave off misunderstandings and willful distortions. Many problems can be avoided if a channel for consultation is in place before actual difficulties arise.

2. *Laying down rules*. While the Chinese custom is to respect the decision of superiors when no written guidelines are available for reference, such decisions are still often the cause of discontent and conflicts.

   To avoid confusion, it is useful to delineate a set of rules governing every possible situation, from the use of company cars to everyday work matters, accounting procedures, and recruitment requirements.

3. *Keeping informed*. It is not uncommon for the Chinese partner of a joint venture to blame everything on authoritative but unpublished "regulations," leaving the foreign partner with little choice but to accept. It is necessary, therefore, to make a constant effort to collect and exchange information so as to keep abreast of the situation.

   Of course, doing this is not always easy. There are, in fact, unwritten rules and rules that are deliberately not made public. There are also cases in which the Chinese are just as uninformed.

4. *Applying external pressure*. In times of real difficulty or when the attitude or behavior of the Chinese side becomes unreasonable, it sometimes helps to speak to responsible officials or members of the government organizations in charge. The Chinese will back down in the face of disapproval from high officials. There has been a case in which a joint venture partner took up a case of blatant abuse in the pages of the *China Daily*. It helped.

Common Irritants Faced by Joint Venture Partners

There are many other differences in practices and attitudes that cause conflicts among Chinese and foreign partners in joint ventures. Some of these differences include the following:

1. *Low valuation of management techniques.* Chinese managers generally do not fully realize the importance of management know-how, such as operational control or the making up of work schedules for the New Century project. For example, the Chinese managers claimed to realize the importance of management know-how, but when one younger worker wanted to take time out from other chores to master the technique, he was told that "such skills" were not so significant.

2. *Fascination with high technology.* There is one incident when Chinese managers demanded the donation of a minicomputer, when a simple word processor was quite adequate for the task in question. Possession of a computer— any computer—was deemed necessary to lend the project a high-tech aura.

3. *Low productivity.* The abundance of bookstores and the popularity of quality control programs on television suggest that there are hard working and conscientious workers in the work force. Still, productivity is generally low, probably due to deep-rooted defects in the system.

4. *Conservatism.* People in power tend to be conservative and uninterested in trying new ways for fear of failure.

5. *Recruitment rules.* It is always necessary to reach a prior agreement on a set of rules regarding recruitment and wages. Otherwise, a project may find itself providing "employment" for people who were not taken on through the normal channels.

6. *Lack of division of labor in the food processing industry.* Hotels must take into consideration the low state of technology and the division of labor in the Chinese food industry. They must make space available and provide processing facilities for, among other things, the dismemberment of entire pig carcasses and the processing of vegetables delivered with soil and dirt still clinging to them.

7. *Relatively high overhead.* With the average staffing level of Chinese hotels running at twenty-two employees per room, the higher wage bill of joint venture hotels can depress profit margins considerably.

8. *Unanticipated expenses.* Frequent changes in government or municipal funding policies can be a serious drain on joint investors. The New Century project saw costs rise considerably with the introduction of compulsory purchase of electricity bonds and the additional utilities fee.

9. *Expenses for petty gifts.* Like the Japanese, Chinese managers and officials are fond of getting presents, particularly cigarettes and liquor. Gifts of these kinds at the right time can help build better ties.

10. *Lack of horizontal coordination and problem-solving initiative.* At one point, construction work on the New Century project came to a virtual halt. When

management took up the matter with the building contractor, the company blamed the raw material supplier for its failure to deliver cement on time. The supplier blamed the cement company. The cement company cited equipment failure, and the local heavy machinery company was blamed for not providing immediate repair. In the end, the complaint had to go to a higher-level government organization, which arranged a consultation session among all ten companies involved. None of them took any initiative to break the knot before the government department took action.

Occasionally, solutions are reached rapidly when a complaint is lodged by foreigners. A solution can be reached sooner if the foreign partner takes up the matter with the authorities.

11. *Problems peculiar to Beijing.* Joint ventures in Beijing often face a unique set of problems. Beijing is by nature more conservative and bureaucratic than other cities. It has a better educated citizenry that looks down on service jobs, and it has generally no manufacturing industries of it own.

Prospects for the Future

In the early years of China's open-door policy, foreign joint venture hotels fared extremely well. They could charge high prices because there was little competition as services at Chinese-owned hotels were too poor to pose any challenge. Overhead costs were also relatively low. But the situation is changing rapidly, due mainly to four factors:

1. A large number of joint venture projects have been approved;
2. The growth in the number of foreign visitors coming to Beijing has slowed;
3. Competition from Chinese-owned hotels where services are improving is growing; and
4. Hotel construction costs are rising significantly.

As quite a few hotels were being built in preparation for the 1990 Asian Games, demand should decrease after the event. Once the building rush ends, if no further new hotels are built, the situation should improve gradually after 1993. During the slump period between 1991 and 1993, however, Beijing hotels will have to compete for guests. Survival depends on the location, service, room charge, and ability to line up tour groups from abroad. Ultimately, much will depend on how well the hotels are managed. In Beijing, as elsewhere, survival will go to "the fittest."

Currently, foreign cash reserves present no immediate problem for New Century, but with rising costs and possible low profit returns, it is doubtful whether the Japanese partners can recoup their investment within the period of the joint venture and pay off the loan within a short time. Moreover, in times of a hard currency crunch, the parent companies of the foreign partners will have to bail the project out by paying the salaries of the Japanese expatriate staff.

Possible conflict over legal interpretations may arise. It is well known that misunderstandings and gaps in perception may grow in times of difficulty. The Japanese partners involved in the New Century project are sometimes bothered by what they see as a lack of reciprocity in their relationship with the Chinese partners. The feeling that the Japanese side has not been given a fair deal in the joint venture is not understood by the Chinese partner. And it can certainly be argued that joint purpose, cooperation, and equal partnership are essential for many joint ventures.

But there are problems involving the Japanese way of conducting business too. It will be necessary for the local representatives to seek sustained cooperation and understanding from their parent companies in Japan while working to solve problems in China.

Proposals for Improvement

After two years, the Japanese partners in the New Century project point to two keys to future smooth progress. First, the Chinese partners and workers should accept that they have much to learn and get on with it. They cannot absorb the know-how and experience of the foreign partners if they insist that this and that foreign approach "won't work in China." Second, the Chinese should understand that in a budding major service industry like hotel operation and building construction they need the more experienced expatriate managers to show them proper methods and should, therefore, welcome their presence.

CASE THREE: THE BABCOCK & WILCOX BEIJING COMPANY LTD.[3]

In early August 1988, Joseph Heart, general manager of Babcock & Wilcox Beijing Company Ltd. (B&WBC), was informed by his American parent company that he would be promoted to head the international division of the parent company. As the first general manager of B&WBC, Heart had been very successful in running the joint venture. Before leaving office, Heart believed it his duty to impart to his successor the experience that he had gained in China over the past few years.

In viewing in retrospect his work as general manager of B&WBC, Heart found that there were indeed many points worth mentioning. He decided to create a memorandum emphasizing such important aspects as what kinds of problems the joint venture might encounter in the future and what possible courses of action might be taken to cope with these problems.

Company Background

B&WBC is a Sino-American equity joint venture company that manufactures boilers for power stations. Set up in 1986, the company is owned 50 percent by the Beijing Boiler Works (BBW) and 50 percent by the Babcock & Wilcox American Company (B&W). The initial investment of the joint venture totaled US $30.96 million, and its registered capital amounted to US $12 million.

Since its establishment in 1867, the Babcock & Wilcox American Company (B&W) has enjoyed a good reputation for producing high-quality boilers and auxiliary equipment. The company has fifteen plants worldwide. In the fiscal year ending March 31, 1986, the company had sales of US $1.45 billion and operating income of US $37.7 million.

B&W principally serves the electric utility industry. In the late 1980s, reduced demand for electricity, excess electricity generating capacity, environmental restraints, and financial pressures on the utility industry in the United States have resulted in a continued delay, suspension, and cancellation of steam systems. Faced with a decreasing market in the United States, the company had to explore market opportunities for its products in other countries.

In 1983, B&W began exploring the possibility of setting up a joint venture in China. Accompanied by Chinese government officials, Heart, along with other American personnel, visited the five largest boiler manufacturers in China: the Harbin Boiler Works, the Dongfang Boiler Works, the Wuhan Boiler Works, the Shanghai Boiler Works, and the Beijing Boiler Works. Among the five leading manufacturers, only the Beijing Boiler Works (BBW) was considered by B&W to be a prospective Chinese partner. Small in size and lacking in technology, BBW was eager to cooperate with B&W. The other boiler factories were not considered prospective partners because they had already introduced technical know-how from another well-known multinational corporation on a license basis. Moreover, the objective of B&W was to establish a small but viable beachhead that could be enlarged in the future as conditions permit. Heart believed that B&W, having established an operations base, could develop firsthand knowledge of the Chinese market, identify new opportunities, and actively participate in the country's growth.

Founded in 1958, BBW had 3,600 people on its payroll by 1985, including approximately 780 managerial and technical personnel. At the end of 1984, BBW had RMB 41.8 million worth of fixed assets with a net value of RMB 25.6 million. BBW was capable of producing medium pressure boilers for power stations, along with other products. However, the designs of its boilers did not include the most recent developments, and BBW had only limited contacts to keep informed about new technology in the dynamic boiler manufacturing field. Faced with ever-intensifying competition from the other four larger boiler manufacturers, BBW's top management recognized the need to upgrade technology and improve efficiency. As a result, BBW was more than willing to join forces with B&W when the latter approached BBW.

Negotiations and Approval of the Joint Venture

Negotiations for the joint venture between B&W and BBW started in May 1985. Both parties finally came to agree that the business scope of their prospective joint venture, B&WBC, would include designing, manufacturing, selling, installing, and repairing boilers for power stations, importing some necessary raw materials and spare parts, and exporting part of the finished products.

From the very beginning, top management of B&W was aware of the very important role that the Chinese government was playing in the process of negotiating and establishing the joint venture—from letter of intent to feasibility study to drafting a contract and having it approved. Since China has basically a planned economy, joint venture project proposals are usually reviewed by the government and, if approved, included in either the local or national economic plan long before contracts are signed with foreign firms.

Getting approval for a proposed project is a cumbersome process that often involves various Chinese organizations with overlapping authority and little, if any, horizontal communication and cooperation. The top management of B&W finally sent James White, a well-informed and patient liaison, to meet with various high-ranking Chinese officials. White told them that the severe shortage of electricity in China had hindered and was hindering the further development of the Chinese economy; therefore, the Chinese government should put top priority on the development of their electric utility industry to improve China's infrastructure and thereby assist in its modernization goals. As an American pioneer in boiler manufacturing for the electric utility industry, B&W was in a position to help China to modernize its boiler industry.

White's visit proved fruitful. Because of B&W's connections with relevant Chinese government organizations, the joint venture was finally approved without much difficulty. The involved government organizations included key project offices under the State Council, the Ministry of Foreign Economic Relations and Trade (MOFERT), the State Planning Commission, the State Economic Commission, the Ministry of Water Conservancy and Electric Power (MOWCEP), the Ministry of Machine Building Industry (MOMBI), and the Beijing municipal government.

Figure 9.1
Babcock & Wilcox Beijing Company Ltd., Organizational Chart

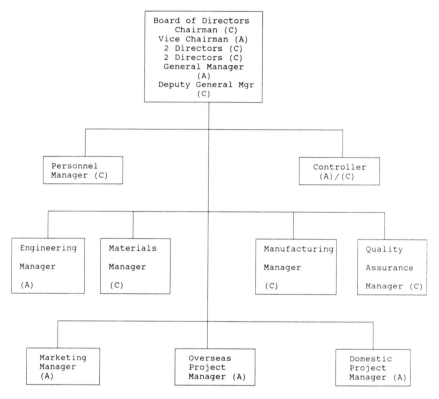

Note: Letters in parentheses are nationality marks, with "A" standing for American and "C" for Chinese.

B&WBC's Initial Operating Experience

B&WBC went into operation on August 3, 1986. Its organization followed the usual pattern for a Sino-foreign equity joint venture. The general manager, Heart, had been a long-serving marketing manager of B&W in the United States. The deputy general manager, Yang Wen, was a design engineer for BBW. Zhang Guohua, former deputy director of BBW, was the joint venture's marketing manager. Figure 9.1 shows the organizational chart of B&WBC.

The start-up phase of operations is a unique stage in the life of any enterprise in any country. Typically, the start-up period is a time when costs are high, efficiency is low, and problems are encountered and solved as the project moves along its learning or experience curve. This has certainly been the case with B&WBC.

During the initial operating stage of B&WBC, several problems surfaced. They included an inadequate supply of power, raw materials, and capital, as well as an inability to generate sufficient foreign exchange revenues to meet foreign exchange expenditures. Since these problems were virtually beyond the power of the joint venture, B&WBC turned to the Chinese government for help.

Coordinated by the State Council, several meetings were held exclusively to deal with the above-mentioned issues, presided over by a ranking government official. Leaders of relevant Chinese government organizations were called upon to solve the problems on the spot. As a result, the MOWCEP guaranteed to supply B&WBC with sufficient power, and the State Planning Commission agreed to include B&WBC in the State plan for allocation of materials. The foreign exchange of US $6 million needed by B&WBC in the first three operating years was shared by the State Economic Commission, the Ministry of Machine Building Industry, and the Beijing municipal government, each offering US $2 million.

The wage structure of a joint venture in China typically consists of a basic wage, a bonus based on performance, and a payment for various subsidies such as housing, transportation, and insurance. The basic wage and bonus usually are paid directly to the employee by the venture, while the subsidy payments are made to either the worker's unit (i.e., the Chinese partner) or the local government. B&WBC followed this general pattern. To achieve the outstanding increases in productivity, Heart used various bonus systems and strict penalties for tardiness and other unacceptable behavior. As a result, productivity increased substantially.

Since the tradition of the "iron rice bowl" (the lifetime employment system) is still strong in China, disciplining workers is difficult. During the early days of B&WBC, American managers had to take turns counting the exact number of people working in three shifts to assure that they were on the job and performing their tasks. On one occasion, Heart dismissed a workshop director for poor performance, and workers at the workshop became so angry that they went on strike.

Conflicts also occurred with regard to management salaries and other issues. Chinese managers complained that they were treated unfairly and demanded that they receive the same salary as expatriate managers under the principle of "equal pay for equal work." Heart argued, however, that Chinese managers ignored the fact that U.S. managers generally are more experienced and better qualified than their Chinese counterparts, at least during the early years of a project, and that expatriate managers require large bonuses to compensate for working abroad. Although the Chinese partners later agreed to pay higher salaries to American managers, the

issue remains unsolved. Jealous of the American's living in high-grade
hotels, higher salaries, private cars, and other privileges, the Chinese
managers are still disgruntled at the high cost of maintaining expatriates
at B&WBC.

At the onset, Chinese managers and some of the workers held an adverse attitude toward the American managers' methods. They complained
that American managers were too aggressive and impatient, while American managers complained of Chinese dilatoriness and irresponsibility.
Chinese managers would inform American counterparts that in China
more haste means less speed, while American managers would attempt
to persuade their Chinese counterparts to think that time is money. Initially morale at B&WBC was quite low. Workers evaluated Chinese managers by a simple standard: whoever quarreled with Americans the most
aggressively would be considered comrade in arms, and whoever coop-
erated with the Americans would be nicknamed "Er Gui Zi" (fake foreigners).

Initially, American managers at B&WBC found that Chinese workers
lacked responsibility and initiative and were unaccustomed to using their
own judgment to solve problems. Hygiene and preventative maintenance
were often neglected by workers. To improve worker performance,
B&WBC spent much time and effort on training and motivating the work
force. In addition to instituting bonus schemes, work rules, and other
material incentive systems, B&WBC strived to give both workers and
managers a sense of self-respect and dignity and continually urged them
to take more responsibility and pride in their work. Consequently, workers
were happy about their high wages. The clean factory and other facilities
also won employee approval. Although workers had difficulty becoming
accustomed to the new rules, such as one hour instead of two for lunch,
a "loving-your-company" spirit was developing. A Chinese employee at
B&WBC once said, "The first time I got my pay from the joint venture
company, I was surprised to find it had almost doubled. I told myself that
I'd better behave well. I have witnessed the remarkable change in this
factory. What the joint venture achieved in one year in terms of output
increases and quality improvements could not have been accomplished
by the Chinese themselves in five or even ten years. Now I regard working
for the company as my glory."

Materials Sourcing

Presently, there are two sets of parallel price systems for raw materials
in China, the State plan price and the market price. Materials sourced
inside the planning system are purchased at State plan prices, which are
always lower than market prices. Materials sourced outside the planning
system, on the other hand, are usually purchased on a contract basis at

a price negotiated between the supplier and the buyer. Joint ventures that source production inputs in China obtain them through a variety of channels. Some ventures are included in the State plan for allocation of materials, while others are not.

The key factor in being included in the State plan is the strength of the relationship ("guanxi") the joint venture or its Chinese partner's organization enjoys with the planning authorities, which often depends on how important the venture is to the central or local government. B&WBC receives 50 percent of its production inputs through State plan allocation due to the support of the State Planning Commission and the Beijing municipal government.

However, a State plan allocation does not necessarily mean that materials will be obtained. Allocations are merely an authorization to buy from State supply bureaus and do not guarantee the actual supply of materials. High-quality materials are often in short supply, and enterprises with allocations must compete for them. Purchasing through the State allocation plan involves following the procedures of the State Planning Commission, the State Bureau of Supplies and Materials, the local municipality, and the local bureau of machinery. With so many government organizations with which to deal, bureaucratic problems often arise.

China's bureaucracy is characterized by personal rule at the top, with a fragmented, segmented, and stratified organization below. Each bureaucratic unit exists in a particular hierarchy, and the various units do not readily cooperate with units outside their chain of command. Horizontal communication is practically nonexistent, and the ability to transcend bureaucratic boundaries is enjoyed only by the leadership. Cooperation at lower levels depends on the relationship ("guanxi") and the ability to bargain for what is wanted.

The bureaucracy can influence a joint venture's operations in a variety of ways. Control over materials, labor, utilities, and other key factors provides the opportunity for direct influence. The vague wording of most of China's laws, compounded by the possibility of varying interpretations and applications by officials, also allows for considerable bureaucratic influence. If there is no overt interference in a plant's operations, officials can create difficulties through less direct methods—even in as trivial an issue as controlling visa approvals for training overseas. Because of their involvement in day-to-day activities, bureaucrats at low levels can especially frustrate operations.

Zhao Weiming, the manager responsible for purchasing materials at B&WBC, complained that some bureaucracies often set obstacles to the joint venture. For instance, all materials purchased by B&WBC have to be delivered to the warehouse of a local bureau of machinery before they can be picked up by B&WBC. In doing so, the local bureau of machinery can charge B&WBC additional money for storage and management fees.

On the average, B&WBC's annual demand for steel is about 50,000 tons, of which 30 to 40 percent needs to be imported because it is either unavailable in China or cannot be found at required quality levels and specifications. Because of the close relationship between B&WBC and the planning authorities, B&WBC is allowed to use RMB to purchase imported materials brought in under the State plan. Purchasing imported materials through State plan allocation, however, frequently causes delays.

According to Zhao, it takes on the average more than ten months for B&WBC to obtain imported materials after placing an order. Even once the delayed materials finally do arrive, they usually cannot be used immediately because different phases of production and different products require different materials. This often leads to unnecessary inventory and a waste of time and materials. Zhao said,

> If we imported materials directly from foreign suppliers, we would have to spend only four to five months to get the materials, and the time of delivery would be guaranteed. The waste of time and materials could thus be avoided. Of course, it all depends on whether or not we can get enough foreign exchange through our export efforts in the future. Right now, we have only limited hard currency, so we have to rely on the State plan allocations for a long time. That means we must do everything possible to keep on good terms with the bureaucracy. By and large, our company has done a good job at that.

Heart learned quickly how to deal with the bureaucracy. He often invited high-ranking officials to play golf with him so that he could build close relationships with these VIPs. According to Heart, to effectively deal with China's bureaucracy, a joint venture should tactfully use both the carrot and the stick. Strong support from a central government ministry or top-level official can contribute to the smoothness of relations and a venture's ability to solve problems. Equally important is the need to identify and become acquainted with the key members of the bureaucratic units with which the joint venture must deal. The value of a good relationship with local officials cannot be stressed enough.

Technology Transfer

Why are U.S. companies investing in China? The answer is simple—the lure of the Chinese market. The owners of U.S. companies believe that investing is the best way to gain access to the Chinese market, either now or in the long term. As can be expected, this motivation is in conflict with Chinese motivations for attracting foreign investment. The Chinese goals for joint ventures are to acquire modern technology and managerial skills to develop the Chinese economy and to earn foreign exchange through the development of export industries. This basic conflict—the foreign partner seeks market access while the Chinese partner seeks advanced technology and exports—is responsible for some of the problems and misunderstandings in B&WBC's operating experience.

As stipulated in the contract, the technology transfer by B&W, the American parent company, should embody the following five aspects:

1. Eight licensed products;
2. Trademark of B&W;
3. Twenty-five technologies, including six design technologies, one automatic control technology, two technology standards, one technology on equipment's purchase, maintenance, and installation, four technologies on purchasing materials, one technology on both boiler adjustment and testing, and seven other technologies;
4. Sixty-nine engineering handbooks; and
5. Thirty-one patents.

These technologies were priced at US $1.2 million; an additional US $500,000 as threshold expense and 3 percent of the selling price as royalty fee were paid to B&W.

Yang Wen, deputy general manager of B&WBC, who has an engineering background, has been dissatisfied with the American attitude toward technology transfer. In his opinion, the American partner lacked sincerity in offering the latest state-of-the-art technology. Yang commented, "The Americans are holding back secrets. To get the most advanced technology out of these stingy Americans, we have no alternative but to fight." His view is shared by Zheng Gang, deputy engineering manager, who said, "Americans are reluctant to help us design new products such as 300 mw boilers, because they are unwilling to see us become their future competitor in the world market. But that's the goal we have been pursuing for so many years. No fights, no gains. My idea is to keep fighting against the Americans for their new technology until we acquire the most advanced technology and become full-fledged. By that time, we can say bye-bye to our American partner."

However, American managers at B&WBC held a different view with regard to the issue of technology transfer. David Dirkson, the resident American engineering manager, said, "In my view, what the Chinese lack most are effective management skills and talent. As for technology, it is absolutely important, but before the management problem gets solved, too much emphasis on transferring up-to-date technology would be of little significance. One must always keep in mind that technology should be compatible with its environment, people who use the technology, management of the people, and market conditions."

Another reason for the Americans' reluctance to transfer technology is China's notoriously inadequate security measures for preventing the illegal proliferation of transferred technology. As Heart pointed out, "Our Chinese partner always complains about being inadequate in technology security measures. I catch sight of our Chinese competitors coming in and going out of our company from time to time."

Heart agreed with Dirkson that management is a far more important issue to be addressed at B&WBC than technology transfer. He thinks that the existing management is less than adequate. Right now there are eight Americans working in the joint venture. Heart intended to have more qualified American managers, but the strong opposition from the Chinese partner concerning the high cost of maintaining expatriates prevented him from doing so. However, when the joint venture elects not to use the state personnel agency to hire, the shortage of qualified management personnel and the problems associated with a local transfer make it rather difficult to acquire new talent within China.

If suitable candidates are found in China, they are invariably attached to another unit or organization that naturally wants to retain its qualified personnel. More often than not, the prospective employee's unit refuses to allow a candidate to transfer freely. Some units refused a transfer outright while others allowed the transfer only after a payment from the joint venture (say, RMB 20,000), creating a sort of "free agent compensation" system for skilled workers in China.

Heart once contracted some MBA students in China who had studied international business management and could communicate with American managers without the language barrier, but he was unable to hire them for a number of reasons. One reason was that those MBA students were assigned by the State upon their graduation. Another reason was that the Chinese partner simply could not accept the practice of promoting from the outside, which was considered contrary to China's time-honored tradition of promoting from within.

Employee transfer is also impeded by the fact that most joint ventures do not provide housing for their workers. Employees supplied by the Chinese partner or local labor bureau will be able to stay in the housing they occupy, but employees hired independently by the joint venture give up the housing supplied by their original unit. Therefore, job candidates are often unwilling to transfer to a joint venture unless housing is provided.

Heart complained that middle management was particularly weak. Part of the problem is that the age group to which most middle managers belong is that group whose education was disrupted during the Cultural Revolution (from 1966 to 1976). Another factor is that managerial appointments are often made on the basis of political connections as opposed to skills. A third contributing factor is that the Western aggressive management style conflicts with the Marxist concept of "workers first." This concept is so deep-rooted in people's minds that Heart found it hard to get managers to push workers and that workers often do not respect managers.

Marketing

Prior to the establishment of B&WBC, Beijing Boiler Works (BBW) was only capable of producing 25 mw (milliwatt) boilers due to outdated equipment and technology. Now the joint venture can produce 200 mw and 300 mw boilers of superior quality, thanks to a greater use of imported materials and better production and managerial expertise brought in by the American partner.

Most products produced by B&WBC have been sold in China for RMB. The major reason the joint venture is making RMB sales is that it cannot yet successfully compete for foreign exchange sales in either the export or domestic market. Any profits earned at this early stage of the project's life are to be reinvested in the venture. B&WBC's financial statements for 1986, 1987, and 1988 are shown in Table 9.1.

Generally speaking, joint venture products sold on the domestic market are subject to the industrial and commercial consolidated tax, a turnover tax on goods passing through the raw material to manufactured to finished goods cycle. B&WBC was awarded a three-year tax exemption in 1986 because it was treated as an enterprise with advanced technology. At the same time, a higher price subsidy was granted to B&WBC than was given to other domestic boiler manufacturers such as the Harbin Boiler Works, the Dongfang Boiler Works, the Shanghai Boiler Works, and the Wuhan Boiler Works. In spite of such favorable treatment, the costs of B&WBC's products are still higher than comparable Chinese products because of higher labor costs, higher design costs, imported materials, and expatriate expenses.

Compared with domestic competitors, B&WBC has many features unique to its products, such as higher reliability and longer product life. However, many Chinese customers do not seem to be willing to pay a premium for the higher quality and superior features. Zhang Guohua, marketing manager of B&WBC, was upset by the situation. He said,

In China, everybody is supposed to be concerned about national interest because China is a socialist country. But in practice many Chinese people are not responsible at all. Take our boilers as an example. Though they are better in performance and stability and have a longer life span, they often do not appeal to Chinese purchasers. Many Chinese purchasing people only consider the price and not the performance and other factors. It is quite common in China that everything is OK so long as the purchased equipment can start operation after having been installed. As for later breakdowns, it

Table 9.1

B&WBC Income Statements as of December 31, 1986, 1987, and 1988 (In Thousands RMB)

	1986	1987	1988
Sales	22,022	230,218	238,783
Cost of sales	18,330	215,442	206,512
Gross Margin	3,692	14,776	32,271
Expenses:			
Selling expenses	94	103	0
General and administrative expenses	5,304	21,138	24,138
Total Expenses	5,398	21,605	24,138
Profit on sales	-1,706	-6,829	8,133
Add: Other Income	359	4,002	9,131
Operating Income	-1,347	-2,827	17,264
Add: Non-operating income	4	115	101
Less: Non-operating expenses	7	960	636
Net Profit	-1,350	-3,672	16,729

Assets	1986	1987	1988
Current Assets:			
Cash	37,392	9,253	7,805
Accounts receivable	3,956	41,237	90,051
Prepayment to supplies	7,101	3,066	4,232
Other receivables	18,761	2,864	7,609
Prepaid expenses	110	784	0
Inventory	113,243	141,026	209,506
Total Current Assets	180,563	198,230	319,203
Property, plant & equipment (net value)	37,705	78,808	78,758
Other Fixed Assets	12,367	14,366	12,877
Total fixed assets	50,072	93,174	91,635
Total Assets	230,635	391,404	410,838
Liabilities & Capital			
Current Liabilities:			
Accounts payable	59,274	64,340	85,480
Advances from customers	35,514	63,008	121,376
Other payable	62,262	45,715	64,072
Total Current Liabilities	157,050	173,063	270,928
Long term debt	38,962	88,320	96,288
Paid-in-capital	36,853	36,853	50,923
Retained earnings	-2,230	-6,832	2,699
Total Liabilities & Capital	230,635	291,404	410,838

is not the responsibility of the person in charge of the purchasing. Obviously, China's irrational economic system is to blame.

In China, the production and selling of large electricity generating equipment are regulated by the government. While boilers smaller than 200 mw are subject to market regulations, the prices for those larger than 200 mw (including 200 mw) are set by three government organizations. The process begins with the Ministry of Water Conservancy and Electric Power, which represents the interests of end users, negotiating a price with the Ministry of Machinery Building Industry, which represents the interests of producers. This tentative price is finally subject to the review and approval of the State Administration of Prices.

NOTES

1. *Jetro China Newsletter*, no. 79 (March-April 1989): pp. 9–14, reprinted with permission.

2. *Jetro China Newsletter*, no. 80 (May-June 1989): pp. 18–25, reprinted with permission.

3. All personal names have been changed. The author is solely responsible for the summaries, paraphrases, and quotations attributed to specific personalities in the case. This case was prepared by Wang Zhengyuan under the supervision of Professor Gao Guopei. Gao Zailang helped in collecting materials. The author appreciates the cooperation rendered by Babcock and Wilcox Beijing Company Limited and the University of International Business and Economics. The case is intended only to be a vehicle for discussion and is not to illustrate the effective or ineffective handling of an administrative situation. Published by permission.

10

Outlook for Foreign Direct Investment in China

The dilemma of the 1990s will be how quickly Chinese leaders can convince foreign investors that business conditions have stabilized and improved within the People's Republic. The challenge for the Chinese leadership is to develop long-term strategies designed to move ahead with economic reform while at the same time preventing social unrest and inflation from bringing chaos. The question remains, will China's leaders be able to bring back the momentum of 1987 through June 1989, whereby investment and trade boomed, without making radical changes in the political environment. Sustained growth in foreign investment during the 1990s will not move forward without returning to the reforms, which were abandoned in mid–1989, and correcting internal business practices and further enhancing the investment climate.

It is important to note that the austerity program, which limited loans and credits, slowed but did not fully destroy the foreign investment momentum. In so doing, China reversed the decentralization of decision-making authority at the provincial and local levels, centralizing more authority in Beijing. While a degree of recentralization was deemed necessary to curb inflation and to channel financial resources (loans and bank guarantees) and scarce materials into projects that were fulfilling national needs, as well as to stop unnecessary, luxury imports from entering the Chinese marketplace, the leadership apparently overreacted.

INVESTMENT PERFORMANCE

Even with the negative impact resulting from the events of June 1989, China has been successful in attracting foreign investment during the initial period of the open-door policy. Almost 26,000 foreign investment contracts have been signed since 1979, and committed investment has reached nearly US $37 million. As noted in chapter 5, equity joint ventures have numbered more than half of the total investment while contractual joint ventures have accounted for approximately almost one third. At the same time, approximately 1,600 wholly foreign-owned enterprises have been established and 59 offshore oil ventures undertaken. These investments have contributed significantly to China's modernization efforts in all sectors of the economy through capital inflows, transfer of technology and managerial expertise, and the expansion of the export base and market.

At the initial phase of the open-door policy, foreign investors preferred contractual joint ventures as a means to enter the Chinese market. As companies gained experience and confidence, interest shifted toward equity investment. From 1985 onward, the number of equity joint ventures has far outpaced those of a contractual nature. While increasing in number, equity joint venture investments tended to be small and averaged less than US $1.5 million, according to data supplied by the Ministry of Foreign Economic Relations and Trade. Asian venture investments, excluding those of Japan and Korea, tend to have a longer life span than those of the United States, Europe, and Australia. Since 1987, South Asian investments have tended to range from twenty-nine to sixty years, whereas those for the United States fall primarily in the ten-to-twenty-year time frame.

While many of the difficulties that exist for foreign equity investments in China can be placed at the doorstep of Chinese authorities, including inadequate legislation, mishandling of the economy, and internal political struggles that cause policies to vacillate, it should be noted that part of the problem has been the naiveté of many Chinese government officials in dealing with the West and with the foreign investors themselves. One must realize that most government officials have been "feeling their way" during the past eleven years of the open-door policy. They will be the first to admit that many mistakes were made as they attempted to move the Chinese economy forward.

There have also been problems that the foreign investors have brought upon themselves. Like their Chinese counterparts, foreign investors have little experience in working in centrally planned economies and virtually none had any experience in China whatsoever prior to the open-door policy. Pioneer investors will also admit that they made too many assumptions, took too much for granted, and were often overly optimistic. One of the most unrealistic assumptions made by Western investors was in terms of the profitability of operations. Having watched the dramatic growth that took place in other Asian economies, they assumed that this would also be the case in China. Furthermore, many believed that once they established operations in China, the Chinese marketplace would automatically open to them. Often their actions were based on impulse rather than on realistic foresight and sound planning.

Managers of many foreign equity joint ventures, made erroneous judgments concerning their partner's ability to secure necessary financing, purchase raw materials, and resolve problems as they arose. The prudent investors, however, either made sure that there were alternative sources of financing or that exports would provide the hard currency necessary to fund operations and provide for repatriation of profits or both.

An equally complicating factor has been the lack of support given by the foreign partner's headquarters to equity joint venture operations in China. A common joke is that no sooner would the ink be dry on the contract, than the U.S. headquarters would be asking about the projected profitability impact on its next quarterly report. Instead of looking toward the long-term viability of the project, emphasis would be placed on short-term returns.

For many foreign companies doing business in China, there has and continues to be a lack of cultural understanding. Not only has this led to a misinterpretation of official statements but to a basic lack of understanding of Chinese culture in a socialist setting. A promise is not a promise to be fulfilled, a "yes" is not necessarily an agreement and understanding, and what is written into law does not always agree with practice. Exacerbating the problem is the fact that many firms chose to use consultants who, because of the foreign managers' naiveté and unfamiliarity with China, misled them. As a result, time was wasted, funds spent unnecessarily, and both progress and profitability delayed.

Furthermore, some firms' reputations suffered in China because of the actions of their foreign consultants who, in many cases, were either of Chinese extraction or had sold themselves as well-connected and informed China consultants. In fact, many of these individuals or consultancy groups led the unsuspecting foreigner to the wrong partner, to the wrong location, or to the wrong type of agreement. These consultants also have added to the corruption problems as they found it expedient to bribe officials to obtain favorable treatment for their clients.

It must be remembered that for every firm that did place an investment in China, there were thousands that explored the Chinese market but did not get to the contract stage. In some cases, they were perhaps better off than if they had signed an agreement, but in many other cases, an opportunity for long-term profitability was missed.

POLITICAL RISK

Investing in any developing country assumes a greater degree of country risk than investing in developed countries. China is no exception. Furthermore, forecasting and managing country risk is never precise.

China is not considered a highly rated country politically by either conventional methods or by financial publications such as *Euro Money* or *Institutional Investor*. The primary reason is that China is a centrally administered nation with differing political philosophies, systems, and structures from those in the West. Some observers believe that in this type of political setting government intervention in political life and in business operations is too aggressive. Therefore, there is a greater likelihood that the government may intervene in foreign investment operations when it is politically expedient, without considering the consequences of intervention to the foreign investor or the outside world. As a result, the probability that foreign investment might be nationalized by the government could remain high.

On the other hand, it can be argued that the likelihood of nationalization in China is not as strong as it might appear. Since 1949, for example, China has not nationalized any foreign investments and certainly did not do so in the period following the Tiananmen Square incident. Shortly after the People's Republic of China was established, the leadership only ordered the branches of foreign banks to leave China. Further, it did so without seizing the foreign banks' assets. Moreover, since 1979 the government has not altered its stance on encouraging foreign investment.

Another factor influencing country risks in China is its relationship with Hong Kong and Taiwan. Although signals are mixed, China is attempting to set good examples and to offer excellent benefits to investors from both economies to demonstrate its sincerity about further liberalization. Any action, such as nationalization or expropriation, would greatly damage China's efforts to unify the nation in the future, as well as drive away any third country investments.

Some social problems in China are also worth consideration. As income levels increase, the issue of the unfairness of income distribution continues to rise. Not only do intellectuals and office workers maintain that they are earning less than farmers and workers, but income gaps are widening in different geographical locations. Workers in coastal areas receive higher pay than workers in the inner regions of the country and unless this issue is resolved, social unrest may be unavoidable.

A related problem concerns inflation. Although Chinese authorities reduced inflation from in excess of 35 percent during 1988 and early 1989 to less than 10 percent in 1990 through the austerity program, a question remains as to how authorities will manage to resume and sustain economic growth without igniting inflationary pressures.

An additional problem is the corruption of some government officials, who use their positions and power to benefit themselves at the expense of the public interest. The public continues to complain that many high officials and/or their children take advantage of their positions and privileges to make money either improperly or illegally. This problem is hurting public confidence in the government, the Chinese political system, and even the economic reforms taking place. Many individuals complain that they were better off before economic reforms took place. If proper measures are not taken to overcome these issues, unrest may well arise in the foreseeable future.

Economic factors may provide an even more complicated picture for investors analyzing country risk in China. China is the largest market in terms of population. It is a country with abundant natural resources that can very well be utilized for generating foreign exchange earnings when needed. On economic policy issues, China has a firm commitment to its modernization programs, to its open-door policy, to foreign direct investment in the country, and to other international economic cooperation programs. Based on these facts, China will likely go forward with its present economic policies and further expand the role of market forces in economic development. In striving to modernize, China will continue to import large amounts of technology, machinery, and other capital goods, as well as daily consumer products. Whether China will be able to generate adequate foreign currency earnings to finance all these expensive imports, in addition to repaying its external borrowings, remains an issue. Furthermore, it remains to be seen whether China will be able to honor its foreign debt obligations that will become due prior to 1995.

IMPROVING THE CLIMATE FOR FOREIGN INVESTMENT IN CHINA

The future of China will depend, to a large degree, on what happens politically and economically during the first five years of the 1990s. Not only will the leadership have to give indications of positive, forward movement and stability, but there must be further refinement of legislation concerning foreign investment. Refinements will need to be made with respect to the types of investments that will be encouraged and given priority. Streamlining the bureaucracy is essential to assure investors that negotiations will always proceed expeditiously and that those responsible for negotiations have full power to do so.

Foreign investment laws per se must be examined. In most cases, the two-year tax holiday is not competitive with those of other foreign countries. For those industries that meet China's requirements, selectivity should be used to extend the period for a longer duration. Furthermore, there should be more flexibility in terms of which industries should have an opportunity to sell on the local market and to what degree. The legal environment must be further improved.

While it is anticipated that China's long-awaited copyright law will be enacted by the standing committee of the National People's Congress in the near future, many of the loopholes must be tightened. This also applies to patent and trademark legislation. Until investors are assured that piracy will not occur, no amount of encouragement from the government will attract foreign investors to the Chinese market.

The authorities must recognize that China is not a low labor cost country even though the average worker's take-home pay is indeed low. First, although foreign firms supposedly have the right to hire employees from the open market, most firms must go through the official government bureau (FESCO) to hire personnel at wage rates that are unrealistic. When this is done, only a small portion of the wages and salaries paid goes to the individual employee; the remaining 85 to 90 percent is paid to the Chinese government. Although the Shanghai government is showing signs of altering this policy, the central government has not.

The second problem lies in the hidden cost that foreign companies must incur on behalf of their Chinese employees. In addition to wages and salaries, one must also add bonuses, insurance, and contributions to labor unions. Even more significant is the fact that in most cases housing must be provided, and this has the effect of tripling labor costs. Furthermore, unless desirable housing is provided, foreign firms do not have the ability to attract the most qualified and productive employees.

The third labor problem is inherent within the Chinese system itself. For the most part, Chinese workers and managers alike lack both the training and experience necessary to be productive in the workplace. The Chinese leadership must understand that joint ventures are not schools but are business entities and must earn a profit. Consequently, the educational system in China must be revamped and more appropriate training provided. The quality of faculty in most business schools and training institutes must be upgraded and curricula focused on Western management, financial, production, and accounting and control procedures to ensure that graduates possess the basic entry-level skills that are needed by industry.

In addition, the work ethic of Chinese employees must be improved. Western firms are plagued by absenteeism, inefficiency in the workplace, and dereliction of duty. Many employees will use any excuse, such as attending school or illness, to be absent from work when in reality they may have a second job. When on the job, many tend to sit around and drink tea, visit with fellow employees, or read a newspaper. Secretaries are not well trained, have poor telephone etiquette, and are rude to both customers and fellow employees. In addition, many Chinese managers develop cliques, creating a communication gap between themselves and the foreign partners. Thus, they do not share information, a practice that inhibits performance. A part of the problem may be attributed to the fact that the Chinese compensation system does not provide financial incentives for employees by rewarding positive performance. The remainder results from vestiges of the old system of Chinese management, which is still prevalent in government organizations, that focuses on the quantity of personnel employed, not on the quality of their output.

The issue of conflicts of interest between joint ventures and the Chinese government must also be addressed. For example, both Chinese partners and labor unions tend to set unrealistically low production goals in order to ensure bonuses. Furthermore, they often attempt to influence the choice of component parts and raw materials suppliers, focusing on cost rather than quality. Also, government bureaus tend to withhold important information, which prevents performance. Laws are passed but are not translated and made public quickly. Important geological surveys are undertaken and the information is not shared with foreign investor companies. Tax laws change so often that managers do not know how to plan and function accordingly. Unless these issues are addressed, the resulting conflicts will further prevent investors from coming to China, as well as continue to hinder the profit performance of existing operations.

Many joint venture firms scaled back production considerably in 1989 and 1990. In some cases, this situation may be attributed to the austerity program and erratic supplies of needed manufacturing inputs; however, a major cause is uncertainty. Combined with the overall downturn in demand within the global economy, companies are in a wait-and-see mode until the situation in China has stabilized and the Chinese government clearly indicates its position on foreign investment for the 1990s.

Consequently, clear-cut policies must be set quickly to assure that the open-door policy will continue, and positive action must be taken to correct the problems that inhibit foreign ventures' performance in China. The longer that China remains partially isolated from the rest of the world, the greater the gap that will emerge between China and other developing nations that are now making rapid progress in upgrading their economies and attracting foreign investment inflows. Most foreign firms already have excess plant capacity in their existing facilities, as well as the ability to place future investments in almost any country in the world.

Maintaining the open-door policy and opening the Chinese market further to foreign investors is essential if future investment inflows are to be attracted. Recent moves by the Soviet Union and other Eastern European countries to open their markets and industries to foreign investment, permitting 100 percent ownership of both factories and land, provide an attractive alternative for foreign investors. They add to the host of nations offering incentives that already have caused many firms to seek investments elsewhere than in China. The big push by foreign firms is now to get a foothold in the unified and rapidly expanding European community before 1993. As a consequence, the Chinese leadership must think hard and act fast if it is even going to make minimal progress toward its modernization goals for the year 2000 and beyond.

APPENDIX I

Sample Contract and Articles of Association for Joint Ventures Using Chinese and Foreign Investment

Sample Contract for Joint Ventures Using Chinese and Foreign Investment

CHAPTER 1. GENERAL PROVISIONS

In accordance with the Law of the People's Republic of China on Joint Ventures Using Chinese and Foreign Investment and other relevant Chinese laws and regulations, ———— Company and ———— Company, adhering to the principle of equality and mutual benefit and through friendly consultations, agree to jointly establish a joint venture enterprise in ———— the People's Republic of China. The contract hereunder is agreed upon.

CHAPTER 2. PARTIES OF THE JOINT VENTURE

Article 1

Parties of this contract are as follows: ———— Company (hereafter referred to as Party A), registered with ———— in China, and its legal address is at ———— (street) ———— (district) ———— (city) ———— China.

Legal representative:

Name:

Position:

Nationality:

———— Company (hereinafter referred to as Party B), registered with ————. Its legal address at ————.

Legal representative:

    Name:

    Position:

    Nationality:

Note: In case there are more than two investors, they will be called Party C, D . . . in proper order.

CHAPTER 3. ESTABLISHMENT OF THE JOINT VENTURE COMPANY

Article 2

In accordance with the Law of the People's Republic of China on Joint Ventures Using Chinese and Foreign Investment and other relevant Chinese laws and regulations, both parties of the joint venture agree to set up ———— joint venture limited liability company (hereafter referred to as the joint venture company.)

Article 3

The name of the joint venture company is ———— Limited Liability Company.

The name in foreign language is ————.

The legal address of the joint venture company is at ———— (street) ————(city) ———— (province).

Article 4

All activities of the joint venture company shall be governed by the laws, decrees, and pertinent rules and regulations of the People's Republic of China.

Article 5

The organizational form of the joint venture company is a limited liability company. Each party to the joint venture company is liable to the joint venture company within the limit of the capital subscribed by said party. The profits, risks, and losses of the joint venture company shall be shared by the parties in proportion to their contributions of the registered capital.

CHAPTER 4. THE PURPOSE, SCOPE, AND SCALE OF PRODUCTION AND BUSINESS

Article 6

The purpose of the parties to the joint venture is in conformity with the wish to enhance the economic cooperation and technical exchanges, to improve the product quality, develop new products, and gain competitive position in the world market in quality and price by adopting advanced and appropriate technology and scientific management methods, so as to raise the economic results and ensure satisfactory economic benefits for each investor.

Note: This article shall be written according to the specific situations in the contract.

Article 7

The productive and business scope of the joint venture company is to produce ——— products, provide maintenance service after the sale of the products, and study and develop new products.
Note: To be written in the contract according to the specific conditions.

Article 8

The production scale of the joint venture company is as follows:

1. The production capacity after the joint venture begins operations is ———.

2. The production scale may be increased up to ——— with the development of pro-duction and operations. The product varieties may be developed into ———.

Note: To be written according to the specific situation.

CHAPTER 5. TOTAL AMOUNT OF INVESTMENT AND THE REGISTERED CAPITAL

Article 9

The total amount of investment of the joint venture company is RMB ——— (or foreign currency agreed upon by both parties).

Article 10

Investment contributed by the parties is RMB ———,which will be the regis-tered capital of the joint venture company.
Of which: Party A shall pay ——— RMB, accounts for ———%; Party B shall pay ——— RMB, accounts for ———%.

Article 11

Both Party A and Party B will contribute the following as their investment:

Party A:

cash ——— RMB

machines and equipment ——— RMB

premises ——— RMB

the right to the use of the site ——— RMB

industrial property ——— RMB

others ——— RMB

——— Total investment in RMB

Party B:

cash ——— RMB

machines and equipment ——— RMB

industrial property ——— RMB

others ——— RMB

——— Total investment in RMB

Note: When contributing capital goods or industrial property as an investment, Party A and Party B shall conclude a separate contract to be a part of this main contract.

Article 12

The registered capital of the joint venture company shall be paid in ——— installments by Party A and Party B according to the respective proportion of their investment.

Each installment shall be as follows:

Note: To be written according to the specific conditions.

Article 13

In case any party to the joint venture intends to assign all or part of its investment subscribed to a third party, consent shall be obtained from the other party to the joint venture, and approval from the examination and approval authority is required.

When one party to the joint venture assigns all or part of its investment, the other party has preemptive right.

CHAPTER 6. RESPONSIBILITIES OF EACH PARTY TO THE JOINT VENTURE

Article 14

Party A and Party B shall be responsible respectively for the following matters:

Responsibilities of Party A:

Handling of applications for approval, registration, business license, and other matters concerning the establishment of the joint venture company with the relevant departments in charge of China;

Processing the application for the right to the use of a site with the authority in charge of the land;

Organizing the design and construction of the premises and other engineering facilities of the joint venture company;

Providing cash, machinery and equipment, and premises—in accordance with the stipulations in article 11;

Assisting Party B in processing import customs declarations for the machinery and equipment contributed by Party B as investment and arranging the transportation within the Chinese territory;

Assisting the joint venture company in purchasing or leasing equipment, materials, raw materials, articles for office use, means of transportation, communication facilities and so on;

Assisting the joint venture company in contacting and arranging for fundamental facilities, such as water, electricity, transportation, and so on;

Assisting the joint venture in recruiting Chinese management personnel, technical personnel, workers, and other needed personnel;

Assisting foreign workers and staff in applying for entry visas, work licenses, and in processing their travel documents;

Responsible for handling other matters entrusted by the joint venture company.

Responsibilities of Party B:

Providing cash, machinery, equipment, and industrial property—in accordance with the stipulations in article 11—shipping capital goods, such as machinery and equipment to the Chinese port, that have been contributed as investment;

Handling the matters entrusted by the joint venture company, such as selecting and purchasing machinery and equipment outside of China, and so on;

Providing the needed technical personnel for the installation, testing, and trial production of the equipment, as well as for production and inspection;

Training technical personnel and workers of the joint venture company;

In the case where Party B is the licensor, it shall be responsible for the stable production of qualified products by the joint venture company based on the design capacity within the stipulated period; and

Responsible for other matters entrusted by the joint venture company.

Note: To be written according to the specific situation.

CHAPTER 7. TRANSFER OF TECHNOLOGY

Article 15

Both Party A and Party B agree that a technology transfer agreement shall be signed between the joint venture company and Party B (or a third party) so as to obtain the advanced production technology needed for realizing the production scale stipulated in chapter 4 of the contract, including product design, manufacturing technology, means of testing, material prescription, standard of quality, and the training of personnel.

Note: To be written according to the specific conditions.

Article 16

Party B offers the following guarantees on the transfer of technology:

Note: This article applies only when Party B is responsible for transferring technology to the joint venture company.

1. Party B guarantees that the overall technology, such as the design, technological processes, tests, and inspection of products will be integrated, precise, and reliable. It is to satisfy the requirements of the joint venture's operation purpose and be able to meet the quality standards and production capacity stipulated in the contract;

2. Party B guarantees that the technology stipulated in this contract and the technology transfer agreement shall be fully transferred to the joint venture company and pledges that the technology provided should be truly advanced;

3. Party B shall compile a detailed list of the technology provided and technological services at various stages, as stipulated in the technology transfer agreement, which will be an appendix to the contract and a guarantee of its performance;

4. The drawings, technological conditions, and other detailed information are part of the transferred technology and shall be offered on time;

5. Within the validity period of the technology transfer agreement, Party B shall provide the joint venture company with improvements on the technology and the improved information and technological materials in time, and it shall not charge separate fees; and

6. Party B shall guarantee that the technological personnel and the workers in the joint venture company can master all of the technology transferred within the period stipulated in the technology transfer agreement.

Article 17

In case Party B fails to provide equipment and technology in accordance with the stipulations in this contract and in the technology transfer agreement or in case any deceiving or concealing actions are found, Party B shall be responsible for compensating the direct losses to the joint venture company.

Article 18

The technology transfer fee shall be paid in royalties. The royalty rate shall be ———% of the net sales value of the products produced.

The term for royalty payment is the same as the term for technology transfer agreement stipulated in article 19 of this contract.

Article 19

The term for the technology transfer agreement signed by the joint venture company and Party B is ——— years. After the expiration of the technology transfer agreement, the joint venture company shall have the right to use, research, and develop the imported technology continuously.

Note: The term for a technology transfer agreement is generally no longer than ten years, and it shall be approved by the Ministry of Foreign Economic Relations and Trade or by other examination and approval authorities entrusted by the Ministry of Foreign Economic Relations and Trade.

CHAPTER 8. SELLING OF PRODUCTS

Article 20

The products of the joint venture company will be sold both on the Chinese market and on the overseas market, the export part accounts for ———%, with ———% for the domestic market.

Note: An annual percentage and amount for outside and inside selling will be written out according to practical situations. In normal conditions, the amount for export shall at least meet the needs of foreign exchange expenses of the joint venture company.

Article 21

Products may be sold in overseas markets through the following channels:

The joint venture company may sell its products directly in international markets, which will account for ———% of production;

The joint venture company may sign sales contracts with Chinese foreign trade companies, entrusting them to be a sales agent or exclusive sales agencies, which may account for ———%; and

The joint venture company may entrust Party B to sell its products, which may account for ———%.

Article 22

The joint venture's products to be sold in China may be handled by the Chinese materials and commercial departments by means of agency or exclusive sales, or they may be sold by the joint venture company directly.

Article 23

In order to provide maintenance service for the products sold both in China or abroad, the joint venture company may set up sales branches for maintenance service both in China or abroad subject to the approval of the relevant Chinese department.

Article 24

The trademark of the joint venture's product is ———.

CHAPTER 9: THE BOARD OF DIRECTORS

Article 25

The date of registration of the joint venture company shall be the date of the establishment of the board of directors of the joint venture company.

Article 26

The board of directors is composed of ——— directors, of which ——— shall be appointed by Party A, ——— by Party B. The chairman of the board shall be appointed by Party A, and its vice-chairman by Party B. The term of office for the directors, chairman, and vice-chairman is four years. Their term of office may be renewed if continuously appointed by the relevant party.

Article 27

The highest authority of the joint venture company shall be its board of directors. It shall decide all major issues concerning the joint venture company. Unanimous approval shall be required before any decisions are made concerning major issues. As for other matters, approval by majority or a simple majority shall be required.
Note: The main contents shall be listed according to article 36 of the Regulations for the Implementation of the Joint Venture Law.

Article 28

The chairman of the board is the legal representative of the joint venture company. Should the chairman be unable to exercise his responsibilities for some reason, he shall authorize the vice-chairman or any other directors to represent the joint venture company temporarily.

Article 29

The board of directors shall hold a meeting at least once every year. The meeting shall be called and presided over by the chairman of the board. The chairman may convene an interim meeting based on a proposal made by more than one-third of the total number of directors. Minutes of the meetings shall be placed on file.

CHAPTER 10. BUSINESS MANAGEMENT OFFICE

Article 30

The joint venture company shall establish a management office that shall be responsible for daily management. The management office shall have a general manager, appointed by party ——; —— deputy general managers, —— by party ——; —— by party ——. The general manager and deputy general managers shall be appointed by the board of directors for terms of —— years, which may be renewed.

Article 31

The responsibility of the general manager is to carry out the decisions of the board and to organize and conduct the daily management of the joint venture company. The deputy general managers shall assist the general manager in his work.

Several department managers may be appointed by the management office. They shall be responsible for the work of their respective departments, follow directives of the general manager and deputy general managers, and report directly to them.

Article 32

In case of graft or serious dereliction of duty on the part of the general manager and/or deputy general managers, the board of directors shall have the power to dismiss them at will.

CHAPTER 11. PURCHASE OF EQUIPMENT

Article 33

In the purchase of required raw materials, fuel, parts, means of transportation, articles for office use, and so on, the joint venture company shall give first priority to source them in China where quality is the equivalent.

Article 34

In case the joint venture company entrusts Party B to purchase equipment from overseas markets, the persons appointed by Party A shall be invited to take part in the purchasing.

CHAPTER 12. PREPARATION AND CONSTRUCTION

Article 35

During the period of preparation and construction, an office shall be set up by the board of directors. This office shall consist of ——— persons, among which ——— persons will be from Party A, ——— persons from Party B. This office shall have one manager recommended by Party ———, and one deputy manager by Party ———. The manager and deputy manager shall be appointed by the board of directors.

Article 36

The preparation and construction office is responsible for the following: examining the project designs; signing project construction contracts, organizing the purchasing and inspection of relevant equipment and materials; developing the project construction schedule; preparing the budget; controlling project expenditures and accounting procedures; and maintaining records of documents, drawings, files, and materials during the construction phase of the project.

Article 37

A technical group shall be organized with several technical personnel appointed by Party A and Party B. This group, under the leadership of the preparation and construction office, is in charge of all aspects of the project, including project design, quality control, as well as equipment, materials, and technology utilized.

Article 38

Remuneration and expenses of the preparation and construction office staff shall be covered in the project budget as agreed upon by both parties.

Article 39

After having completed the project, the preparation and construction office shall be dissolved by the board of directors.

CHAPTER 13. LABOR MANAGEMENT

Article 40

The labor contract covering the recruitment, employment, dismissal and resignation, wages, labor insurance, welfare, rewards, penalty, and other matters concerning the staff and the workers of the joint venture company shall be drawn up between the joint venture company and the trade union of the joint venture company as a whole or with individual employees in accordance with the Regulations of the People's Republic of China on Labor Management in Joint Ventures Using Chinese and Foreign Investment and Its Implementation Rules.

After being signed, the labor contracts shall be filed with the local labor management department.

Article 41

The appointment of high-ranking administrative personnel recommended by both parties and their salaries, social insurance, welfare, and standards for traveling expenses shall be decided by the board of directors.

CHAPTER 14. TAXES, FINANCE, AND AUDIT

Article 42

The joint venture company shall pay taxes in accordance with Chinese laws and other relative regulations.

Article 43

Staff members and workers of the joint venture company shall pay individual income taxes according to the Individual Income Tax Law of the People's Republic of China.

Article 44

Allocations for reserve and expansion funds of the joint venture company, as well as welfare funds and bonuses for staff and workers, shall be set aside in accordance with the stipulations in the Law of the People's Republic of China on Joint Ventures Using Chinese and Foreign Investment. The annual proportion of allocations shall be decided by the board of directors according to the business situation of the joint venture company.

Article 45

The fiscal year of the joint venture company shall be from January 1 to December 31. All vouchers, receipts, statistical statements, reports, and account books shall be written in Chinese.
Note: A foreign language may be used concurrently with mutual consent.

Article 46

The examination of the joint venture's finances shall be conducted by an auditor registered in China and the reports shall be submitted to the board of directors and general manager.

In case Party B considers it necessary to employ a foreign auditor registered outside of China to undertake the annual financial audit, Party A shall give its consent. However, all associated expenses shall be borne by Party B.

Article 47

In the first three months of each fiscal year, the manager shall prepare the previous year's balance sheet, profit and loss statement, and a proposal regarding the disposal of profits, and he will submit them to the board of directors for examination and approval.

CHAPTER 15. DURATION OF THE JOINT VENTURE

Article 48

The duration of the joint venture company is ——— years. The establishment of the joint venture company shall start from the date of issuance of the business license of the joint venture company.

An application for extension of the duration, proposed by one party and unanimously approved by the board of directors, shall be submitted to the Ministry of Foreign Economic Relations and Trade (or the examination and approval authority entrusted by it) six months prior to the expiration date of the joint venture.

CHAPTER 16. THE DISPOSAL OF ASSETS AFTER EXPIRATION OF THE DURATION

Article 49

Upon the expiration of the joint venture agreement (or termination before the date of expiration), liquidation shall be carried out according to relevant laws. The liquidated assets shall be distributed in accordance with the proportion of investment contributed by Party A and Party B.

CHAPTER 17. INSURANCE

Article 50

The insurance policies carried by the joint venture company for various kinds of risks shall be underwritten by the People's Insurance Company of China. The type, value, and duration of the insurance shall be determined by the board of directors in accordance with the stipulations of the People's Insurance Company of China.

CHAPTER 18. AMENDMENTS, ALTERATIONS, AND DISCHARGE OF THE CONTRACT

Article 51

Amendments of the contract shall come into force only after a written agreement is signed by Party A and Party B and approved by the original examination and approval authority.

Article 52

In case of an inability to fulfill the contract, or to continue operations due to heavy losses in successive years as a result of a force majeure, the duration of the joint venture and the contract may be terminated prior to the time of expiration after unanimous agreement of the board of directors and approval by the original examination and approval authority.

Article 53

Should the joint venture company be unable to continue its operations or achieve the business purpose stipulated in its contract, due to the fact that one of the contracting parties fails to fulfill the obligations prescribed by the contract and articles of association or seriously violates the stipulations of the contract and articles of association, that party shall be deemed in breach of the contract. The other party shall have the right to terminate the contract and to claim damages in accordance with the provisions of the contract after approval by the original examination and approval authority. In case Party A and Party B of the joint venture company agree to continue the operation, the party that fails to fulfill the obligations shall be liable for the economic losses thus suffered by the joint venture company.

CHAPTER 19. LIABILITIES FOR BREACH OF CONTRACT

Article 54

Should either Party A or Party B fail to pay contributions on schedule as defined in chapter 5 of this contract, the breaching party shall pay to the other party ———% of the contribution starting from the first month after the expiration of the time limit. Should the breaching party fail to pay after three months, ———% of the contribution shall be paid to the other party, which shall have the right to terminate the contract and to claim damages from the breaching party in accordance with the stipulations in article 53 of the contract.

Article 55

Should all or part of the contract and its appendices be unfulfilled, owing to the fault of one party, the breaching party shall bear the responsibilities thus caused. Should it be the fault of both parties, they shall bear their respective responsibilities accordingly.

Article 56

In order to guarantee the performance of the contract and its appendices, both Party A and Party B shall provide each other with bank guarantees for their respective contribution to the contract.

CHAPTER 20. FORCE MAJEURE

Article 57

Should either of the parties to the contract be prevented from executing the contract by force majeure, such as an earthquake, typhoon, flood, fire, war, or other unforeseen events, this party shall notify the other party by cable without delay and within fifteen days thereafter provide detailed information of the events and a notarized document explaining the reason for the party's inability to execute or delay in executing all or part of the contract. Both parties shall decide through consultations whether to terminate the contract, to exempt part of the obligations for implementation of the contract, or to delay the execution of the contract according to the effects of the events on the performance of the contract.

CHAPTER 21. APPLICABLE LAW

Article 58

The formation of this contract, its validity, interpretation, execution, and settlement of disputes shall be governed by the related laws of the People's Republic of China.

CHAPTER 22. SETTLEMENT OF DISPUTES

Article 59

Any disputes arising from the execution of (or in connection with) the contract shall be settled through friendly consultation between both parties. In case no settlement can be reached through consultations, the dispute shall be submitted for arbitration to the Foreign Economic and Trade Arbitration Commission of the China Council for the Promotion of International Trade in accordance with established rules of procedure. The arbitral award is final and binding upon both parties.

OR

Any disputes arising from the execution of (or in connection with) the contract shall be settled through friendly consultation between both parties. In case no settlement can be reached, the dispute shall be submitted to ——— Arbitration Organization in ——— for arbitration in accordance with its rules of procedure. The arbitral award is final and binding upon both parties.

OR

Any disputes arising from the execution of (or in connection with) the contract shall be settled through friendly consultation between both parties. In case no settlement can be reached through consultation, the dispute shall be submitted for arbitration.

Arbitration shall take place in the defendant's country. If in China, arbitration shall be conducted by the Foreign Economic and Trade Arbitration Commission of the China Council for the Promotion of International Trade in accordance with its rules of procedure.

If in ———, arbitration shall be conducted by ——— in accordance with its rules of procedure.

The arbitral award is final and binding on both parties.

Note: When formulating contracts, only one of the above-mentioned provisions can be used.

Article 60

During arbitration, the contract shall be executed continuously by both parties except for matters in dispute.

CHAPTER 23. LANGUAGE

Article 61

The contract shall be written in Chinese and in ———. Both languages are equally authentic. In the event that any discrepancy arises between the two afore-mentioned versions, the Chinese version shall prevail.

CHAPTER 24. EFFECTIVENESS OF THE CONTRACT AND MISCELLANEOUS

Article 62

The appendices drawn up in accordance with the principles of this contract are an integral part of this contract, including: the project agreement, technology transfer agreement, and sales agreement.

Article 63

The contract and its appendices shall come into force beginning from the date of approval of the Ministry of Foreign Economic Relations and Trade of the People's Republic of China (or its entrusted examination and approval authority).

Article 64

Should notices in connection with any party's rights and obligations be sent by either Party A or Party B by telegram, telex, or facsimile, a written letter shall be required immediately afterward. The legal addresses of Party A and Party B listed in this contract shall be the posting address.

Article 65

This contract is signed in ———, China, by the authorized representatives of both parties on ———, 19———.

For Party A   For Party B

(Signature)   (Signature)

Sample Articles of Association for Joint Ventures Using Chinese and Foreign Investment

CHAPTER 1. GENERAL PROVISIONS

Article 1

In accordance with the Law of the People's Republic of China on Joint Ventures Using Chinese and Foreign Investment and the contract signed by ——— com-pany (hereinafter referred to as Party A) and ——— company (hereinafter referred to as Party B), the articles of association are hereby formulated.

Article 2

The name of the joint venture company shall be ——— Limited Liability Company.

Its name in foreign language is ———.

The legal address of the joint venture company is ———.

Article 3

The names and legal addresses of the parties to the joint venture are as follows:

Party A: ——— Company at ———.

Party B: ——— Company at ———.

Article 4

The joint venture company is a limited liability company.

Article 5

The joint venture company has the status of a legal person and is subject to the jurisdiction and protection of legal systems of the People's Republic of China. Its activities shall be governed by Chinese laws, decrees, and other pertinent rules and regulations.

CHAPTER 2. PURPOSE AND SCOPE OF BUSINESS

Article 6

The purpose of the joint venture company is to produce and sell ——— products and to reach ——— level for obtaining satisfactory economic benefits for the parties to the joint venture company.

Note: Each joint venture company may specify items and amounts according to its own conditions.

Article 7

The business scope of the joint venture company is to design, manufacture, and sell ——— products and provide postsale services.

Article 8

The scale of production of the joint venture company is as follows:

——— year ———(unit of quantity)

——— year ———

——— year ———

Article 9

The joint venture company may sell its products in the Chinese domestic market and in international markets, as follows:

———— (year): ————% for export;

————% for the domestic market.

———— (year): ————% for export;

————% for the domestic market.

CHAPTER 3. THE TOTAL AMOUNT OF INVESTMENT AND REGISTERED CAPITAL

Article 10

The total amount of investment of the joint venture company is RMB ————. Its registered capital is RMB ————.

Article 11

The investment contributed by each party is as follows:

Party A: Investment subscribed is RMB ————, and accounts for ————% of the registered capital, to include:

Cash ————,

Machinery and equipment ————,

Premises ————,

Land use right ————,

Industrial property ————,

Other ————.

Party B: Investment subscribed is RMB ————, and accounts for ————% of the registered capital, to include:

Cash ————,

Machinery and equipment ————,

Industrial property ————,

Other ————.

Article 12

The parties to the joint venture shall contribute all forms of investment subscribed according to the time limit stipulated in the contract.

Article 13

After the investment is paid by the parties to the joint venture, a Chinese registered accountant shall be invited by the joint venture company to verify it and provide a certificate of verification. According to this certificate, the joint venture shall issue an investment certificate that includes the following items: name of the joint venture, date of the establishment of the joint venture, names of the parties and the investment contributed, date of the contribution of the investment, and the date of issuance of the investment certificate.

Article 14

During the term of the joint venture, the joint venture company shall not reduce its registered capital.

Article 15

Should one party assign all or part of its investment subscribed, consent must be obtained from the other party to the joint venture. When one party assigns its investment, the other party has preemptive rights.

Article 16

Any increase in or assignment of the registered capital for the joint venture company must be approved by the board of directors and submitted to the original examination and approval authority for approval. The registration procedures for changes shall be dealt with at the original registration and administration office.

CHAPTER 4. THE BOARD OF DIRECTORS

Article 17

The joint venture shall establish a board of directors, which is the highest authority of the joint venture company.

Article 18

The board of directors shall decide all major issues concerning the joint venture company. Its functions and powers are as follows:

• Deciding and approving important reports submitted by the general manager (for insurance, production plans, annual business reports, funds, loans, etc.);

• Approving annual financial reports, budgets for receipts and expenditures, and plan for the distribution of annual profits;

• Adopting major rules and regulations of the company;

• Deciding to set up branches;

• Amending the articles of association of the company;

• Discussing and deciding the termination of production, termination of the company, or merger with another economic organization;

• Deciding the hiring policy for retaining senior officials, such as the general manager, chief engineer, treasurer, auditor, and others;

• Providing for liquidation upon the expiration of the joint venture company; and

• Handling other major issues as determined by the board of directors.

Article 19

The board of directors shall consist of ―――― directors, of which ―――― shall be appointed by Party A and ―――― by Party B. The term of office for the directors is four years and may be renewed.

Article 20

A chairman of the board shall be appointed by Party A and a vice-chairman of the board by Party B.

Article 21

When appointing and replacing directors, a written notice shall be submitted to the board.

Article 22

The board of directors shall convene for ——— meeting(s) every year. An interim meeting of the board of directors may be held based on a proposal made by more than one-third of the total number of directors.

Article 23

The board meeting will normally be held on the premises of the company.

Article 24

The board meeting shall be called and presided over by the chairman. Should the chairman be absent, the vice-chairman shall call and preside over the board meeting.

Article 25

The chairman shall give each director written notice thirty days prior to the date of the board meeting. The notice shall include the agenda, time, and place of the meeting.

Article 26

Should a director be unable to attend the board meeting, he may present a proxy in written form to the board. In case a director neither attends nor entrusts others to attend the meeting, he will be regarded as being in abstention.

Article 27

The board meeting requires a quorum of over two-thirds of the total number of directors. When the quorum is less than two-thirds, the decisions adopted are invalid.

Article 28

Detailed written records shall be made for each board meeting and signed by all the directors present or by any proxy present. The record shall be made in Chinese and ——— and shall be filed with the company.

Article 29

The following issues must be agreed upon unanimously by the board of directors:
Note: To be stipulated according to each company's situation.

Article 30

The following issues must be passed by over two-thirds of the total number of directors or by over half of the total number:
Note: To be stipulated according to each company's situation.

CHAPTER 5. BUSINESS MANAGEMENT ORGANIZATION

Article 31

The joint venture company shall establish a management organization, consisting of production, technology, marketing, finance, and administration offices, etc.
Note: To be stipulated according to each company's situation.

Article 32

The joint venture company shall have one general manager and ——— deputy general manager(s) who are retained by the board of directors. The first general manager shall be recommended by Party ———, deputy general manager(s) by Party ———.

Article 33

The general manager is responsible directly to the board of directors. He shall carry out the decisions of the board of directors and organize and conduct the daily operations and management of the joint venture company. The deputy general managers shall assist the general manager, and during his absence they shall exercise the functions of the general manager.

Article 34

Decisions on the major issues concerning the daily work of the joint venture company shall be signed jointly by the general manager and the deputy general managers, after which these decisions shall be effective. Issues that need co-signatures shall be specifically stipulated by the board of directors.

Article 35

The term of office for the general manager and deputy general managers shall be ——— years and may be renewed at the invitation of the board of directors.

Article 36

At the invitation of the board of directors, the chairman, vice-chairman and/or directors of the board may concurrently be the general manager, deputy general managers, or other high-ranking personnel of the joint venture company.

Article 37

The general manager or deputy general managers shall not hold posts concurrently as general manager or deputy general managers of other economic organizations in commercial competition with their own joint venture company.

Article 38

The joint venture company shall have one chief engineer, one treasurer, and one auditor engaged by the board of directors.

Article 39

The chief engineer, treasurer, and auditor shall be under the authority of the general manager.

The treasurer shall exercise leadership in financial and accounting affairs, develop appropriate accounting procedures, and implement information control systems.

The auditor shall be in charge of auditing the joint venture company, examining and checking all financial receipt and expenditure accounts, and submitting written reports to the general manager and the board of directors.

Article 40

The general manager, deputy general managers, chief engineer, treasurer, auditor, and other high-ranking personnel who wish to resign shall submit their written requests to the board of directors in advance of terminating their service to the company.

In case any one of the above-mentioned persons is found guilty of graft or serious dereliction of duty, that person may be dismissed at any time by the board. Those who violate any criminal law shall be placed under criminal sanction.

CHAPTER 6. FINANCE AND ACCOUNTING

Article 41

The finance and accounting procedures of the joint venture company shall be handled in accordance with the Stipulations of the Finance and Accounting System of the Joint Ventures Using Chinese and Foreign Investment formulated by the Ministry of Finance of the People's Republic of China.

Article 42

The fiscal year of the joint venture company shall coincide with the calendar year, that is, from January 1 to December 31 of the Gregorian calendar.

Article 43

All vouchers, account books, statistic statements, and reports of the joint venture company shall be written in Chinese.

Article 44

The joint venture company will adopt RMB as its accounts keeping unit. The conversion of RMB into other currency shall be in accordance with the exchange rate of the converting day published by the State Administration of Exchange Control of the People's Republic of China.

Article 45

The joint venture company shall open accounts in RMB and foreign currency with the Bank of China or other banks specified by the Bank of China.

Article 46

Accounting for the joint venture company shall be based on the internationally accepted accrual basis and utilize the debit and credit accounting system.

Article 47

The following items shall be covered in the financial accounts books:

1. The amount of overall cash receipts and expenses of the joint venture company;
2. All materials purchased and sold by the joint venture company;
3. The registered capital and debts of the joint venture company;
4. The time of payment, increases, and assignment of the registered capital of the joint venture company.

Article 48

The joint venture company shall develop a statement of assets and liabilities and losses and gains for the past year within the first three months of each fiscal year and, after being examined and signed by the auditor, submit it to the board for its approval.

Article 49

Parties to the joint venture have the right to invite an external auditor to undertake a separate examination at their own expense. The joint venture company shall provide the necessary records for this examination.

Article 50

The depreciation period for the fixed assets of the joint venture company shall be decided by the board of directors in accordance with the Rules for the Implementation of the Income Tax Law of the People's Republic of China Concerning Joint Ventures with Chinese and Foreign Investment.

Article 51

All matters concerning foreign exchange shall be handled in accordance with the Provisional Regulations for Exchange Control of the People's Republic of China and other pertinent regulations, as well as the stipulations of the joint venture contract.

CHAPTER 7. PROFIT SHARING

Article 52

The joint venture company shall draw reserve funds, expansion funds, bonuses, and welfare funds for staff and workers after payment of taxes. The proportion of allocation is decided by the board of directors.

Article 53

After paying taxes in accordance with the law and allocating money to the various funds, the remaining profits will be distributed according to the proportion of each party's investment in registered capital.

Article 54

The joint venture company shall distribute its profits. The profit distribution plan and the amount of profit distributed to each party shall be published within the first three months following each fiscal year.

Article 55

The joint venture company shall not distribute any profits unless any losses of the previous fiscal year have been reimbursed. Should any profits remain from the previous year, they may be distributed together with that of the current year.

CHAPTER 8. STAFF MEMBERS AND WORKERS

Article 56

The employment, recruitment, dismissal, and resignation of staff members and workers for the joint venture company and their salary, welfare benefits, labor insurance, labor protection, labor discipline, and other matters shall be handled according to the Regulations of the People's Republic of China on Labor Management in Joint Ventures Using Chinese and Foreign Investment and its implementation rules.

Article 57

The required staff members and workers to be recruited by the joint venture company will be recommended by the local labor department or the joint venture will recruit employees through public selection examinations and employ those who are qualified with the consent of the labor department.

Article 58

The joint venture company has the right to take disciplinary action, record demerits, and reduce salaries for staff members and workers who violate the rules and regulations of the joint venture company and the labor authorities. Those involved in serious violations may be dismissed. A notice of termination of workers shall be filed with the labor and personnel department in the locality.

Article 59

The salary for staff members and workers shall be set by the board of directors according to the specific situation of the joint venture, with reference to pertaining Chinese stipulations, and shall be specified in detail in the labor contract.

The salary and wages of staff members and workers shall be increased according to the production efficiency and the increasing skill levels of the staff members and workers.

Article 60

Matters concerning welfare funds, bonuses, labor protection, and labor insurance shall be stipulated in various regulations of the joint venture company to ensure that the staff members and workers are protected.

CHAPTER 9. THE TRADE UNION ORGANIZATION

Article 61

The staff members and workers of the joint venture company have the right to establish trade unions and carry out activities in accordance with the stipulations of the Trade Union Law of the People's Republic of China.

Article 62

The trade union in the joint venture company represents the interests of the staff members and workers. The tasks of the trade union are as follows: to protect the democratic rights and material interests of the staff members and workers pursuant to the law; to assist the joint venture company in arranging and making rational use of welfare funds and bonuses; to organize political, professional, scientific, and technical studies; to carry out literary, art, and sports activities; and to educate staff and workers to observe labor discipline and strive to fulfill the economic tasks of the joint venture company.

Article 63

The trade union of the joint venture company will sign labor contracts with the joint venture company on behalf of the staff members and workers and supervise the implementation of the contracts.

Article 64

Persons in charge of the trade union of the joint venture company have the right to attend, as nonvoting members, and to report the opinions and demands of staff members and workers, meetings of the board of directors. They have the right to discuss such issues as development plans, production practices, and operational activities of the joint venture.

Article 65

The trade union shall take part in the mediation of disputes arising between the staff members and workers and the joint venture company.

Article 66

The joint venture company shall allot an amount of money totaling 2 percent of all the salaries of the staff members and workers of the joint venture company to the trade union fund, which shall be used by the trade union in accordance with the Managerial Rules for Trade Union Funds formulated by the All China Federation of Trade Unions.

CHAPTER 10. DURATION, TERMINATION, AND LIQUIDATION

Article 67

The duration of the joint venture company shall be ———— years, beginning from the day when the business license is issued.

Article 68

An application for the extension of duration of the joint venture, as proposed by both parties and approved at a board meeting, shall be submitted to the original examination and approval authority six months prior to the expiration date of the joint venture. Only upon their approval may the duration be extended, and the joint venture company shall go through registration formalities for the alteration at the original registration office.

Article 69

The joint venture may be terminated before its expiration if the parties to the joint venture agree unanimously that the termination of the joint venture is in the best interest of both parties.

To terminate the joint venture before the term expires requires a decision by the board of directors through a plenary meeting, and the request shall be submitted to the original examination and approval authority for approval.

Article 70

Either party shall have the right to terminate the joint venture in case one of the following situations occurs:

Note: *To be stipulated according to each joint venture company's situation.*

Article 71

Upon the expiration or termination of the joint venture before its term ends, the board of directors shall delineate procedures and principles for liquidation, nominate candidates for the liquidation committee, and set up the liquidation committee to dissolve the joint venture company's assets.

Article 72

The tasks of the liquidation committee are as follows: to conduct a thorough check of the property of the joint venture company and its claims and indebtedness, to compile the statement of assets and liabilities and lists of property, and to formulate a liquidation plan. All of these activities shall be carried out upon approval of the board of directors.

Article 73

During the liquidation process, the liquidation committee shall represent the company to sue and be sued.

Article 74

The liquidation expenses and remuneration to the members of the liquidation committee shall be paid in priority from the existing assets of the joint venture company.

Article 75

The remaining property, after the clearance of debts of the joint venture company, shall be distributed among the parties to the joint venture according to the proportion of each party's investment in registered capital.

Article 76

Upon completion of the liquidation, the joint venture company shall submit a liquidation report to the original examination and approval authority, nullify its registration in the original registration office, relinquish its business license, and, at the same time, publically announce its termination.

Article 77

After terminating the joint venture company, its account books shall be left in the care of the Chinese partner.

CHAPTER 11. RULES AND REGULATIONS

Article 78

Following are the rules and regulations formulated by the board of directors of the joint venture company.

1. Management regulations, including the powers and functions of the managerial branches, and the company's working rules and procedures;
2. Rules for the staff members and workers;
3. Systems of labor and salary;
4. System of work attendance record, promotion, and awards and penalties for staff members and workers;
5. Detailed rules for staff members' and workers' welfare;
6. Financial system;
7. Liquidation procedures upon the dissolution of the joint venture company; and
8. Other necessary rules and regulations.

CHAPTER 12. SUPPLEMENTARY ARTICLES

Article 79

The amendments to the Articles of Association shall be unanimously agreed upon by the board of directors and submitted to the original examination and approval authority for approval.

Article 80

The Articles of Association shall be written in the Chinese language and the ———— language. Both languages shall be equally authentic. In the event of any discrepancy between the two above-mentioned versions, the Chinese version shall prevail.

Article 81

The Articles of Association shall come into effect upon receiving approval by the Ministry of Foreign Economic Relations and Trade of the People's Republic of China (or its entrusted examination and approval authority). The same applies in the event of amendments.

Article 82

The Articles of Association is signed in ———, China, by the authorized representatives of both parties on ———, 19———.

For Party A   For Party B

(Signature)   (Signature)

Source: Bureau of Laws and Regulations, Ministry of Foreign Economic Relations and Trade, Beijing, China.
Note: This translation is by the authors and, therefore, unofficial.

APPENDIX II

Regulations for the Development and Opening of the Shanghai Pudong New Area

Regulations of the Shanghai Municipality for the Encouragement of Foreign Investment in the Pudong New Area

Article 1

The regulations are formulated in accordance with the decisions of the State Council concerning the development and opening of Pudong and the relevant State laws and regulations in order to provide a better environment to attract foreign investment and speed up the construction of the Pudong New Area (hereafter referred to as the New Area).

Article 2

Foreign corporations, enterprises, and other economic organizations or individuals (hereafter referred to as foreign investors) are encouraged to set up the following Sino-foreign equity joint ventures, Sino-foreign cooperative joint ventures, and enterprises operated exclusively with foreign capital (hereafter referred to as foreign-invested enterprises) in the New Area and are granted preferential treatment. Included are:

1. Those that establish manufacturing enterprises, especially export enterprises and technologically advanced enterprises;
2. Those that invest for development and operation of tracts of land together with projects thereon in accordance with the consolidated planning of the New Area; and

3. Those that are engaged in the exploitation of energy resources and the construction of transportation.

Article 3

Foreign investors shall be allowed to run tertiary industries in the New Area. Upon the approval of the State Council, financial operations, commercial retail sales, and other enterprises involving investment by foreign businessmen shall be permitted to be undertaken.

Article 4

A free trade zone shall be established in the New Area, in which foreign investors shall be permitted to set up trade institutions to engage in entrepot trade or to act as an agent for foreign-invested enterprises within the New Area to import raw materials and spare parts and to export their finished products upon approval of the competent departments of the State Council.

Article 5

The enterprise income tax on the income derived from production, operation, and other sources of manufacturing enterprises with foreign investment shall be levied at the reduced rate of 15 percent. After the enterprise applications are approved by the tax organization, those enterprises with a period of operation over ten years may be exempt from income tax in the first and the second profit-making years and allowed a 50 percent reduction from the third to the fifth years.

In accordance with State regulations, when the period of enterprise income tax exemption expires, export enterprises with foreign investment shall pay at a reduced rate of 10 percent of the enterprise income tax when the annual value of export goods amounts to more than 70 percent of total annual value of production; technologically advanced enterprises may pay the enterprise income tax with a reduced rate of 10 percent for another three years when the period of enterprise income tax exemption expires.

Foreign-invested enterprises engaged in airport, port, railway, highway, power station, and other energy resources or transportation construction projects shall pay at the rate of 15 percent of the enterprise income tax. After the enterprise applications are approved by the tax organization, those enterprises with a period of operation over fifteen years may be exempt from enterprise income tax starting from the first profit-making year. They shall be granted this for five (5) consecutive years and allowed a 50 percent reduction from the sixth to tenth years.

Article 6

Foreign investors may, in the New Area, invest in the development of tracts of land in accordance with the consolidated planning and may participate in the development of infrastructure projects and the operation of real estate businesses on such land.

The foreign-invested enterprises that participate in the construction of infrastructure facilities together with projects in such land may enjoy the same treatment described in the first paragraph of article 5 hereof after the enterprise applications are approved by the tax organization.

Article 7

After their applications are approved by the tax organization, such financial organizations as foreign-invested banks, Chinese-foreign jointly invested banks, and finance companies (with paid-in capital according to the regulations and working funds alloted to branches of foreign-invested banks from their head offices totaling over US $10 million with a business period exceeding ten years) shall pay at the reduced rate of 15 percent of the enterprise income tax. They shall be exempt from the income tax in the first profit-making year and pay a 50 percent reduction for the second and third years if their paid-in capital or working funds will not be decreased in a period of ten years.

Article 8

Financial organizations such as foreign banks, branches of foreign-invested banks, and Chinese-foreign jointly invested banks and finance companies shall pay the consolidated industrial and commercial tax at the rate of 3 percent on income from loan business and at the rate of 5 percent on income from other financial business.

Article 9

Foreign investors who reinvest their share of profits earned in their enterprises or in other foreign-invested enterprises to set up new foreign-invested enterprises for a business period not less than five years shall be refunded 40 percent of the enterprise income tax paid on the reinvested amount; those who reinvest their profits to set up or extend their export enterprises or technologically advanced enterprises for a business period no less than five years shall receive a full refund of the enterprise income tax paid on the reinvested amount.

Article 10

Foreign investors of a Sino-foreign equity joint venture may remit out of the territory of China their share of profits earned from the enterprise. The remittance shall be exempt from the income tax.

Article 11

Foreign investors without establishments in China shall all pay at the reduced rate of 10 percent of income tax on dividends, interests, rents, royalties, and other income earned in the New Area, except those who are exempt from income tax by law. However, those who supply funds or equipment at favorable rates or transfer advanced technology may be granted a greater reduction, even exemption from income tax upon approval of the Municipal People's Government.

Article 12

Foreign-invested enterprises in the New Area shall be exempt from local income tax until the end of the year 2000.

Article 13

Newly constructed buildings in the New Area either self-built or purchased for private use by foreign-invested enterprises shall be exempt from house property tax for five years beginning from the month the construction is completed or the purchase is made.

Article 14

Export products manufactured by foreign-invested enterprises, except crude oil, refined oil, and those products under other existing regulations otherwise stipulated by the State, may be exempted from the consolidated industrial and commercial tax.

Article 15

Export products manufactured by foreign-invested enterprises in the New Area, except those under other existing regulations stipulated by the State, shall be exempt from customs duty.

Article 16

Building materials, equipment, and spare parts for production and management use, means of communication, office appliances, and raw and auxiliary materials for production imported by foreign-invested enterprises for their own use shall be exempt from customs duty and the consolidated industrial and commercial tax.

Customs duty and the consolidated industrial and commercial tax shall be repaid on imported duty-free materials, such as raw and auxiliary materials, and spare parts and components used to process the products that are later to be sold on the domestic market. Those restricted for import by State regulations shall require applying to the relevant departments to obtain import licenses.

Article 17

Household wares and traffic vehicles brought to China in reasonable quantities by foreign employees of foreign-invested enterprises for their own use in setting up a new home shall be exempt from customs duty and the consolidated industrial and commercial tax.

Industrial income tax on wages or salaries of foreign employees shall be allowed a 50 percent reduction.

Article 18

Machinery, equipment, vehicles, and materials for capital construction that are needed for construction in the New Area shall be imported free of customs duty and the consolidated industrial and commercial tax.

Article 19

Foreign-invested enterprises may not apply for examination and approval to obtain import licenses when they need to import machinery, equipment, vehicles for production use, raw materials, fuel, bulk parts, machine parts, components and fittings (including those restricted by the State) in order to implement their product export contracts. These imports shall be supervised and cleared by the Customs Department on the strength of enterprise contract or import and export contract.

Article 20

Foreign-invested enterprises may sell certain quantities of their products manufactured as substitutes for imports on domestic markets on approval of the relevant department and after paying customs duties and the consolidated industrial and commercial tax according to relevant regulations. A portion of foreign currencies may be obtained when necessary.

Article 21

Foreign-invested enterprises in need of short-term working capital in the course of production and circulation may be given priority in receiving such loans upon the examination and approval of the bank or other financial institution with which they have opened accounts.

Article 22

Foreign employees of foreign-invested enterprises may apply for multiple entry and exit visas as needed.

Article 23

Foreign-invested enterprises may decide on their own organizational structure and personnel system as needed by their production and management systems. The staff members and workers needed by the enterprises should be recruited from the public within the territory of Shanghai and may also be recruited outside Shanghai with the approval of the municipal labor and personnel department. The original organization where the recruited staff members or workers have been working should cooperate and allow its employees to be transferred. In case of disputes, the labor and personnel department shall coordinate and arbitrate.

The employees recruited by foreign-invested enterprises shall work under the labor contract system.

The employment, recruitment, dismissal, or discharge of staff members or workers by foreign-invested enterprises shall be filed with the municipal labor and personnel department for record.

Article 24

The wage standard, form of pay, reward, allowance, and other employee systems of foreign-invested enterprises are to be decided by the enterprise itself.

Article 25

Foreign investors in the New Area may be granted particularly preferential treatment if their invested projects are especially encouraged in Shanghai after their applications have been examined and submitted by the Shanghai Foreign Investment Commission to obtain thereafter the approval from the Shanghai Municipal People's Government.

Article 26

The regulations are applicable to enterprises and projects invested in the New Area by corporations, enterprises, and other economic organizations or individuals from Hong Kong, Macao, and Taiwan in accordance with the regulations by analogy.

Article 27

Matters not stipulated in the regulations shall be handled according to the relevant laws, regulations, and rules of the State and the Shanghai Municipality.

Article 28

The Shanghai Foreign Economic Relations and Trade Commission and the Shanghai Foreign Investment Commission are responsible for the interpretation of the regulations.

Article 29

The regulations shall come into effect as of the date of approval and promulgation.

Note: Promulgated by the Shanghai Municipal People's Government on September 10, 1990.

Examination and Approval Measures for Foreign-Funded Enterprises in the Shanghai Pudong New Area

With a view to improving the investment environment, promoting work efficiency, and facilitating investments by foreign business people in the Pudong New Area, the present examination and approval measures of foreign-funded enterprises in the Shanghai Pudong New Area are especially formulated hereby in accordance with the laws, rules and regulations, and related policies of the People's Republic of China.

1. Requirements for Application

   Each of the Sino-foreign equity joint ventures, Sino-foreign cooperative ventures and enterprises operated exclusively with foreign capital (hereafter referred to as foreign-invested enterprises) that apply for establishment in the Pudong New Area shall meet the requirements of the overall planning and investment direction of the Pudong New Area.

2. Examination and Approval Departments and the Limits of Authority

   The Shanghai Foreign Investment Commission (hereafter referred to as the SFIC) shall be responsible for examining and approving the following projects:

   - A project whose total amount of investment is between US $5 million and US $30 million
   - A restricted project whose total amount of investment is under US $5 million
   - A project operated exclusively with foreign capital
   - Any project with key development areas at the city level, such as the Waigaoqiao Free Trade Zone, the Lujiazui Finance and Trade Area, the Jinqiao Export Processing Area, and so on.

   The projects involving energy and raw materials that are needed to balance nationwide supply or the projects involving the administration of quotas and licenses shall be reported to the relevant State department for approval or for the record.

A nonrestricted project whose total amount of investment is less than US $5 million shall be examined and approved by the relevant bureaus or people's governments at the district or country level.

Any manufacturing project whose total amount of investment is over US $30 million and any nonmanufacturing project that needs to be approved by the competent departments of the State Council shall be preliminarily examined by the SFIC and all related departments and then it shall be submitted to the appropriate departments of the State Council for examination and approval.

3. Examination and Approval Procedures
The procedures hereunder shall be followed for establishing foreign-invested enterprises:

- Present a project proposal
- Submit the feasibility study report, contract, and articles of association
- Apply for the issuance of approval certificate
- Apply for a business license

Foreign business people and Chinese investors shall, according to the amounts and contents of their investment projects, respectively submit their project proposals, feasibility study reports, contracts, and articles of association (hereafter referred to as documents for approval) to the SFIC or the relevant bureaus and people's governments at the district or country level.

Chinese investors are responsible for the submission of documents for approval of Sino-foreign equity joint ventures and Sino-foreign cooperative ventures, while documents for approval of enterprises operated exclusively with foreign capital are submitted by the consultant agencies entrusted by foreign business people in Shanghai.

Certificates of approval shall be granted by the SFIC after the contracts and articles of association of the foreign-invested enterprises are approved.

For foreign-invested enterprises in the Pudong New Area, whose examination and approval is the responsibility of the Shanghai Municipality, the time limit for examination and approval upon receipt of the related documents is twenty days for a project proposal; thirty days for the feasibility study report, contract, and articles of association; seven days for the issuance of an approval certificate; and fifteen days for checking and granting a business license.

4. Other Items

The present measures are applicable to all projects invested by companies, enterprises, other economic organizations or individuals from Hong Kong, Macao, and Taiwan in the Pudong New Area.

Items not listed in the present measures shall be handled according to the relevant regulations of the State and the Shanghai Municipality.

Note: Ratified by the Shanghai Municipal People's Government on September 6, 1990.

Regulations on the Reduction and Exemption of Enterprise Income Tax and the Industrial and Commercial Consolidated Tax to Encourage Foreign Investment in the Shanghai Pudong New Area

Article 1

To expand economic cooperation and technology transfer, absorb foreign investment, introduce advanced technology, and speed up development and construction within the Shanghai Pudong New Area (hereafter referred to as the New Area), the present regulations are especially formulated hereby.

Article 2

The enterprise income tax on the income derived from the production, operation, and other sources of manufacturing enterprises with Sino-foreign equity joint ventures, Sino-foreign cooperative joint ventures, and manufacturing enterprises operated exclusively with foreign capital in the New Area shall be levied at the reduced rate of 15 percent. After the enterprise applications are approved by the tax authority, those enterprises with a period of operation over ten years may be exempt from income tax in the first and the second profit-making years and allowed a 50 percent reduction from the third to the fifth years.

Article 3

In accordance with the State regulations, when the period of enterprise income tax exemption expires, export enterprises with foreign investment shall pay at a reduced rate of 10 percent of the enterprise income tax when their annual value of export goods amounts to more than 70 percent of the total annual value of production; technologically advanced enterprises may pay the enterprise income tax with a reduced rate of 10 percent for another three years when the period of enterprise income tax exemption expires.

Article 4

Foreign-invested enterprises engaged in airport, port, railway, highway, power station and other energy resources, or transportation construction projects shall pay at the rate of 15 percent of the enterprise income tax. `After the enterprise applications are approved by the tax organization, those enterprises with a period of operation over fifteen years may be exempted from enterprise income tax starting from the first profit-making year. This shall be granted for five consecutive years, and a 50 percent reduction is allowed from the sixth to tenth years.

Article 5

The foreign-invested enterprises that participate the construction of infrastructure facilities may enjoy the same treatment as the manufacturing enterprises described in article 1 hereof after the enterprise applications are approved by the tax authority.

Article 6

After their applications are approved by the tax authority, such financial organizations as branches of foreign-invested banks, Chinese-foreign jointly invested banks, and finance companies (with paid-in capital by foreign investors or working funds alloted to branches of foreign-invested banks from their head offices totaling over US $10 million with a business period exceeding ten years) shall pay at the reduced rate of 15 percent of the enterprise income tax. They shall be exempt from the income tax in the first profit-making year and pay a 50 percent reduction for the second and third years.

Article 7

Financial organizations such as foreign-invested banks, branches of foreign-invested banks, and Chinese-foreign jointly invested banks and finance companies shall pay the consolidated industrial and commercial tax at the rate of 3 percent on income from loan business and at the rate of 5 percent on income from other financial business.

Article 8

Foreign investors who reinvest their share of profits in their enterprises or other foreign-invested enterprises to set up new foreign-invested enterprises for a business period of not less than five years shall be refunded 40 percent of the enterprise income tax paid on the reinvested amount after their applications are checked and ratified by the tax authority; those who reinvest their profits to set up or extend export enterprises or technologically advanced enterprises with a business period no less than five years shall receive a full refund of the enterprise income tax paid on the reinvested amount.

Article 9

Foreign investors of a Sino-foreign equity joint venture may remit out of the territory of China their share of profits earned from the enterprise. The remittance shall be exempt from income tax.

Article 10

Foreign investors without establishments in China shall all pay at the reduced rate of 10 percent of income tax on dividends, interests, rents, royalties, and other income earned in the New Area, except those who are exempt from income tax by law. However, those who supply funds or equipment at favorable rates or transfer advanced technology may be granted a greater reduction, even exempted upon decision of the Municipal People's Government.

Article 11

Export products manufactured by foreign-invested enterprises, except crude oil, refined oil, and those products under other existing regulations stipulated by the State, may be exempted from the consolidated industrial and commercial tax.

Article 12

Building materials, equipment, and spare parts for production and management use, means of communication, office appliances, and raw materials for production imported by foreign-invested enterprises for their own use shall be exempt from the consolidated industrial and commercial tax.

The consolidated industrial and commercial tax shall be repaid on imported duty-free materials, such as raw and auxiliary materials, spare parts, components, packing materials, and other materials used to process the products that are later to be sold on the domestic market.

Article 13

Household wares and traffic vehicles brought to China in reasonable quantities by foreign employees of enterprises living and working in the New Area for their own use in setting up a new home shall be exempt from the consolidated industrial and commercial tax.

Article 14

The Shanghai Municipal People's Government will exempt or reduce the local income tax for foreign-invested enterprises and the house property tax for newly constructed buildings either self-built or purchased for private use by employees of foreign-invested enterprises.

Article 15

The regulations are applicable to enterprises and projects invested in the New Area by corporations, enterprises, and other economic organizations or individuals from Hong Kong, Macao, and Taiwan in accordance with the regulations by analogy.

Article 16

The State Tax Bureau is responsible for the interpretation of the present regulations.

Article 17

The regulations shall come into effect on October 1, 1990.

Provisions of Land Administration in the Shanghai Pudong New Area

Article 1

These regulations are formulated in accordance with relevant laws and regulations, such as the Law of the People's Republic of China on Land Administration, to consolidate the administration of land in the Pudong New Area, make appropriate use of land resources, and speed up the New Area's development and construction.

Article 2

As required by the economic and social development plans for the Pudong New Area, the land in this area shall be subject to rational development, utilization, and operation according to urban planning policies.

Article 3

Systems such that land-use rights may be obtained subject to payment of a consideration shall be implemented for the state-owned land within the Pudong

New Area. Land-use rights may be obtained by a user by transfer or payment of a land-use fee. The granting of land-use rights shall be carried out by the Municipal Land Administration Bureau.

Article 4

Unless otherwise regulated by laws, corporations, enterprises, other organizations, and individuals inside or outside of the People's Republic of China may obtain land-use rights according to the Provisional Regulations of the People's Republic of China for Granting and Transfering the Right to Use State-Owned Urban Land, the Provisional Procedures for the Administration of Development and Operation of Tracts of Land by Foreign Investors, and the Measures of the Shanghai Municipality for the Transfer of Land-use Rights upon Payment of a Consideration.

Enterprises invested by foreign investors in industry, agriculture, energy, transportation, and infrastructure facilities may also obtain land-use rights according to the Measures of the Shanghai Municipality for the Administration of Land Used by Joint Ventures Using Chinese and Foreign Investment.

The use of land for urban roads, bridges, railways, tunnels, greenbelts, and other public facilities shall be subject to the separate stipulations of the Municipal People's Government.

Article 5

Land-use rights may be obtained for either land equipped with public utilities or tracts of land pending development.

Article 6

After the land users develop and construct the land plots according to the terms and conditions of the contract for granting of land-use rights, such land-use rights may be lawfully transferred, leased, secured, and inherited or be used for other economic activities permitted by law within a stipulated term.

The right to use the land in tracts subject to development may also be transferred according to the projected purpose, so long as its development and construction have been completed as provided for in the contract for granting land-use rights.

Land-use rights obtained in a manner other than through granting or transfer shall not be transferred, secured, or leased.

Article 7

The maximum term for the granting of land-use rights is as follows:

1. Land for commercial, tourist, and recreational purposes: forty years;
2. Land for industrial purposes: fifty years;
3. Land for the purposes of education, scientific research, culture, public health, and sports: fifty years;
4. Land for residential purposes: seventy years; and
5. Land for comprehensive use or other development purposes: fifty years.

Terms for use of land developed and operated in tracts shall be determined according to the purposes.

Article 8

The granting of land-use rights shall be effected through public bidding, auction, or negotiation. Such granting with respect to land used for the purposes of commerce, tourism, recreation, finance, real estate development, and other projects shall be effected generally through public bidding and auction. In the case of land-use rights granted through negotiation, the grantor and the grantee shall agree upon the fee for such granting on the basis of different land development costs, land benefits, location classifications, purposes, project parameters, land-use terms, and other conditions.

Article 9

The fees for land-use rights granting shall be paid in currency or foreign currency by foreign business people.

Article 10

Upon the expiration of the term of land-use rights, a land user may apply for an extension of such terms according to the regulations.

Article 11

Land users in the Pudong New Area who have obtained land-use rights gratis by means of governmental assignments and so on shall pay urban land-use taxes. Land used for the purposes of administrative institutions financially supported by fiscal allotment and military facilities shall be administered by the existing regulations.

Article 12

Land users who have obtained land-use rights by means of governmental assignment may transfer, lease, or secure their land-use rights, provided that approval is received for relevant applications, a contract granting land-use rights is executed, and fees for such granting are paid.

With respect to land for which usage rights have been obtained gratis according to the law by means of governmental assignment, if the original purpose for the use of such land is changed or if the right to use such land is transferred as a result of buying and selling related to the housing thereupon, other than private housing for personal use, a contract for the granting of land-use rights shall be executed. Fees for such granting shall be paid, with the exception of the land otherwise stipulated according to the construction of the Pudong New Area by the Shanghai Municipal People's Government.

Fees for granting land-use rights may be paid upon the execution of the contract effecting such granting.

Article 13

Chinese enterprises that have obtained land-use rights gratis according to the law by means of governmental assignment shall be encouraged to use such land-use rights, according to municipal planning, as a condition of investment and cooperation for the establishment of joint ventures with foreign businesses. Such land-use rights shall be converted to revenue of the government in the joint venture, part of which may be assigned to the original land user. With respect to development in conjunction with foreign businesses in such industrial sectors as agriculture, energy, transportation, and infrastructure facilities, as an alternative, land-use fees shall be paid according to the Measures of the Shanghai Municipality for Administration of Land Used by Joint Ventures Using Chinese and Foreign Investment.

Article 14

In case a land user that has obtained land-use rights gratis according to the law by means of governmental assignment ceases to use the land as a result of removal, dissolution, disbandment, or other causes, the municipal government shall revoke its land-use rights and may lawfully grant the same. Part of the fees granted for land-use rights to a removed enterprise as the original land user shall be used to meet the demands of the enterprise in connection with its removal.

Article 15

As required by the State, the municipal government may revoke land-use rights originally obtained gratis according to the law by means of governmental assignment. Appropriate compensation shall be made for the buildings and other attachments on such land according to real conditions.

Article 16

The revenues sourced from the land use at a consideration in the Pudong New Area shall be put into the financial budget as a special fund. It shall be used primarily for the land development and urban construction of the Pudong New Area.

Article 17

Users of State-owned land and proprietors or users of collectively owned land must follow relevant regulations to report and register their ownership and land-use rights and register any alteration thereof.

The granting of land-use rights and the subsequent transfer, lease, exchange, inheritance, endowment, securing, and termination thereof shall be registered with the Shanghai Real Estate Registration Office.

Article 18

The land used for State construction, township and village enterprises, and institution construction within the planned urbanized areas in the Pudong New Area shall be examined and approved by the municipal government, while governments of districts or counties shall be responsible for the examination and approval of land used for local house building.

Land used for nonagricultural construction within the boundary of the Pudong New Area shall remain subject to current limits of authority regarding examination and approval.

Article 19

Chinese and foreign consultant and service agencies may be set up in the Pudong New Area to serve the real estate market.

Article 20

The Municipal Land Administration Bureau is responsible for the interpretation of these regulations.

Article 21

These regulations shall come into force as of the date of approval and promulgation.

Note: Promulgated by the Shanghai Municipal People's Government on September 10, 1990.

Guidance of Industries and Investment of the Shanghai Pudong Zone

These guidelines for development of industries and investment are especially formulated on the basis of the industrial policies of the State and the overall planning for economic and social development of Shanghai with a view to building the Pudong New Area into a modernized new area with a rational industrial structure. The People's Government and its functional departments will constantly use economic plans, economic policies, and market guidance mechanisms to guide the development of industries in the New Area. Pursuant to such guidelines, domestic and overseas enterprises and other economic organizations can invest in and operate business in the scope permitted by related regulations.

1. Principles for Development of Industries in the Pudong New Area Shall be Such that Development Must Benefit the:

   Absorption of domestic and overseas capital and investment,

   Expansion of international trade and participation in the international division of labor and international competition,

   Acquisition of international advanced technology and development of industries that mainly produce export products or import-substitution products,

   Supplementation, coordination, and integration of industries between Pudong and Puxi, and

   Development of Shanghai into a multi-functional economic, trading, and financial center of the nation

2. Development of the Following Major Industries Will Be Encouraged in the New Area:

   Energy and Transportation

   - Power plants, transmission and transformer facilities, and integrated thermal supply facilities
   - Development, transportation, storage, and processing of oils and natural gas
   - Ports, piers, warehouses, and accessories
   - Railroads and highways

   Urban Infrastructure Facilities

- Gas
- Water supply and drainage
- Roads and bridges
- Postal and telecommunication facilities
- Environmental protection facilities for sewerage treatment, etc.

Undertakings That Spur Export and Import Substitution (including those in industry and agriculture):

- Communication equipment
- Computers
- Electronic components and devices
- Semiconductor components
- Other electronic products
- Precision instruments and meters
- Precision machinery and high-efficiency forging equipment
- Precision medical and clinical diagnostic equipment
- Office automation equipment
- Precision machinery elements
- Precision molds
- Electric motors
- Automobile parts and components
- Specialized large-scale, complete sets of equipment
- Other integrated equipment for electric machinery
- Semisynthetic antibiotics and other new pharmaceuticals
- Medium- and high-grade dyes and auxiliaries
- High-efficiency agrochemicals with low toxicity
- Food and fodder additives
- Chemical reagents and biochemical reagents
- Other precision products and delicate chemicals with high yields and low pollution
- Updated household electrical appliances
- High-efficiency energy-saving lights and lighting equipment
- High-grade cosmetic product lines
- Medium- and high-grade apparel and high fashions of elite brands and designs
- High-grade decorative textiles
- Other export-oriented light industry products and textiles
- Engineering plastics and special resins and products
- Special synthetic fibers

- Updated construction materials
- Other updated materials
- Biotechnical engineering products
- Laser technique engineering products
- Other emerging technology products
- Farm and sideline products to generate foreign exchange

3. Industries in Which Development is Restricted or Prohibited in the Pudong New Area:

Industries in which development is restricted or prohibited by the industrial policies of the State

Industries that produce substantial amounts of wastes and fail to meet environmental protection requirements for wastes discharged after pollution control efforts are made

Industries engaged in pornographic, obscene, or activities involving State security, or those that are detrimental to the economic and social development of the State.

These guidelines shall be implemented under the joint supervision and execution of the Planning Commission of the Shanghai Municipality and the Pudong Development Office of the Shanghai Municipality. The Planning Commission of the Shanghai Municipality is responsible for the explanantion.

Note: Ratified by the Shanghai Municipal People's Government on September 6, 1990.

Appendix III

Detailed Rules for the Implementation of the Law of the People's Republic of China on Wholly Foreign-Owned Enterprises in China

Approved by the State Council of the People's Republic of China on October 28, 1990. Promulgated by the Ministry of Foreign Economic Relations and Trade on September 12, 1990.

CHAPTER 1. GENERAL PROVISIONS

Article 1

The Detailed Rules are formulated in accordance with the provisions of Article 23 of the Law of the People's Republic of China on Wholly Foreign-Owned Enterprises in China (hereinafter referred to as wholly foreign-owned enterprises.)

Article 2

The wholly foreign-owned enterprises are subject to the jurisdiction and protection of Chinese laws. The business activities conducted by a wholly foreign-owned enterprise within the territory of China must observe the Chinese laws and regulations without injury to the public interests of China.

Article 3

A wholly foreign-owned exterprise to be established must be beneficial to the development of the Chinese national economy, be able to gain remarkable economic results and meet at least one of the following requirements:

1. Adopting advanced technology and equipment which can help develop new products, save energy and raw materials, upgrade existing products, and substitute importation;

2. The annual output value of the export products accounts for 50 percent or more of the total output value of all products of that year with a balance or surplus in the foreign exchange revenues and expenditures.

Article 4

The establishment of a wholly foreign-owned enterprise is prohibited in the following lines of business:

1. News, publication, broadcast, television, film,

2. Domestic commerce, foreign trade, insurance,

3. Posts and telecommunications, and,

4. Any others prohibited by the provisions of the Chinese government.

Article 5

The establishment of a wholly foreign-owned enterprise is restricted in the following lines of business:

1. Public utilities,

2. Communications and transportation,

3. Real estate,

4. Trust investment, and

5. Lease.

An application for establishing a wholly foreign-owned enterprise in the lines of business described in the preceding paragraph is subject to approval by the Ministry of Foreign Economic Relations and Trade of the People's Republic of China (hereinafter referred to as Ministry of Foreign Economic Relations and Trade), unless otherwise stipulated in the Chinese laws and regulations.

Article 6

An application for establishing a wholly foreign-owned enterprise shall not be approved if the enterprise involves any of the following circumstances:

1. Detriment to China's sovereignty or public interests,

2. Endangerment to the security of China,

3. Violation of Chinese laws and regulations,

4. Nonconformity with the requirements of the development of China's national economy, or

5. Possibility of environmental pollution.

Article 7

A wholly foreign-owned enterprise, within the approved scope of operation, is entitled to do business independently without interference whatever.

CHAPTER 2. ESTABLISHMENT PROCEDURES

Article 8

After the examination and approval of applications for the establishment of wholly foreign-owned enterprises by the Ministry of Foreign Economic Relations and Trade, certificates of approval shall be granted by the Ministry.

The State Council may authorize the people's governments in provinces, autonomous regions, municipalities directly under the central government, special cities with independent plan and special economic zones to examine and approve the applications for establishing wholly foreign-owned enterprises under the following situations, and certificates of approval are granted by such people's governments after the approval:

1. The total amount of investment is within the authorization for approval as set by the State Council, and

2. No allocations of raw materials by the State are required and the national overall balance of energy resources, transportation, and quotas for export are not affected.

The approval of the establishment of a wholly foreign-owned enterprise by the people's government in a province, autonomous region, municipality directly under the central government, special city with independent plan, and special economic zone within the authorization for approval set by the State Council shall be filed with the Ministry of Foreign Economic Relations and Trade within fifteen days of approval. (The Ministry of Foreign Economic Relations and Trade and the people's governments in the provinces, autonomous regions, municipalities directly under the central government, special cities with independent plans, and special economic zones shall be hereinafter referred to as "the examination and approval authority.")

Article 9

A wholly foreign-owned enterprise applying for the establishment shall, according to the authorization for approval, obtain the consent of the departments concerned of foreign economic relations and trade in advance, if the products of such an enterprise involve the export licenses, export quotas, import licenses, or are restricted for import by the state.

Article 10

Before applying for the establishment of a wholly foreign-owned enterprise, a foreign investor shall submit to the local people's government, at county level or above where the enterprise will be located, a report covering the following items: objective of the enterprise to be established; scope and scale of operation; products; technology and equipment to be adopted; the sale ratio of products in domestic and international markets; acreage and requirement of the land to be used; conditions and quantity of water required, electric power, coal, gas, or other energy resources to be used; requirements for public facilities, etc.

The local people's government at county level or above shall answer the foreign investor in written form within thirty days from the date of receiving the report submitted by the foreign investor.

Article 11

A foreign investor shall, through the local people's government at county level or above where the wholly foreign-owned enterprise will be established, submit the application for establishing the wholly foreign-owned enterprise with the following documents to the examination and approval authority:

1. Application for establishing a wholly foreign-owned enterprise,
2. Feasibility study report,
3. Articles of association of the enterprise,
4. List of legal representatives of the enterprise (or the candidates for the board of directors),
5. Documents of testimonial and financial credit of the foreign investors,
6. Written reply of local people's government at county level or above where the wholly foreign-owned enterprise will be established,
7. List of goods and materials needed to be imported, and
8. Other documents needed to be submitted.

The documents in the preceding items (1) and (3) shall be written in Chinese, while documents in items (2), (4), and (5) may be written in foreign languages with Chinese translation attached.

Where two or more foreign investors jointly apply for establishing a wholly foreign-owned enterprise, they shall submit the duplicate of the contract signed between them to the examination and approval authority for the record.

Article 12

The examination and approval authority shall decide whether to approve or disapprove the application for the establishment of a wholly foreign-owned enterprise within ninety days from the date of receiving all the documents. Should anything imperfect or inappropriate be found in the aforementioned documents, the examination and approval authority may demand a supplement or amendment to them within a limited period of time.

Article 13

After the application for establishing a wholly foreign-owned enterprise is approved by the examination and approval authority, the foreign investor shall, within thirty days from the date of receiving the certificate of approval, apply to the administrations for industry and commerce for registration and a business license. The date of issuance of the business license for a wholly foreign-owned enterprise shall be the date of its establishment.

If the foreign investor fails to apply to the administration for industry and commerce for registration after thirty days from the date of receiving the certificate of approval, the certificate of approval shall automatically become invalid.

The enterprise shall go through the formalities for tax registration with the tax authority within thirty days of its establishment.

Article 14

A foreign investor may entrust organizations specially serving foreign-funded enterprises in China or other economic organizations to handle the matters stipulated in Article 9, Paragraph 1 of Article 10, and Article 11. A contract of mandate shall be signed between the foreign investor and the organizations mentioned above.

Article 15

The application for establishing a wholly foreign-owned enterprise shall include the following items:

1. Names, residence, places of registration of the foreign investors, and names, nationalities, and titles of the legal representatives,
2. Name and legal address of the wholly foreign-owned enterprise to be established,
3. Scope of operation, variety of products, and scale of production,
4. Total amount of investment, registered capital, source of funds, ways and time limit of contribution to the wholly foreign-owned enterprise to be established,
5. Form of organization or mechanism and legal representative of the enterprise,
6. Main production equipment to be adopted and its present condition, production technologies, levels of the technologies, and their source of supply,
7. Districts for sale, ways and means of sales, and the ratio of products to be sold on the domestic and international markets,
8. Arrangements for revenues and expenditures of foreign currency,
9. Arrangements for staff and organization, employment, training, salaries and wages, welfare benefits, labor insurance, labour protection, and other matters of staff and workers,
10. Possibility or degree of environmental pollution and the measures for solution,
11. Choice and acreage of the land to use,
12. Funds, energy, and raw materials necessary for capital construction and production and the measures for solution,
13. Progress schedule of project, and
14. Term of operation of the enterprise to be established.

Article 16

Articles of association of a wholly foreign-owned enterprise shall include the following items:

1. Name and legal address of the enterprise,
2. Objective and scope of operation,
3. Total amount of investment, registered capital and time limit of contribution,
4. Form of organization,
5. Internal organizations and their functions of the enterprise, and rules for han-

dling routine affairs, the responsibility and authority of legal representative, general manager, general engineer, general accountant, and other high-ranking executive officers,

6. Principles and systems governing finance, accounting, and auditing,
7. Labor management,
8. Duration, dissolution, and liquidation of the enterprise, and
9. Procedures for amendment of the articles of association.

Article 17

The articles of association shall come into force after being approved by the examination and approval authority. The same applies in the event of amendments.

Article 18

When a wholly foreign-owned enterprise is split up, merged with others, or faced with important changes that have taken place on the capital for some reason, it shall apply to the examination and approval authority for approval with a certificate of verification provided by an accountant registered in China. Then registration procedures for changes shall be followed at the administrations for industry and commerce.

CHAPTER 3. FORM OF ORGANIZATION AND REGISTERED CAPITAL

Article 19

A wholly foreign-owned enterprise shall take the form of a limited liability company. It may also take other forms of organization with approval.

Where a wholly foreign-owned enterprise is a limited liability company, the foreign investor shall be liable to the enterprise within the limit of the capital subscribed by it.

Where a wholly foreign-owned enterprise takes other forms of organization, the liability of the foreign investor to the enterprise shall be determined according to the Chinese law and regulations.

Article 20

The total amount of investment of a wholly foreign-owned enterprise refers to the sum of funds for operating the enterprise, that is, the sum total of capital construction funds and working capital necessary for reaching the production scale of the enterprise.

Article 21

The registered capital of a wholly foreign-owned enterprise refers to the total amount of capital registered at the administrations for industry and commerce when applying for the establishment of the enterprise, that is, all the capital subscribed by the foreign investor.

The registered capital of a wholly foreign-owned enterprise shall be appropriate to its business scale, and the ratio is registered capital and total amount of investment shall be in conformity with the relevant provisions of China.

Article 22

A wholly foreign-owned enterprise shall not reduce its registered capital during its term of operation.

Article 23

Any increase or assignment of the registered capital of a wholly foreign-owned enterprise shall be approved by the examination and approval authority and then go through the procedures for alteration of registration with the administrations for industry and commerce.

Article 24

Where a wholly foreign-owned enterprise mortgages or assigns its property, or rights and interests, the enterprise shall submit it to the examination and approval authority for approval and then file it with the administrations for industry and commerce for the record.

Article 25

A legal representation of a wholly foreign-owned enterprise is a person in charge who exercises his functions and powers on behalf of the enterprise in line with the enterprise articles of association.

When the legal representative is unable to perform his functions and powers, he shall entrust an agent in written form to exercise his functions and powers.

CHAPTER 4. WAYS AND TIME LIMIT FOR CONTRIBUTING INVESTMENT

Article 26

The investment contributed by a foreign investor may be provided in freely convertible foreign currency or by machinery, equipment, and industrial property right and know-how, which are evaluated.

With the approval of the examination and approval authority, a foreign investor may also contribute his profits in RMB yielded from his other enterprises operating in the territory of China.

Article 27

The machinery or equipment contributed as investment by a foreign investor shall meet the following conditions:

1. Necessary for the production of the wholly foreign-owned enterprise, and

2. Unable to be manufactured in China, or though able, their technical performance or time of supply do not meet the demand.

The pricing of such machinery or equipment shall not be higher than the normal prices of similar machinery or equipment in the international market.

A list of the machinery or equipment contributed as investment shall be made out in detail, including items, assortments, quality, pricing and submitted as annex to the application for establishing a foreign-owned enterprise to the examination and approval authority.

Article 28

The industrial property right or know-how contributed as investment by a foreign investor shall meet the following conditions:

1. It is owned by the foreign investor, and
2. New products urgently needed in China or export products easily sold in the world market can be manufactured with such industrial property or know-how.

The pricing of such industrial property right or know-how shall be in conformity with the international principle in valuation and its total value shall be no more than 20 percent of the registered capital of the enterprise.

Detailed information shall be provided pertaining to the industrial property right or know-how contributed as investment, including copies of the ownership certificate, state of validity, technical characteristics, practical value, the basis and standard on which the valuation is made, and submitted as annex to the application for establishing a wholly foreign-owned enterprise to the examination and approval authority.

Article 29

When machinery or equipment contributed as investment arrives at a Chinese port, the wholly foreign-owned enterprise shall apply for inspection to the Chinese commodity inspection organization, which will issue the inspection report to that effect.

Where the assortment, quality, and quantity of such machinery or equipment are inconsistent with those described in the list of contributed investment that was submitted to the examination and approval authority, the authority has the power to require the foreign investor to make corrections within a given time.

Article 30

After the industrial property right or know-how contributed as investment is put into use, the examination and approval authority has the power to check. If such industrial property right or know-how is not in conformity with the original document submitted by the foreign investor, the examination and approval authority has the right to require the foreign investor to make corrections within a given time.

Article 31

The time limit for a foreign investor to subscribe the capital shall be stipulated in the application for establishing the wholly foreign-owned enterprise. The foreign investor may subscribe the capital by installments. However, the last installment shall be paid within three years from the date of the issuance of the business license. The first installment by a foreign investor shall be no less than 15 percent of all of his capital subscribed and paid within ninety days from the date on which the enterprise's business license is issued.

In case a foreign investor fails to subscribe the first installment of capital within the period stipulated in the preceding paragraph, the certificate of approval for the enterprise will become invalid automatically. The enterprise shall then go through the procedures of nullifying its registration with the administrations for industry and commerce and hand in its business license for cancellation; in case a wholly foreign-owned enterprise fails to handle the procedures of nullification and cancellation, the administrations for industry and commerce shall withdraw the business license of the enterprise and make an announcement.

Article 32

A foreign investor shall pay each installment of capital on schedule after the first installment is made. If any installment is overdue by more than thirty days without appropriate reason, it shall be handled according to the provisions of paragraph 2, Article 31 of these Detailed Rules.

Where a foreign investor has appropriate reasons for the delay of its contribution, it shall, with the consent of the examination and approval authority, report it to the administrations for industry and commerce for the record.

Article 33

After each installment of capital is paid by the foreign investor the wholly foreign-owned enterprise shall employ an accountant registered in China for verification and to issue a report after the verification. The report shall be filed with the examination and approval authority and the administrations for industry and commerce.

CHAPTER 5. USE OF LAND AND ITS FEE

Article 34

The use of land by a wholly foreign-owned enterprise shall be reviewed and arranged by the people's government at county level or above where the enterprise is to be located according to the circumstances of its own district.

Article 35

A wholly foreign-owned enterprise shall with its certificate of approval and business license handle the procedures with the land administrative department of the local people's government at county level or above where the enterprise is to be located and obtain a certificate of land within thirty days from the date of issuing its business license.

Article 36

A certificate of land is a legal document against which the wholly foreign-owned enterprise is entitled to use the land. Without approval, the enterprise shall not assign its right to use the land during its term of operation.

Article 37

A wholly foreign-owned enterprise shall pay the land use fees to the department in charge of land in locality upon the time it receives the certificate of land.

Article 38

A wholly foreign-owned enterprise shall pay the land development fees if the land for which the enterprise is entitled to use has been developed.

The land development fees referred to in the preceding paragraph includes expenses for requisition, demolition and resettlement, and expenses for infrastructure provided for the wholly foreign-owned enterprise. The land development fees may be charged in one lump sum or yearly by the land development unit.

Article 39

If the land to be used by a wholly foreign-owned enterprise is undeveloped, the enterprise may develop it by itself or entrust a relevant Chinese unit to do the job. The construction of basic facilities shall be arranged under unified management of the people's government at county level or above where the enterprise is located.

Article 40

The standard for the land use fees and land development fees shall be fixed in accordance with the relevant provisions of China.

Article 41

The period for use of land by a wholly foreign-owned enterprise extends as long as its approved term of operation.

Article 42

A wholly foreign-owned enterprise may acquire the right to use the land according to either the provisions of the present Chapter or other law and regulations of China.

CHAPTER 6. PURCHASE AND SALE

Article 43

A wholly foreign-owned enterprise shall make and implement its production and operation plan by itself. The plan shall be filed with the local department that is in charge of the enterprise's line of business.

Article 44

A wholly foreign-owned enterprise has the right to make decisions of its own to purchase machinery, equipment, raw materials, fuel, parts, fittings, components, means of transport and stationery, etc. (hereinafter referred to as "goods and materials") for its own use.

In purchasing goods and materials in China, a wholly foreign-owned enterprise shall enjoy the same treatment as the Chinese enterprises under the like conditions.

Article 45

In selling products in the Chinese market, a wholly foreign-owned enterprise shall follow its approved sale ratio.

In case a wholly foreign-owned enterprise intends to sell more of its products than the approved sale ratio in the Chinese market, an approval is required from the examination and approval authority.

Article 46

A wholly foreign-owned enterprise has the right to export its own products by itself and it may entrust a Chinese foreign-trade corporation or corporation outside China for sales on commission.

A wholly foreign-owned enterprise has the right to sell its products by itself in China in line with the approved sale ratio or may entrust a Chinese commercial agency for sales on commission.

Article 47

For machinery or equipment contributed as investment by a foreign investor and for which the import license is required according to Chinese laws, the enterprise shall, with the list of import equipment and materials that has been approved, apply to the issuing authority for import license by itself or through an agency.

Within the approved scope of operation, a wholly foreign-owned enterprise shall make out an annual plan for importing goods and materials that are necessary for the production of the enterprise, and if import licenses for such goods and materials are required according to the provisions of China, the enterprise shall apply for such licenses to the issuing authority every six months.

A wholly foreign-owned enterprise shall make out an annual plan for export products if the export licenses for such products are required according to the provisions of China and shall apply for export licenses to the issuing authority every six months.

Article 48

The prices for goods, materials, technologies, and services imported by a wholly foreign-owned enterprise shall not be higher than the normal prices of similar goods, materials, technologies, and services on the international market. The enterprise may decide the prices of its products for export by itself with reference to the prices on international market, but the prices shall not be lower than the reasonable prices for export. If a wholly foreign-owned enterprise evades tax by means of import at higher price and export at lower price or other methods, the tax authority has the power to investigate its legal responsibility according to the laws.

The prices for products sold in the Chinese market by a wholly foreign-owned enterprise in line with the approved sale ratio shall follow the provisions of the price control regulations in China.

Article 49

A wholly foreign-owned enterprise shall provide statistical information and submit statistical statements and reports in accordance with the Law of Statistics of the People's Republic of China and the provisions of statistical system concerning foreign investment in China.

CHAPTER 7. TAXATION

Article 50

A wholly foreign-owned enterprise shall pay taxes in accordance with related laws and regulations of China.

Article 51

Staff and workers in a wholly foreign-owned enterprise shall pay individual income taxes in accordance with the provisions of related Chinese laws and regulations.

Article 52

A wholly foreign-owned enterprise shall be exempted from customs duty and industrial and commercial consolidated tax for the following goods and materials imported by it:

1. Machinery, equipment, parts, building materials related and materials required for installation, and reinforcement of machinery that are contributed as investment by the foreign investor,
2. Machinery, equipment, parts, means of import transport by the enterprise for its own use in production and management with part of the investment funds, and
3. Raw materials, auxiliary materials, components, parts, and packing materials imported by the enterprise for production of export goods.

Taxes shall be levied and pursued according to the Chinese tax laws if the imported goods and materials mentioned in the preceding paragraph are approved for sale in China or for manufacturing products to be sold in China.

Article 53

The export products, except those restricted by China for export, of a wholly foreign-owned enterprise shall be exempted from customs duty and industrial and commercial consolidated tax in accordance with the tax law of China.

CHAPTER 8. FOREIGN EXCHANGE CONTROL

Article 54

A wholly foreign-owned enterprise shall handle its foreign exchange transactions in accordance with the laws and regulations on exchange control of China.

Article 55

With the business license issued by the administrations for industry and commerce, a wholly foreign-owned enterprise may open a foreign exchange account with a bank that is permitted to handle foreign exchange transactions in the territory of China, and the supervision of receipts and payments shall be carried out by the bank with which the account is opened.

The foreign exchange income of a wholly foreign-owned enterprise shall be deposited into the foreign exchange account in the bank with which the account is opened, and the expenditures in foreign exchange by the wholly foreign-owned enterprise shall be made out of the foreign exchange account.

Article 56

A wholly foreign-owned enterprise shall keep the balance of its foreign exchange revenues and expenditures by itself.

Where a wholly foreign-owned enterprise is unable to keep the balance of its foreign exchange revenues and expenditure by itself, the foreign investor shall state it expressly in its application for establishing the enterprise and put forward a concrete proposal of solution. The examination and approval authority shall give a reply after consulting with the departments concerned.

Where it is stated expressly in the application that the wholly foreign-owned enterprise can keep the balance of its foreign exchange revenues and expenditures by itself, no governmental department is responsible for solving any problem on the balance of its foreign exchange revenues and expenditures.

In case the products made by a wholly foreign-owned enterprise are needed urgently in China and able to be used as the import substitution, they can be sold in China with permission, and the foreign exchange may be collected upon the approval of the authority for exchange control of China.

Article 57

If a wholly foreign-owned enterprise needs to open a foreign exchange account with a bank outside China as required for its production and operation, it shall obtain permission from the authority for exchange control of China, and report regularly its foreign exchange revenues and expenditures with its bank statement according to the provisions of the authority for exchange control.

Article 58

Staff and workers from foreign countries or from Hong Kong, Macao, or Taiwan, working in a wholly foreign-owned enterprise, may, after due payments of income taxes according to the tax law of China, remit freely their salaries and wages and other legitimate income.

CHAPTER 9. FINANCIAL AFFAIRS AND ACCOUNTING

Article 59

A wholly foreign-owned enterprise shall, in accordance with the Chinese laws, regulations, and provisions of the finance authority, set up its financial and accounting system and report it to the local finance and tax authorities for the record.

Article 60

The fiscal year of a wholly foreign-owned enterprise shall begin from January 1 and end on December 31 of the Gregorian calendar.

Article 61

The profit of a wholly foreign-owned enterprise after payment of income tax according to the tax law of China shall be allocated for reserve funds, bonuses, and welfare funds for staff and workers. The proportion of allocation for reserve funds shall be no less than 10 percent of the profit after tax until the accumulative amount of allocation for reserve funds reaches 50 percent of the registered capital, and then no more allocation for reserve may be made. The proportion of allocation for bonuses and welfare funds for staff and workers shall be decided by the enterprise itself.

No profit shall be distributed unless the losses suffered by a wholly foreign-owned enterprise from the previous accounting years are recovered; the profit retained by the enterprise and carried over from the previous accounting years may be distributed together with the distributable profit of the current accounting year.

Article 62

The accounting vouchers, books, statements, and financial reports prepared by a wholly foreign-owned enterprise shall be written in Chinese. In case of being written in foreign languages, they shall be supplemented with Chinese translations.

Article 63

A wholly foreign-owned enterprise shall conduct independent accounting.

A wholly foreign-owned enterprise shall compile its annual accounting statement and statement on liquidation in accordance with the provisions of the finance and tax authorities of China.

A wholly foreign-owned enterprise using a foreign currency as its bookkeeping base shall compile not only the accounting statement in the foreign currency, but also the separate accounting statement in RMB equivalent to the foreign currency.

A wholly foreign-owned enterprise shall employ an accountant registered in China to verify its annual accounting statement and statement on liquidation and render a certificate of verification.

The annual accounting statement and statement of liquidation of a wholly foreign-owned enterprise mentioned in the second and third paragraphs shall be, with the certificate rendered by the accountant registered in China, submitted to the finance and tax authorities in the set time, as well as to the examination and approval authority and the general administrations for industry and commerce for the record.

Article 64

A foreign investor may employ a Chinese or foreign accountant to audit the account books of its enterprise. The expenses thereon shall be borne by the foreign investor.

Article 65

A wholly foreign-owned enterprise shall submit its annual balance sheet and its profit and loss statement to the finance and tax authorities as well as to the examination and approval authority and the administrations for industry and commerce for the record.

Article 66

A wholly foreign-owned enterprise shall set an account book in its location, and accept the supervision of the finance and tax authorities.

In case that a wholly foreign-owned enterprise violates the aforesaid provisions, the finance and tax authorities may impose a fine on the enterprise, and the administrations for industry and commerce may suspend its business or revoke its business license.

CHAPTER 10. STAFF AND WORKERS

Article 67

In the employment of staff and workers in the territory of China, a wholly foreign-owned enterprise shall sign labor contracts with its staff and workers according to the laws and regulations of China, and matters such as employment, dismissal, renumeration, labor protection, labor insurance, etc. shall be expressly stipulated in the contracts.

A wholly foreign-owned enterprise is prohibited to employ child labor

Article 68

A wholly foreign-owned enterprise shall take the responsibility for professional and technical training of its staff and workers, and set up system of examining its staff and workers, thus enabling them to meet the requirements of development in production and managerial skills.

CHAPTER 11. TRADE UNION

Article 69

Staff and workers in a wholly foreign-owned enterprise have the right to establish grass-roots trade unions and carry out trade union activities in accordance with the Trade Union Law of the People's Republic of China (hereinafter referred to as the Trade Union Law).

Article 70

The trade union as representative of staff and workers in a wholly foreign-owned enterprise is empowered to sign labor contracts with the enterprise on behalf of the staff and workers and supervise over the execution of those contracts.

Article 71

The basic tasks of the trade union in a wholly foreign-owned enterprise are to protect the lawful rights and interests of the staff and workers pursuant to the laws and regulations of China; to assist the enterprise in rational use of welfare and bonus funds; to organize political, professional, scientific, and technical studies and to carry out literary, arts, and sports activities for staff and workers; to educate staff and workers, and to observe labor discipline and exert themselves to fulfill the productive tasks of the enterprise.

The representatives of the trade union have the right to attend as nonvoting members the meetings held by a wholly foreign-owned enterprise to decide matters concerning staff and workers on awards and penalties, salaries and wages, welfare benefits, labor protection, labor insurance, etc. A wholly foreign-owned enterprise shall pay attention to the opinions of the trade union for its cooperation.

Article 72

A wholly foreign-owned enterprise shall actively support the work of the trade union and provide necessary space and facilities for the trade union for the purpose of office, meeting, and collective activities of welfare, culture, and sports in accordance with the provisions of the Trade Union Law.

A wholly foreign-owned enterprise shall allot monthly an amount of money in proportion to 2 percent of the total salaries and wages actually paid to its staff and workers as funds for the trade union. The funds shall be used by the trade union in that enterprise according to the relevant managerial rules for trade union funds formulated by the A110-China Federation of Trade Union.

CHAPTER 12. DURATION, TERMINATION, AND LIQUIDATION

Article 73

The term of operation of a wholly foreign-owned enterprise shall be, according to its particular line of business and its concrete conditions, stipulated by the foreign investor in its application for establishing the enterprise, and approved by the examination and approval authority.

Article 74

The term of operation of a wholly foreign-owned enterprise shall begin from the date on which the business license of the enterprise is issued.

In case an extension for term of operation is required upon the expiration, a wholly foreign-owned enterprise shall submit an application for extension of the term to the examination and approval authority 180 days before the expiration. The examination and approval authority shall decide the approval or disapproval within thirty days from the date of receiving the application for extension.

Upon the approval of extension of the term, the enterprise shall go through formalities for the alteration of registration with the administrations for industry and commerce within thirty days from the date of receiving the approval document.

Article 75

A wholly foreign-owned enterprise shall be terminated for any of the following situations:

1. Expiration of the term of operation,
2. Dissolution decided by the foreign investor due to the poor operation and heavy losses,
3. Inability to continue the operation due to heavy losses caused by force majeure, such as natural calamity, war, etc.,
4. Bankruptcy,
5. Revocation made by the authorities concerned due to the violation of Chinese laws and regulations and harm to the public interests, or
6. Occurrence of other reasons of dissolution stipulated in the articles of association of the enterprise.

In case a wholly foreign-owned enterprise is involved in the situations described in (2), (3), and (4) of the preceding paragraph, the enterprise shall submit an application for termination by itself to the examination and approval authority for verification and approval. The date of termination shall begin from the date of verification and approval by the examination and approval authority.

Article 76

In case a wholly foreign-owned enterprise is terminated under the provisions of (1), (2), (3), and (6) in Article 75, the enterprise shall make a public announcement and notify the creditors within fifteen days from the date of termination. It shall, within fifteen days from the day on which the announcement of termination is issued, put forward the procedures and principles for liquidation, nominate the candidates for the liquidation committee, and submit them to the examination and approval authority, and then carry out liquidation after examination and verification by the authority.

Article 77

The liquidation committee shall be composed of the legal representatives of a wholly foreign-owned enterprise, and representatives of the creditors and the competent authorities concerned. It shall also employ an accountant registered in China and a lawyer as its members.

The liquidation expenses shall be paid first from the existing assets of the enterprise.

Article 78

The liquidation committee shall exercise its functions and powers as follows:

1. To convene the meeting of creditors,

2. To take over and sort out the property of the enterprise and work out a balance sheet and a list of property,

3. To put forward a basis on which the property is evaluated and calculated,

4. To formulate a liquidation program,

5. To collect claims and clear debts,

6. To recover the amount of money which should be, but fail to be, contributed by shareholders,

7. To allocate the property left over after the clearance of all debts, and

8. To sue and be sued on behalf of the wholly foreign-owned enterprise.

Article 79

Before the completion of the liquidation of a wholly foreign-owned enterprise, the foreign investor shall not remit or carry the funds of the enterprise outside China and not dispose of the property of the enterprise by itself.

If the net assets and remaining property exceed the registered capital of a wholly foreign-owned enterprise upon completion of the liquidation, the exceeding part is regarded as the profit on which income taxes shall be levied in accordance with the tax law of China.

Article 80

Upon the completion of liquidation of a wholly foreign-owned enterprise, the foreign investor shall go through the formalities for nullifying its registration and cancelling its business license with the administrations for industry and commerce.

Article 81

When a wholly foreign-owned enterprise is disposed of its property upon the liquidation, any Chinese-owned enterprises or other economic organizations have the priority of purchase under the like conditions.

Article 82

In case a wholly foreign-owned enterprise is terminated pursuant to (4) of Article 75, the liquidation shall be conducted with reference to the related laws and regulations of China.

In the event that a wholly foreign-owned enterprise is terminated according to (5) of Article 75, the liquidations shall be carried out in accordance with the relevant provisions of China.

CHAPTER 13. SUPPLEMENTARY PROVISIONS

Article 83

All the insurance coverage of a wholly foreign-owned enterprise shall be furnished by insurance institutions within the territory of China.

Article 84

Economic Contract Law of the People's Republic of China shall apply to the economic contracts concluded between a wholly foreign-owned enterprise and any other Chinese-owned enterprises or economic organizations.

Foreign Economic Contract Law of the People's Republic of China shall apply to the economic contracts concluded between a wholly foreign-owned enterprise and a foreign company, enterprise, or individual.

Article 85

If a company, enterprise, other economic organization, or individual in Hong Kong, Macao, and Taiwan, and a Chinese citizen inhabiting abroad establishes a wholly foreign-owned enterprise by itself in the mainland, it shall be handled with reference to the present Detailed Rules.

Article 86

Staff and workers from foreign countries or Hong Kong, Macao, and Taiwan working in a wholly foreign-owned enterprise may bring in a rational number of self-use means of transport and articles for daily use and go through formalities for the importation according to the provisions of China.

Article 87

The Ministry of Foreign Economic Relations and Trade is responsible for the interpretation of the present Detailed Rules.

Article 88

The present Detailed Rules shall enter into force from the date of promulgation.

Further Reading

Almanac of China's Foreign Economic Relations and Trade, 1980–1989

Asia Week

Asian Wall Street Journal

Balance of Payments Yearbook. Washington, D.C.: International Monetary Fund, 1979–1980.

Brown, David G. *Partnership with China: Sino-Foreign Joint Ventures in Historical Perspective*. Boulder, Colo.: Westview Press, 1986.

Browning, Graeme. *If Everybody Bought One Shoe: American Capitalism in Communist China*. New York: Hill and Wang, 1989.

Business International, Joint Ventures in the People's Republic of China: A Corporate Guide. Hong Kong: Business International, 1985.

Cheng, Chu-Yuan. "China's Economy at the Crossroads." *Current History: A World Affairs Journal*. September 1987: pp. 252–256.

China Business Review

China: Country Economic Memorandum—Between Plan and Market. Washington, D.C.: World Bank, May 1990.

China Daily

China Economic Daily

China Newsletter

China Trade

Chu, David K. W., and Gordon W. K. Wong. "Foreign Direct Investment in China's Shenzhen Special Economic Zone: The Strategies of Firms from Hong Kong, Singapore, USA, and Japan." *Issues in International Business*. Summer-Fall 1986: pp. 35–42.

Cohen, Jerome Alan. "Equity Joint Ventures." *The China Business Review*. November/December 1982: pp. 23–30.

Cohen, Jerome Alan, and Charles H. Harris. "Equal Pay for Equal Work: Remuneration for Equal Work: Remuneration for High-Level Management in

Chinese-Foreign Equity Joint Ventures." *The China Business Review*. January/February 1986: pp. 10–13.

Daniels, John D., Jeffrey Krug, and Douglas Nigh. "US Joint Ventures in China: Motivation and Management of Political Risk." *California Management Review*. Summer 1985: pp. 46–58.

Doing Business in Asia: A Handbook of Checklists and Essential Facts for Corporate Managers. New York: Business International. 1988.

Economist

Eiteman, David. "American Executives' Perceptions of Negotiating Joint Ventures with the People's Republic of China, Lessons Learned," *The Columbia Journal of World Business*. Winter 1990: pp. 59–67.

Falkenheim, Victor. "Fujian's Open Door Experiment: Pace-Setting Province Tackles Foreign Investment Problems." *The China Business Review*. May-June 1986: pp. 38–42.

Far Eastern Economic Review

"Foreign Direct Investment in the People's Republic of China: Report of the Round Table Organized by the United Nations Centre on Transnational Corporations, in Cooperation with the Ministry of Foreign Economic Relations and Trade, People's Republic of China, Beijing, 25 and 26 May, 1987." New York: United Nations, 1988.

"Fujian's Environment for Taiwan *Investment*." Intertrade. June 1990: pp. 18–19.

Grow, Roy F. "Japanese and American Firms in China: Lessons of a New Market." *The Columbia Journal of World Business*. Spring 1986: pp. 49–56.

Grub, Phillip Donald. *United States-People's Republic of China Trade: A More Sober Appraisal in China, the USSR, and Eastern Europe*. Edited by John K. Ryans, Jr. Kent, Ohio: Kent State University Press, 1974.

———. "A Yen for Yuan: Trading and Investing in the China Market." *Business Horizons*. Bloomington, Ind.: Graduate School of Business, Indiana University, July 1987.

Grub, Phillip Donald, and Bryan L. Sudweeks. *Foreign Direct Investment: Country Profiles and Cases*. Rockville, Md.: Mercury Press/Fairchild Publications, 1986.

———. "Securities Markets and the People's Republic of China." *Journal of Economic Development*. June 1988: pp. 51–69.

Grub, Phillip Donald, and Jian Hai Lin. *Foreign Investment in the People's Republic of China: A Study of Investment Incentives and Environment in the Shenzhen Special Economic Zone*. Washington, D.C.: Office of Research Support and Continuing Professional Education, George Washington University, 1985.

———. "Open Door or Squeezing Through the Keyhole: US Joint Venture Experience in China," *The Mid-Atlantic Journal of Business*. January 1989: pp. 21–34.

———. "Foreign Investment in China: Myths and Realities," *Journal of Economic Development*. December 1988: pp. 17–40.

———. "The Shenzhen Special Economic Zone: Investment Incentives and Environment," *Economia Aziendale*. November 1985: pp. 313–343.

Henley, John S., and Mee-Kau Nyaw. "Reforming Chinese Industrial Management." *Euro-Asia Business Review.* July 1986: pp. 10–15.

Hong Kong Standard

Hsu, John C. *China's Foreign Trade Reforms: Impact on Growth and Stability.* New York: Cambridge University Press, 1990.

Hu, Renkuan, and Stephen C. Yam. "Income Tax Law and Accounting for Joint Ventures Using Chinese and Foreign Investment: An Analysis." *The Securities Bulletin*, no. 32. December 1988.

Intertrade

International Financial Statistics. Washington, D.C.: International Monetary Fund, 1979–1990.

The Journal of Commerce

Korea Economic Herald

Lee, Sue-Jean, and Andrew Ness. "Investment Approval: A Step-by-Step Guide to Finalizing a Contract in China." *The China Business Review.* May-June 1986: pp. 14–18

Li, Zhaoxi. "Joint Venture Management and Mutual Adaptability." *Intertrade.* June 1990: pp. 6–10.

Lin, Jian Hai, and Phillip Donald Grub. "Open Door or Squeezing through the Keyhole: U.S. Joint Venture Experience in China." *The Mid-Atlantic Journal of Business.* December 1988: pp. 21–34.

Ma, Rongjie. "China Opens for Business." *California Lawyer.* August 1985: pp. 34–37, 67.

Mann, Jim. *Beijing Jeep: The Short, Unhappy Romance of American Business in China.* New York: Simon and Schuster, 1990.

Mathur, Igbal, and Chen Jai-Sheng. *Strategies for Joint Ventures in the People's Republic of China.* New York: Praeger, 1987.

Miljus, Robert, and William Moore. "Economic Reform and Workplace Conflict Resolution in China." *The Columbia Journal of World Business.* Winter 1990: pp. 49–58.

National Council for US-China Trade. *US Joint Ventures in China: A Progress Report.* Washington, D.C.: U.S. and Foreign Commercial Service, International Trade Administration, U.S. Department of Commerce. March 1987.

"The New Legal Framework for Joint Ventures in China: Guidelines for Investors." *Law and Policy in International Business* 16, no. 3. 1984: pp. 1005–1050.

New York Times

Pomfret, Richard. "Jiangsu's New Wave in Foreign Investment." *The China Business Review.* November/December 1989: pp. 10–15.

Rines, Melvin. "Managing a Growing Debt." *The China Business Review.* May/June 1989: pp. 16–18.

Schnepp, Otto, Mary Ann Von Glinow, and Arvind Bhambri. *United States-China Technology Transfer.* Englewood Cliffs, N.J.: Prentice-Hall, 1990.

Simon, Denis Fred. "After Tiananmen: What is the Future for Foreign Business in China?" *California Management Review.* Winter 1990: pp. 106–123.

The South China Morning Post

Stevens, Joseph P. "The New Foreign Contract Law in China." *Law and Policy in International Business* 18, no. 2. 1986: pp. 455–474.

Takai, Kiyoshi. "Current Reforms in China and the Outlook for the Future." *China Newsletter*, no. 87: pp. 17–22.

Teng, Weizao, ed. *Transnational Corporations and China's Open-Door Policy.* Lexington, Mass.: Lexington Books, 1988.

Torbert, Preston M. "Wholly Foreign-Owned Enterprises Come of Age: New Law Protects Nascent Form of Investment." *The China Business Review.* July/August 1986: pp. 50–53.

Tsao, James T. H. *China's Development Strategies and Foreign Trade.* Lexington, Mass.: Lexington Books, 1987.

Verzariu, Pompiliu, and Daniel B. Stein. "Joint Venture Considerations." *Joint Venture Agreements in the People's Republic of China.* November 1982: pp. 7–9, 18.

The Wall Street Journal

Wang, N. T. *China's Modernization and Transnational Corporations.* Lexington, Mass.: D.C. Heath, 1984.

Wang, Rongjun. "Management Based on Diverse Cultural Background." *Intertrade.* June 1990: pp. 11–13.

Wang, Zheng Xian. "Multinational Enterprise and China's Economic Development: Problems of FIDI." Unpublished Manuscript, Zhongshan University, Guangzhou, People's Republic of China.

———. "On the Development Strategy of China's Foreign Economic Relations." *Journal of Sun-Yat Sen University (Zhongshan University), Social Science Edition*, no. 2. Guangzhou, People's Republic of China, 1985.

The Washington Post

The Washington Times

The World Economic Herald, various issues, 1985–1989

Worth, Ford. "Doing Business in China Now." *Fortune, Pacific Rim.* 1989: pp. 21–24.

Wu, Chung-Tong. "China's Re-Entry Into the World System: Regional Impacts of Foreign Investments." Paper presented to the Conference on Transnational Capital and Urbanization on the Pacific Rim. Los Angeles, University of California at Los Angeles, March 26–28, 1987.

Zeng, Changling. "Booming Sino-Foreign Joint Ventures." *China's Foreign Trade* 7. 1985: pp. 18–19.

Zimmerman, Alan S. "Marketing in the People's Republic of China: A Survey," *Issues in International Business.* Summer/Fall 1986: pp. 27–34.

Index

About the Authors

PHILLIP DONALD GRUB is Professor of International Business and holder of the Aryamehr Chair of Multinational Management at The George Washington University, Washington, D.C.

JIAN HAI LIN is an Economist with the International Monetary Fund and formerly a Professor of Economics at the University of International Business and Economics, Beijing.